SAS® Programming II:
Manipulating Data with the
DATA Step

Course Notes

SAS® Programming II: Manipulating Data with the DATA Step Course Notes was developed by Jemshaid Cheema and Melinda Thielbar. Additional contributions were made by Michelle Buchecker, Ted Meleky, Warren Repole, and Jim Simon. Editing and production support was provided by the Curriculum Development and Support Department.

SAS® Programming II: Manipulating Data with the DATA Step Course Notes

Book code PROG2, course code 57691, prepared date 24Aug01.

Table of Contents

Course Description

This Level III course is designed for experienced SAS programmers who want to build on the skills acquired in the SAS® Programming I: Essentials course. The course focuses on how to manage SAS data set input and output, work with different data types, and manipulate data.

After completing this course, you should be able to
- read and write different types of data
- combine SAS data sets
- summarize data
- perform data manipulation and transformations using SAS functions
- process data iteratively
- use arrays
- understand DATA step processing.

To learn more...

SAS Education

A full curriculum of general and statistical instructor-based training is available at any of the Institute's training facilities. Institute instructors can also provide on-site training.

For information on other courses in the curriculum, contact the SAS Education Division at 1-919-531-7321, or send e-mail to training@sas.com. You can also find this information on the Web at www.sas.com/training/ as well as in the Training Course Catalog.

SAS Publishing

For a list of other SAS books that relate to the topics covered in this Course Notes, USA customers can contact our SAS Publishing Department at 1-800-727-3228 or send e-mail to sasbook@sas.com. Customers outside the USA, please contact your local SAS office.

Also, see the Publications Catalog on the Web at www.sas.com/pubs for a complete list of books and a convenient order form.

Prerequisites

Before attending this course, you should have completed the SAS® Programming I: Essentials course or have at least six months of experience writing SAS programs.

Specifically, you should be able to

- understand file structures and write system commands to create and access files on your operating system
- write DATA and PROC steps
- understand error messages in the SAS log and debug your program
- understand programming logic concepts (IF/THEN logic)
- create a SAS data set from an external file
- use SAS software to access SAS data libraries
- use TITLE statements
- read a SAS data set using a SET statement
- perform a simple merge using a MERGE statement
- use DROP= and KEEP= data set options
- create and use SAS date values.

You can gain this recommended knowledge of the SAS System from the SAS® Programming I: Essentials course.

General Conventions

This section explains the various conventions used in presenting text, SAS language syntax, and examples in this book.

Typographical Conventions

You will see several type styles in this book. This list explains the meaning of each style:

UPPERCASE ROMAN   is used for SAS statements, variable names, and other SAS language elements when they appear in the text.

italic   identifies terms or concepts that are defined in text. Italic is also used for book titles when they are referenced in text, as well as for various syntax and mathematical elements.

bold   is used for emphasis within text.

`monospace`   is used for examples of SAS programming statements and for SAS character strings. Monospace is also used to refer to field names in windows, information in fields, and user-supplied information.

<u>select</u>   indicates selectable items in windows and menus. This book also uses icons to represent selectable items.

Syntax Conventions

The general forms of SAS statements and commands shown in this book include only that part of the syntax actually taught in the course. For complete syntax, see the appropriate SAS reference guide.

```
PROC CHART DATA= SAS-data-set;
    HBAR | VBAR chart-variables </ options>;
RUN;
```

This is an example of how SAS syntax is shown in text:

- **PROC** and **CHART** are in uppercase bold because they are SAS keywords.
- DATA= is in uppercase to indicate that it must be spelled as shown.
- *SAS-data-set* is in italic because it represents a value that you supply. In this case, the value must be the name of a SAS data set.
- **HBAR** and **VBAR** are in uppercase bold because they are SAS keywords. They are separated by a vertical bar to indicate they are mutually exclusive; you can choose one or the other.
- *chart-variables* is in italic because it represents a value or values that you supply.
- *</ options>* represents optional syntax specific to the HBAR and VBAR statements. The angle brackets enclose the slash as well as *options* because if no options are specified you do not include the slash.
- **RUN** is in uppercase bold because it is a SAS keyword.

Chapter 1   Introduction

1.1 Overview

Objectives

- Explore the functionality of the DATA step.

3

Why the DATA Step?

The DATA step permits true programming functionality.
It is

- flexible
- accessible.

The DATA step is part of base SAS software, making it available on all operating systems and for all SAS users.

4

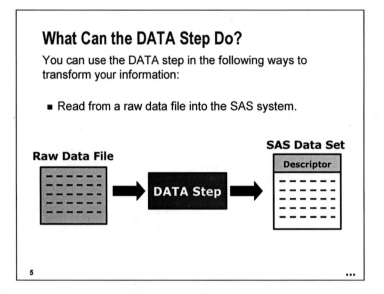

What Can the DATA Step Do?

You can use the DATA step in the following ways to transform your information:

- Read from a raw data file into the SAS system.

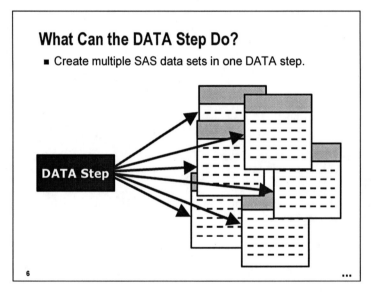

What Can the DATA Step Do?

- Create multiple SAS data sets in one DATA step.

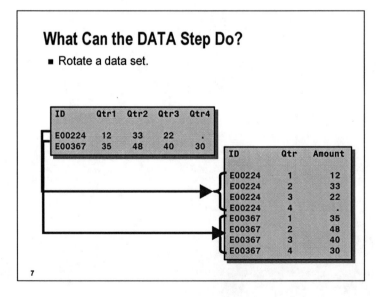

What Can the DATA Step Do?

- Rotate a data set.

What Can the DATA Step Do?

- Combine existing data sets.

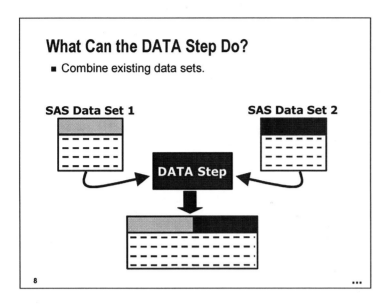

8   ...

What Can the DATA Step Do?

You can also add or augment information in a variety of ways.

- Create accumulating totals.

SaleDate	Sale Amt	Mth2Dte
01APR2001	498.49	498.49
02APR2001	946.50	1444.99
03APR2001	994.97	2439.96
04APR2001	564.59	3004.55
05APR2001	783.01	3787.56

9   ...

What Can the DATA Step Do?

- Manipulate numeric values.

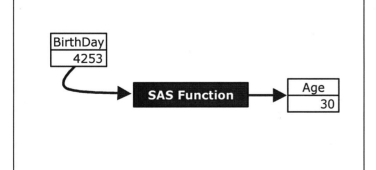

10   ...

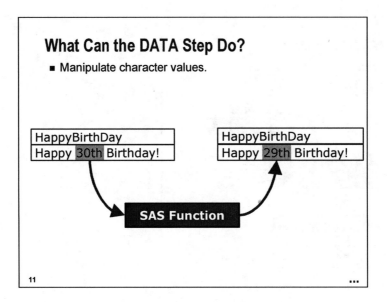

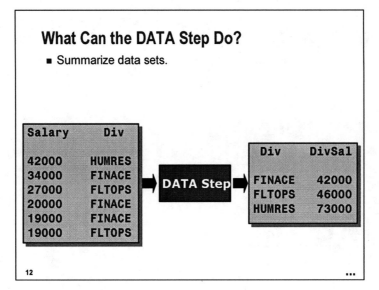

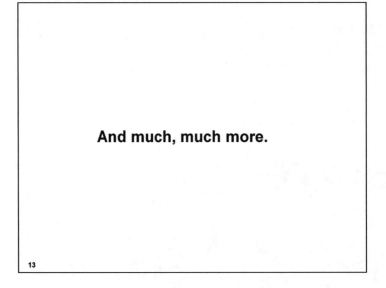

1.2   Review of SAS Basics

Objectives

- Review fundamental SAS concepts.
- Review creating a SAS data set from a raw data file.

15

Industry Terminology Comparison

Data Processing	SAS System	SQL
file	data set	table
record	observation	row
field	variable	column

16

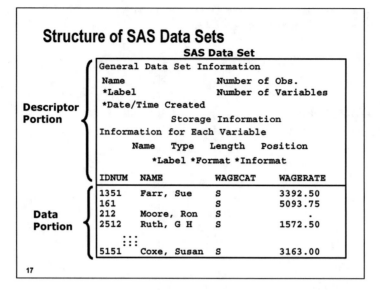

Structure of SAS Data Sets

SAS Data Set

Descriptor Portion

```
General Data Set Information

Name                      Number of Obs.
*Label                    Number of Variables
*Date/Time Created

          Storage Information
Information for Each Variable

     Name    Type    Length    Position
        *Label *Format *Informat
```

IDNUM	NAME	WAGECAT	WAGERATE

Data Portion

IDNUM	NAME	WAGECAT	WAGERATE
1351	Farr, Sue	S	3392.50
161		S	5093.75
212	Moore, Ron	S	.
2512	Ruth, G H	S	1572.50
...			
5151	Coxe, Susan	S	3163.00

17

Attributes of SAS Variables

All SAS variables have three required attributes:

- name
- type
- length.

18

Variable Names

The rules for naming SAS data sets and variables are the same.

Names

- must be 1 to 32 characters in length
- must start with a letter (A-Z) or an underscore (_)
- can continue with any combination of numbers, letters, and underscores.

19

In Version 8 and higher, SAS variable names are displayed in the case that they are created; however, as in all versions of SAS, variable names are **not** case-sensitive within the program. This allows you to create variable names that are easier to read in reports without worrying about case-sensitivity within your SAS programs.

Variable Type and Length

Variables can be

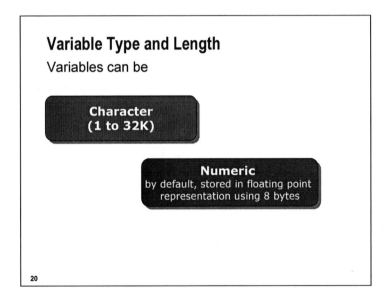

**Character
(1 to 32K)**

Numeric
by default, stored in floating point
representation using 8 bytes

20

✎   It is possible to store numeric variables using fewer than 8 bytes. However, reducing the length of numeric variables decreases their precision and can yield unexpected results.

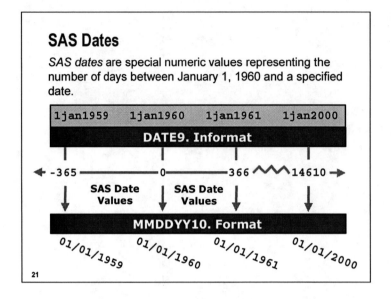

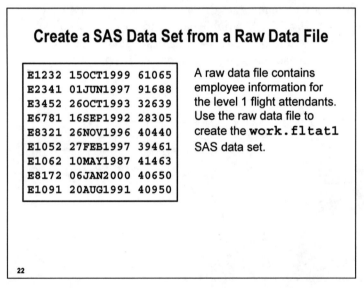

This is a fixed-column raw data file. Each data field starts in the same position, respectively, in every record of the file. You can read fixed-column raw data files with either column or formatted input.

Desired Output

Obs	EmpID	Hire Date	Salary	Bonus
1	E1232	14532	61065	3053.25
2	E2341	13666	91688	4584.40
3	E3452	12352	32639	1631.95
4	E6781	11947	28305	1415.25
5	E8321	13479	40440	2022.00
6	E1052	13572	39461	1973.05
7	E1062	9991	41463	2073.15
8	E8172	14615	40650	2032.50
9	E1091	11554	40950	2047.50

23

In addition to the fields in the raw data file, the desired output has a bonus for each employee, which is 5% of the employee's salary.

The DATA Statement

A DATA step always begins with a DATA statement.
General form of a DATA statement:

> **DATA** *SAS-data-set*;

The DATA statement starts the DATA step and names the SAS data set being created.

24

The DATA statement is a writing instruction. Options in the DATA statement affect how the output data set is created but **not** how the data is read.

The INFILE Statement

If you are reading data from a raw data file, you need an INFILE statement.

General form of an INFILE statement:

> **INFILE** '*raw-data-file*' <*options*>;

The INFILE statement points to the raw data file being read. Options in the INFILE statement affect how SAS reads the raw data file.

25

The INPUT Statement

When you are reading from a raw data file, the INPUT statement follows the INFILE statement.

General form of an INPUT statement:

> **INPUT** *variable-specification* ...;

The INPUT statement describes the raw data fields and specifies how you want them converted into SAS variables.

26

Formatted Input

The input style tells SAS where to find the fields and how to read them into SAS.

> **INPUT** @*n variable-name informat*. ...;

@*n*   moves the pointer to the starting point of the field.

variable-name names the SAS variable being created.

informat   specifies how many positions to read and how to convert the raw data into a SAS value.

27

The INPUT Statement

Common SAS informats:

$w.   reads a standard character field, where *w* specifies the width of the field in bytes.

w.   reads a standard numeric field, where *w* specifies the width of the field in bytes.

DATE9.   reads dates in the form 31DEC2012.

28

An informat is a reading instruction. The informat used depends on the form of the field in the raw data file. For a complete list of SAS informats, see the *SAS Language Reference: Dictionary, Version 8*. Unless these attributes are specified elsewhere, SAS uses the informat to set the type and length of the variables you are reading from the SAS data set.

The Assignment Statement

To create a new variable in the DATA step, use an assignment statement:

> *variable-name=expression*;

The assignment statement creates a SAS variable and specifies how to calculate that variable's value.

29

SAS uses the *expression* to set the type and length for the new variable unless those attributes are specified elsewhere.

Create a SAS Data Set from a Raw Data File

```
data work.fltat1;
   infile 'raw-data-file';
   input @1 EmpID $5.
         @7 HireDate date9.
         @17 Salary 5.;
   Bonus=.05*Salary;
run;
```

30

Create a SAS Data Set from a Raw Data File

Partial Log

```
NOTE: 9 records were read from the infile
      'fltat1.dat'.
      The minimum record length was 21.
      The maximum record length was 21.
NOTE: The data set WORK.FLTAT1 has
      9 observations and 4 variables.
```

31   c01s2d1.sas

1.3   Review of DATA Step Processing

Objectives

- Review the two phases of DATA step processing.

33

Create a SAS Data Set from Raw Data

```
data work.fltat1;
   infile 'raw-data-file';
   input @1 EmpID $5.
         @7 HireDate date9.
         @17 Salary 5.;
   Bonus=.05*Salary;
run;
```

34

Processing the DATA Step

The SAS System processes the DATA step in two phases:

- compilation
- execution.

35

Compilation

During compilation, SAS

- checks code for syntax errors
- translates code to machine code
- establishes an area of memory called the *input buffer* if reading raw data
- establishes an area of memory called the *Program Data Vector* (PDV)
- assigns required attributes to variables
- creates the descriptor portion of the new data set.

36

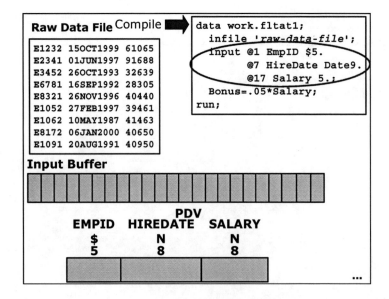

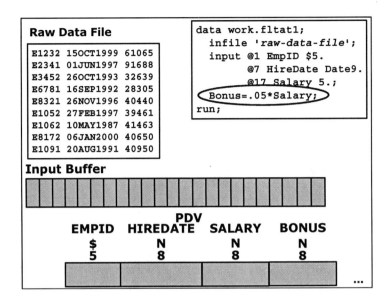

The INPUT statement creates the variables **EmpID**, **Salary**, and **HireDate** and assigns type and length for each variable. The assignment statement creates **Bonus** and sets its type and length. If a variable is referenced multiple times in a DATA step, the attributes are set at the first encounter.

Execution

During the execution phase, SAS

- initializes the PDV to missing
- reads data values into the PDV
- carries out assignment statements and conditional processing
- writes the observation in the PDV to the output SAS data set at the end of the DATA step (by default)
- returns to the top of the DATA step
- initializes any variables that are not read from a SAS data sets to missing (by default)
- repeats the process.

39

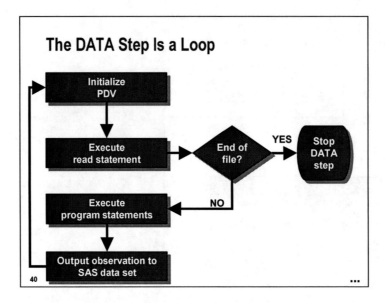

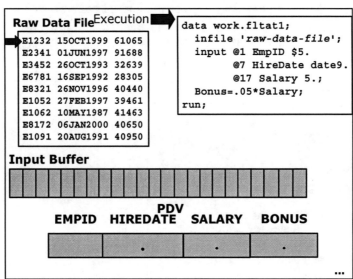

Before the first execution of the DATA step, SAS initializes all variables to missing.

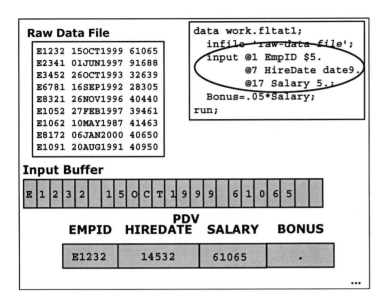

The INPUT statement

1. loads a record into the input buffer

2. reads the specified fields into the PDV.

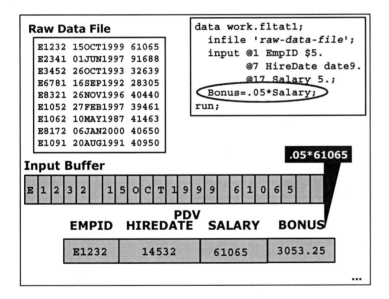

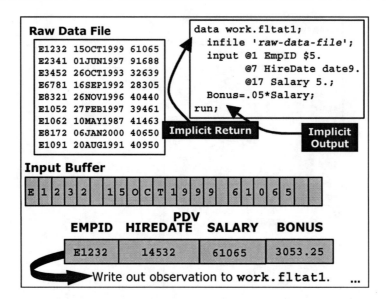

There is an implicit output at the bottom of the DATA step. By default, SAS outputs one observation every time the DATA step executes.

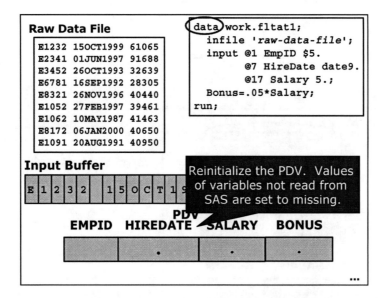

At every execution after the first, all variables not read from SAS are set to missing. This includes variables read with an INPUT statement and variables created with an assignment statement.

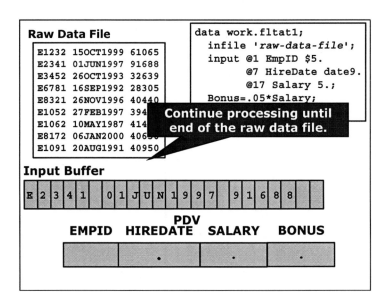

Raw Data File

```
E1232 15OCT1999 61065
E2341 01JUN1997 91688
E3452 26OCT1993 32639
E6781 16SEP1992 28305
E8321 26NOV1996 40440
E1052 27FEB1997 394
E1062 10MAY1987 414
E8172 06JAN2000 406
E1091 20AUG1991 40950
```

```
data work.fltat1;
   infile 'raw-data-file';
   input @1 EmpID $5.
         @7 HireDate date9.
         @17 Salary 5.;
   Bonus=.05*Salary;
```

Continue processing until
end of the raw data file.

Input Buffer

| E | 2 | 3 | 4 | 1 | | 0 | 1 | J | U | N | 1 | 9 | 9 | 7 | | 9 | 1 | 6 | 8 | 8 | | |

PDV

EMPID	HIREDATE	SALARY	BONUS
	.	.	.

1.4   Review of Displaying SAS Data Sets

Objectives

- Review procedures that display SAS data sets.

57

Create a SAS Data Set from Raw Data

```
data work.fltat1;
    infile 'raw-data-file';
    input @1 EmpID $5.
          @7 HireDate date9.
          @17 Salary 5.;
    Bonus=.05*Salary;
run;
```

58

Create a SAS Data Set from Raw Data

Partial Log

```
NOTE: 9 records were read from the infile
      'fltat1.dat'.
      The minimum record length was 21.
      The maximum record length was 21.
NOTE: The data set WORK.FLTAT1 has
       9 observations and 4 variables.
```

59

Viewing a SAS Data Set

You can use the

- CONTENTS procedure to display the descriptor portion of a SAS data set
- PRINT procedure to display the data in a SAS data set.

60

General form of a PROC CONTENTS step:

PROC CONTENTS DATA= *SAS-data-set*;
RUN;

General form of a PROC PRINT step:

PROC PRINT DATA=*SAS-data-set*;
RUN;

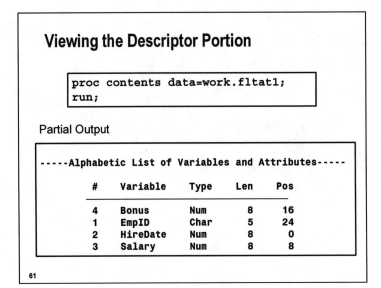

Viewing the Descriptor Portion

```
proc contents data=work.fltat1;
run;
```

Partial Output

```
-----Alphabetic List of Variables and Attributes-----

        #    Variable    Type    Len    Pos

        4    Bonus       Num      8     16
        1    EmpID       Char     5     24
        2    HireDate    Num      8      0
        3    Salary      Num      8      8
```

61

Viewing the Data Portion

```
proc print data=work.fltat1;
run;
```

Partial Output

```
            Hire
Obs   EmpID  Date     Salary     Bonus

 1    E1232  14532     61065    3053.25
 2    E2341  13666     91688    4584.40
 3    E3452  12352     32639    1631.95
 4    E6781  11947     28305    1415.25
 5    E8321  13479     40440    2022.00
```

62

PROC PRINT produces a *list report*, a report with a line for every observation in the data set. By default, all variables and all observations are displayed.

The NOOBS Option

The NOOBS option in the PROC PRINT statement suppresses the observation numbers in the list report.

General form of the NOOBS option:

PROC PRINT DATA=*SAS-data-set* NOOBS;
    <additional SAS statements>
RUN;

63

Viewing the Data Portion

```
proc print data=work.fltat1 noobs;
run;
```

Partial PROC PRINT Output

EmpID	Hire Date	Salary	Bonus
E1232	14532	61065	3053.25
E2341	13666	91688	4584.40
E3452	12352	32639	1631.95
E6781	11947	28305	1415.25

64

The values of **HireDate** are displayed as the number of days since January1, 1960.

The FORMAT Statement

The FORMAT statement applies a SAS format to specified variables. A format controls how data values are displayed.

General form of a FORMAT statement:

> **FORMAT** *SAS-variable(s) format-name. ...;*

You can format as many variables as you need using one FORMAT statement.

65

SAS Formats

General form of a SAS format:

> *<$>FORMAT-NAMEw.<d>;*

- $ indicates a character format.
- *FORMAT-NAME* is the name of the format.
- *w* specifies the total number of characters available for displaying the value.
- . is the required delimiter.
- *d* specifies the number of decimal places to be displayed for a numeric value.

66

Common SAS Formats

Examples of formats are

COMMA*w.d*   adds commas to numeric values.
Example: 46,543

DOLLAR*w.d*   adds commas and a dollar sign to numeric values.
Example: $46,543

MMDDYY10.   writes dates in the form 12/31/2012.

67

```
proc print data=work.fltat1 noobs;
   format HireDate mmddyy10.
          Salary Bonus dollar7.;
run;
```

EmpID	HireDate	Salary	Bonus
E1232	10/15/1999	$61,065	$3,053
E2341	06/01/1997	$91,688	$4,584
E3452	10/26/1993	$32,639	$1,632
E6781	09/16/1992	$28,305	$1,415
E8321	11/26/1996	$40,440	$2,022
E1052	02/27/1997	$39,461	$1,973
E1062	05/10/1987	$41,463	$2,073
E8172	01/06/2000	$40,650	$2,033
E1091	08/20/1991	$40,950	$2,048

Formats assigned in a procedure are temporary; they last only for that procedure. A FORMAT statement in a DATA step assigns the format permanently, making it available whenever the data set is used.

For example, the following code assigns permanent formats to the variables **Salary**, **Bonus**, and **HireDate**:

```
data work.fltat1;
   infile 'raw-data-file';
   input @1 EmpID $5. @7 HireDate date9. @17 Salary 5.;
   Bonus=Salary*.05;
   format HireDate mmddyy10. Salary Bonus dollar7.;
run;
```

The VAR Statement

To control which variables are displayed and the order in which they are displayed, use the VAR statement.

General form of a VAR statement:

> **VAR** *SAS-variable* ...;

69

```
proc print data=work.fltat1 noobs;
   format Salary Bonus dollar7.;
   var EmpID Bonus Salary;
run;
```

EmpID	Bonus	Salary
E1232	$3,053	$61,065
E2341	$4,584	$91,688
E3452	$1,632	$32,639
E6781	$1,415	$28,305
E8321	$2,022	$40,440
E1052	$1,973	$39,461
E1062	$2,073	$41,463
E8172	$2,033	$40,650
E1091	$2,048	$40,950

c01s4d1.sas

1.5   Working with Existing SAS Data Sets

Objectives

- Review the concept of SAS data libraries.
- Review the LIBNAME statement.
- Review creating a new SAS data set from an existing data set.
- Review conditional processing.

72

SAS Files

SAS data sets and other files are stored in SAS data libraries.

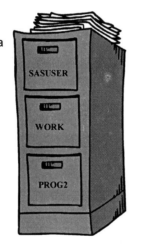

73

SAS Data Libraries

A *SAS data library* is a collection of SAS files that are recognized as a unit by SAS on your operating environment.

- WORK - temporary library

- SASUSER - permanent library

You can create and access your own permanent libraries.

- PROG2 - permanent library

74

SAS Data Libraries

The physical structure of a SAS data library depends on your operating system.

Directory-based operating systems (Windows or UNIX)
- any folder or sub-directory

OS/390 systems
- specially formatted sequential file

75

The LIBNAME Statement

The LIBNAME statement establishes the library reference (or *libref*), which is an alias for the SAS data library.

General form of the LIBNAME statement:

> **LIBNAME** *libref* '*SAS-data-library*' *<options>*;

The *libref* must be 8 characters or fewer.

76

Except for the 8-character length limit, the library reference follows the naming conventions for SAS data sets and variables. Specifically, it must

- begin with a letter or underscore

- include no special characters other than the underscore.

The LIBNAME Statement: Examples

OS/390 Batch and TSO
```
libname prog2 'edu.prog2.sasdata' disp=shr;
```

Windows, DOS, and OS/2
```
libname prog2 'c:\prog2';
```

UNIX
```
libname prog2 '/user/prog2';
```

77

Two-Level SAS Data Set Names

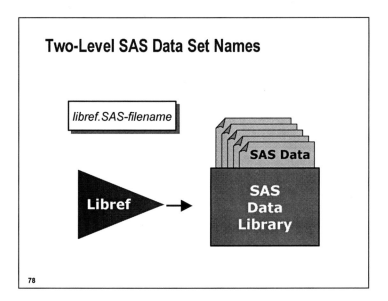

78

The WORK Library

The WORK library is the default library. If you do not specify a library reference on a SAS data set name, SAS assumes the libref is `work`.

`work.fltat1` ◀━━▶ `fltat1`

79

Accessing a Permanent SAS Data Set

There are two steps when accessing a permanent SAS data set:

1. Use a LIBNAME statement to set up a libref that points to the location of the data set.

2. Reference the data set using the libref as the first part of the data set name.

If the libref has already been assigned in the SAS session, you do **not** need to assign it again.

80

Viewing a Permanent SAS Data Set

Windows

```
libname prog2 'c:\workshop\winsas\prog2';

proc print data=prog2.test noobs;
run;
```

81

✏ Except for the name of the SAS data library, the SAS code does not change across operating systems.

Viewing a Permanent SAS Data Set

LName	Score
SMITH	0.90
JONES	0.57
MOORE	0.85
LEE	0.98
LONG	0.67
GREEN	0.70
FOREMAN	0.69

82

Viewing a Permanent SAS Data Set

UNIX

```
libname prog2 '/users/prog2';

proc print data=prog2.test noobs;
run;
```

83   ...

Viewing a Permanent SAS Data Set

LName	Score
SMITH	0.90
JONES	0.57
MOORE	0.85
LEE	0.98
LONG	0.67
GREEN	0.70
FOREMAN	0.69

84

Viewing a Permanent SAS Data Set

OS/390

```
libname prog2 '.prog2.sasdata';

proc print data=prog2.test noobs;
run;
```

85   ...

The period at the beginning of the OS/390 filename concatenates the userid to the front.

Viewing a Permanent SAS Data Set

```
LName       Score

SMITH        0.90
JONES        0.57
MOORE        0.85
LEE          0.98
LONG         0.67
GREEN        0.70
FOREMAN      0.69
```

86

Creating a Permanent SAS Data Set

There are two steps when creating a permanent SAS data set:

1. Use a LIBNAME statement to set up a libref that points to the location you want to save to.

2. Use the libref as the first level of the SAS data set name.

If the libref has already been assigned in the SAS session, you do **not** need to assign it again.

87

Creating a Permanent SAS Data Set

Windows

```
libname prog2 'c:\workshop\winsas\prog2';

data prog2.fltat1;
   infile 'fltat1.dat';
   input @1 EmpID $5.
         @7 HireDate date9.
         @17 Salary 5.;
   Bonus=.05*Salary;
run;
```

88   ...

Creating a Permanent SAS Data Set

UNIX

```
libname prog2 '/users/prog2';

data prog2.fltat1;
   infile 'fltat1.dat';
   input @1 EmpID $5.
         @7 HireDate date9.
         @17 Salary 5.;
   Bonus=.05*Salary;
run;
```

89   ...

Creating a Permanent SAS Data Set

OS/390

```
libname prog2 '.prog2.sasdata';

data prog2.fltat1;
    infile '.prog2.rawdata(fltat1)';
    input @1 EmpID $5.
          @7 HireDate date9.
          @17 Salary 5.;
    Bonus=.05*Salary;
run;
```

90

Create a SAS Data Set with SAS Data

LName	Score
SMITH	0.90
JONES	0.57
MOORE	0.85
LEE	0.98
LONG	0.67
GREEN	0.70
FOREMAN	0.69

The scores from a final exam are stored in the SAS data set `prog2.test`. The professor needs to assign each student a passing grade if the score is 0.7 or above and a failing grade otherwise. The variable `Score` should not appear in the output data set.

92

Desired Output

The data set **work.fnlscores** should contain only the variables **LName** and **Grade**.

LName	Grade
SMITH	Pass
JONES	Failed
MOORE	Pass
LEE	Pass
LONG	Failed
GREEN	Pass
FOREMAN	Failed

93

The SET Statement

Use a SET statement to read a SAS data set.

General form of a SET statement:

> **SET** *SAS-data-set <options>*;

The SET statement points to the SAS data set(s) to be read. Options in the SET statement affect how the data is read.

94

IF-THEN ELSE Statements

One method used to assign values or execute statements conditionally is IF-THEN ELSE statements.

> **IF** *condition* **THEN** *statement*;
>   **<ELSE IF** *condition* **THEN** *statement*;**>**
>   ...
>   **<ELSE** *statement*;**>**

95

The LENGTH Statement

When creating character variables with conditional logic or functions, it is usually a good idea to assign the lengths explicitly using a LENGTH statement.

General form of a LENGTH statement:

> **LENGTH** *variable-name <$> length-specification ...*;

96

SAS sets type and length the first time these attributes are referenced in the program. Once set, they cannot be changed. When using a LENGTH statement, be certain that it is the first statement to reference the variable.

The DROP Statement

To drop variables that are read or created during the DATA step, use a DROP statement.

General form of a DROP statement:

> **DROP** *SAS-variable(s)*;

Variables dropped with a DROP statement are read into the PDV but are not output to the new SAS data set. They are available for processing during the DATA step.

97

A KEEP statement is also valid for selecting variables to output to a SAS data set:

> **KEEP** *SAS-variable(s)*;

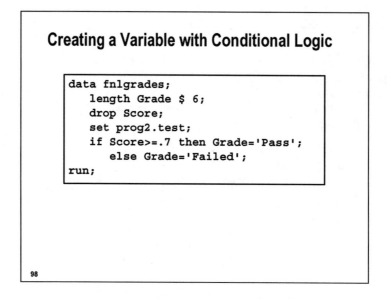

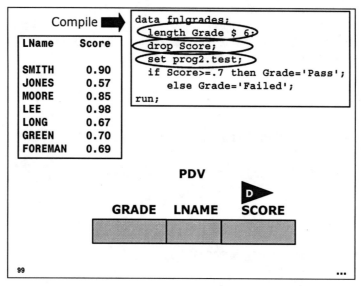

The placement of the LENGTH statement in the DATA step determines the position of the new variable in the PDV and the default order in the output data set. Because the LENGTH statement appears before the SET statement, **Grade** precedes the variables obtained from the **prog2.test** data set. Moving the LENGTH statement after the SET statement would add **Grade** to the end of the PDV.

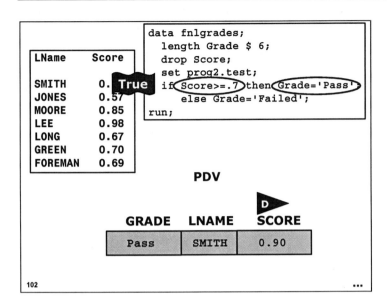

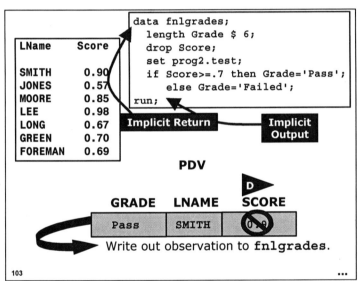

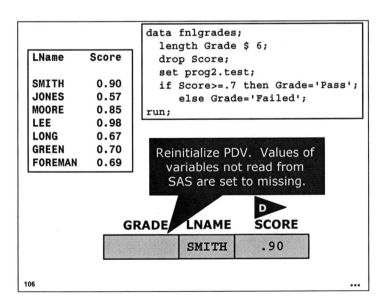

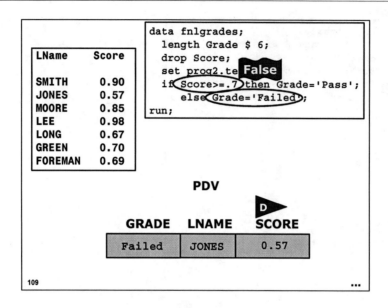

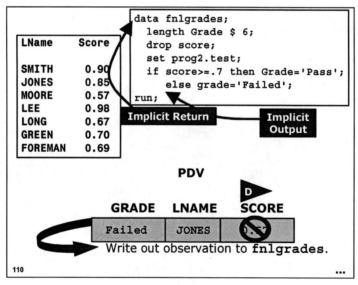

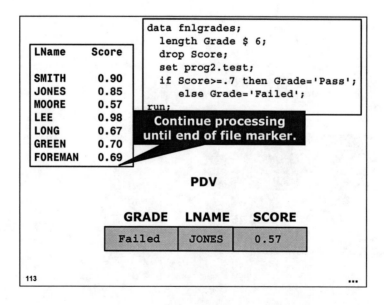

SAS data sets contain an end of file marker that signals the end of the data file. When SAS encounters the end of file marker, SAS stops the DATA step and goes on to the next step.

The VAR Statement

To control which variables are displayed and the order in which they are displayed, use the VAR statement.

General form of the VAR statement:

VAR *SAS-variable … ;*

115

Using the VAR Statement

```
proc print data=fnlgrades noobs;
   var LName Grade;
run;
```

LName	Grade
SMITH	Pass
JONES	Failed
MOORE	Pass
LEE	Pass
LONG	Failed
GREEN	Pass
FOREMAN	Failed

116   c01s5d2.sas

1.6   Prerequisite Syntax

The following is a syntax guide to statements and procedures you should know before starting this class.

Statements Valid Only in a DATA Step

To start the DATA step and name the data set being created:

> **DATA** *SAS-data set*;

To use a raw data file as input:

> **INFILE** '*raw-data-file*' *<options>*;

and

> **INPUT** *variable-specifications*;

To use a SAS data set as input:

> **SET** *SAS-data-set <options>*;

To create a new variable (assignment statement):

> *variable-name=expression*;

To perform conditional processing:

> **IF** *condition* **THEN** *statement*;
>   *<***ELSE IF** *condition* **THEN** *statement;>*
>
>   …
>   *<***ELSE** *statement;>*

DATA Step Compile-Time-Only Statements

To explicitly set the length of a variable:

> **LENGTH** *variable-name <$> length-specification ...;*

To drop a variable or variables on output:

> **DROP** *SAS variable(s) to be dropped;*

or

> **KEEP** *SAS variable(s) to be kept;*

Procedures

To display the descriptor portion of a SAS data set:

> **PROC CONTENTS** DATA=*SAS-data-set;*
> **RUN;**

To create a list report of a SAS data set:

> **PROC PRINT** DATA=*SAS-data-set* <NOOBS>;
> **RUN;**

To control which variables are shown in the PROC PRINT and their order:

> **VAR** *SAS-variable(s);*

Statements Valid in a Procedure or DATA Step

To apply a format to a variable or variables:

> **FORMAT** *variable-name format. ...;*

General form of a format name

> *<$>FORMAT-NAMEw.<d>*;

where

$	indicates a character format.
FORMAT-NAME	is the name of the format.
w	specifies the total characters available for displaying the value.
.	is the required delimiter.
d	specifies the number of decimal places to be displayed for a numeric value.

Common Numeric Formats

COMMA*w.d*	adds commas to the value.
DOLLAR*w.d*	adds dollar signs and commas to the value.
MMDDYY10.	displays SAS dates in the form: 12/31/2012.
DATE9.	displays SAS dates in the form: 31DEC2012.

Global Statements

To assign a library reference to a SAS data library:

> **LIBNAME** *libref* '*operating-system-location*';

To assign a header to SAS output:

> **TITLE***n* '*header*';

You can specify up to 10 titles. TITLE is equivalent to TITLE1.

✎ When a title has been set, it stays in effect until it is changed or canceled, or until the SAS session is ended.

1.7   Navigating the SAS Windowing Environment (Self-Study)

These instructions are intended for students navigating the SAS windowing environment on SAS classroom machines. They may not be appropriate for all sites.

Navigating the SAS Windowing Environment on Windows

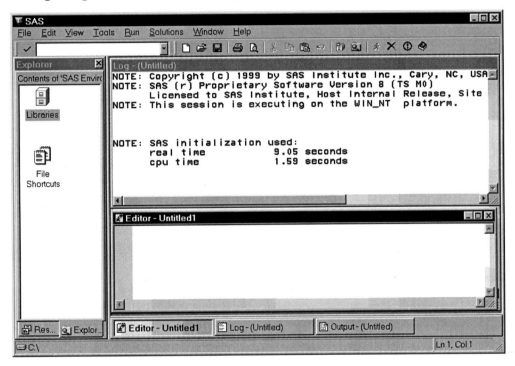

The Enhanced Editor (the default editor on Windows) provides many helpful features. The Enhanced Editor is not automatically cleared when code is submitted. You can use the Program Editor (the default editor in Version 6 and earlier) by selecting **View** ➪ **Program Editor**.

Navigating the Windows

To navigate to any window, do one of the following:

- Select its button at the bottom of the screen (if the window is open).
- Select the window name from the View pull-down menu.
- Type the name of the window at the command box and press Enter.

To close any window, do one of the following:

- Select ☒ in the upper-right corner of the window.
- Issue the END command in the command box.

Opening a SAS Program

To open a SAS program, the Program Editor or the Enhanced Editor must be the active window.

1. Select **File** ⇨ **Open** or click on [icon]. A Windows dialog box appears.

2. Navigate through the folders and highlight the program.

3. Select **OK**.

Submitting a SAS Program

To submit a program, the Program Editor or the Enhanced Editor must be the active window, and the code to be submitted must be in the window.

1. Highlight the code you want to submit. (This is not necessary if you are submitting the entire contents of the window.)

2. Issue the SUBMIT command by clicking on [icon], pressing the F3 key, or selecting **Run** ⇨ **Submit**.

Recalling Submitted Code

The Program Editor is cleared automatically every time code is submitted from it. To recall submitted code, make the Program Editor the active window, and do one of the following:

*   Select **Run** ⇨ **Recall**.
*   Issue the RECALL command from the command box.
*   Use the F4 shortcut key.

Saving a SAS Program

To save a SAS program, the Program Editor or the Enhanced Editor must be the active window, and the code you want to save must be in the window.

1. Select **File** ⇨ **Save As...** . A Windows dialog box appears.

2. Navigate to the folder in which you want to save the program.

3. Type a name for the program in the appropriate box.

4. Select **OK**.

Clearing Windows

To clear a window, do one of the following:

- Activate the window, type `clear` in the command box, and press Enter.
- Activate the window and select **Edit** ⇨ **Clear All**.
- Type `clear` and the name of the window in the command box and press Enter.

Issuing Multiple Commands at Once

To issue more than one command at once, type the commands in the command box separated by semicolons.

For example, to clear both the Log and Output windows, type the following in the command box:

```
clear log; clear output
```

Navigating the SAS Windowing Environment on UNIX

In the UNIX environment, SAS windows are floating, not docked. There is a floating toolbar with a command box and shortcut icons. Pull-down menus are at the top of each window.

Navigating the Window

To activate any window, do one of the following:

- Select its icon at the bottom of the screen.
- Select its name from the View pull-down menu.
- Type its name in the command box and press the Enter key.

Submitting a Program

To submit a SAS program, the Program Editor must be the active window and contain the code you want to submit. Do any of the following to submit the contents of the Program Editor:

- Issue the SUBMIT command from the command box.
- Use the F3 shortcut key.
- Select [⚘] from the toolbar.
- Select **Run** ⇨ **Submit**.

Recalling Submitted Code

The Program Editor is cleared automatically every time code is submitted from it. To recall submitted code, make the Program Editor the active window, and do one of the following:

- Select **Run** ⇨ **Recall**.
- Issue the RECALL command from the command box.
- Use the F4 shortcut key.

Saving a SAS Program

To save a SAS program, the Program Editor must be the active window, and the code you want to save must be in the window.

1. Select **File** ⇨ **Save As...** . A dialog box appears.

2. Navigate to the directory in which you want to save the program.

3. Type a name for the program in the appropriate box.

4. Select **OK**.

Clearing Windows

To clear a window, do one of the following:

- Activate the window, type `clear` in the command box, and press Enter.
- Activate the window and select **Edit** ⇨ **Clear All**.
- Type `clear` and the name of the window at the command box, and press Enter.

Issuing Multiple Commands at Once

To submit more than one command at once, type the commands in the command box separated by semicolons and press Enter.

For example, to clear both the Log and Output windows, type the following in the command box:

```
clear log; clear output
```

Navigating the SAS Windowing Environment on OS/390

The first time you log on:

1. Open the Output window by typing **output** on any command line and pressing Enter.

2. Issue the following command from the command line of the Output window. This prevents suspended output.

   autoscroll 0; wsave

Navigating the Windows

- Each window contains a command line.
- You can open any window by typing its name on any command line and pressing Enter.
- The PgUp and PgDwn keys on your keyboard move you from one open window to another.
- F7 and F8 enable you to scroll up and down within a window
- To close any window and return to the Program Editor, issue the END command or use the F3 key. If the Program Editor is active, the F3 key submits the code in the window.
- To maximize a window, type **Z** on the command line and press Enter. To restore the window to normal size, type **Z** on the command line of the maximized window and press Enter.

Including a SAS Program

To include a SAS program in your session, the Program Editor must be the active window.

1. Type **include 'name-of-SAS-program'** on the command line of the Program Editor window.

2. Press Enter.

Submitting a Program

To submit a SAS program, the Program Editor must be the active window and contain the code you want to submit. To submit code, do one of the following:

- Issue the SUBMIT command from the command line of the Program Editor.
- Use the F3 shortcut key.

Recalling Submitted Code

The Program Editor is cleared automatically every time code is submitted from it. To recall submitted code, make the Program Editor the active window and do one of the following:

- Issue the RECALL command from the command line.
- Use the F4 shortcut key.

Saving a SAS Program

To save a SAS program, the Program Editor must be the active window.

1. Type **file 'name-of-SAS-program'** on the command line of the Program Editor window.

2. Press Enter. A note appears at the bottom of the window.

Clearing Windows

To clear a window, do one of the following:

- Type **clear** on the command line of that window and press Enter.
- Type **clear** and the name of the window to be cleared at any command line and press Enter.

Editing SAS Program Code in the UNIX and OS/390 Environments

Program Editor Line Number Commands

The Program Editor in the UNIX and OS/390 environments uses line number commands. Use these commands to copy, paste, or delete program code.

I	inserts one line (after) the current line.
I*n*	inserts n lines (after) the current line.
IB	inserts one line (before) the current line.
IB*n*	inserts *n* lines (before) the current line.

D	deletes the current line.
D*n*	deletes *n* lines.
DD	deletes a block of lines. Type **dd** on the first and last lines of the block.

R	repeats the current line once.
R*n*	repeats the current line *n* times.
RR	repeats a block of lines once. Type **rr** on the first and last lines of the block.

Moving and Copying Code

To copy or move one line:

1.   Type **c** (to copy) or **m** (to move) the line you want to copy or move.

2.   Type **a** (for after) or **b** (for before) on the appropriate line to indicate where you want to copy or move the specified line to.

To copy or move a block of lines:

1.   Type **cc** or **mm** on the first line you want to copy or move.

2.   Type **cc** or **mm** on the last line you want to copy or move.

3.   Type **a** (for after) or **b** (for before) on the appropriate line to indicate where you want to copy or move the block of lines to.

Chapter 2   Controlling Input and Output

2.1 Outputting Multiple Observations

Objectives

- Explicitly control the output of multiple observations to a SAS data set.

3

A Forecasting Application

The growth rate of each division of International Airlines is forecast in **prog2.growth**. If each of the five divisions grows at its respective rate for the next three years, what will be the approximate size of each division at the end of each of the three years?

Partial Listing of **prog2.growth**

Division	Num Emps	Increase
APTOPS	205	0.075
FINACE	198	0.040
FLTOPS	187	0.080

4

A Forecasting Application

The output SAS data set, `forecast`, should contain 15 observations.

Partial Listing of **forecast**

Division	Increase	Year	New Total
APTOPS	0.075	1	220.38
APTOPS	0.075	2	236.90
APTOPS	0.075	3	254.67
FINACE	0.040	1	205.92
FINACE	0.040	2	214.16

5

The values of `NewTotal` can be displayed as whole numbers by using a SAS format.

Implicit Output (Review)

By default, every DATA step contains an implicit OUTPUT statement at the end of each **iteration** that tells the SAS System to write observations to the data set or data sets that are being created.

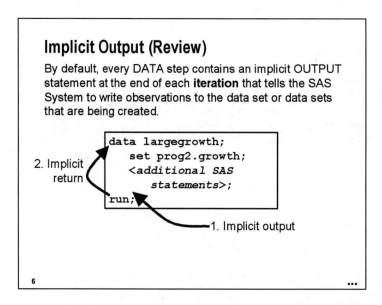

2. Implicit return

```
data largegrowth;
    set prog2.growth;
    <additional SAS
        statements>;
run;
```

1. Implicit output

6   ...

✎   An *iteration* is one execution of a sequence of computer operations or instructions that are performed a specified number of times or until a condition is met.

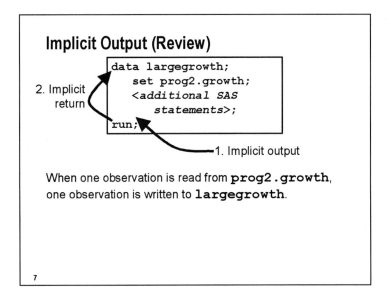

Implicit Output (Review)

2. Implicit return

```
data largegrowth;
    set prog2.growth;
    <additional SAS
       statements>;
run;
```

1. Implicit output

When one observation is read from **prog2.growth**,
one observation is written to **largegrowth**.

7

The OUTPUT Statement

The explicit OUTPUT statement writes the current
contents of the PDV to a SAS data set.

Placing an explicit OUTPUT statement in a DATA step
overrides the implicit output, and SAS adds an
observation to a data set only when an explicit OUTPUT
statement is executed.

> **OUTPUT** *<SAS-data-set-1 ...SAS-data-set-n>*;

8

Using an explicit OUTPUT statement without arguments causes the current
observation to be written to all data sets that are named in the DATA statement.

You can use the explicit OUTPUT statement to

- create two or more SAS observations from each line of input data
- write observations to multiple SAS data sets in one DATA step
- write observations to a SAS data set without any input data.

✎   Implicit return to the beginning of the DATA step occurs after the bottom of
the step is reached, not when an explicit OUTPUT statement is executed.

A Forecasting Application

```
data forecast;
   drop NumEmps;
   set prog2.growth;
   Year=1;
   NewTotal=NumEmps*(1+Increase);
   output;
   Year=2;
   NewTotal=NewTotal*(1+Increase);
   output;
   Year=3;
   NewTotal=NewTotal*(1+Increase);
   output;
run;
```

9

In years two and three, the existing value of **NewTotal** is used to calculate the new value of **NewTotal**.

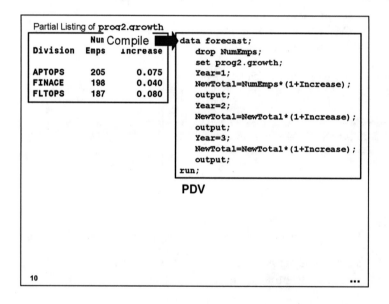

10   ...

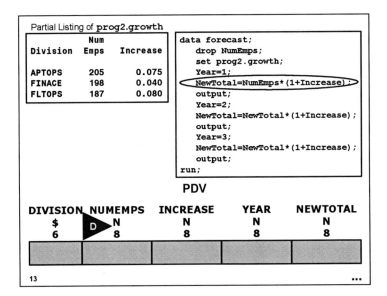

The `forecast` data set contains four variables: `Division`, `Increase`, `Year`, and `NewTotal`. The `Increase` variable is not displayed in the representations of `forecast`.

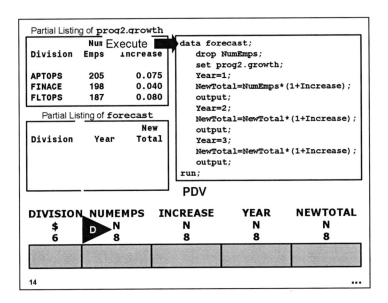

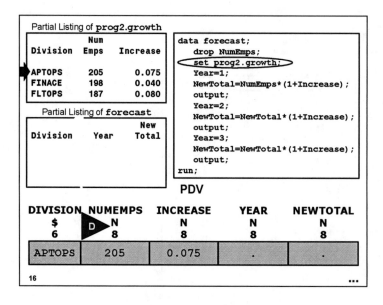

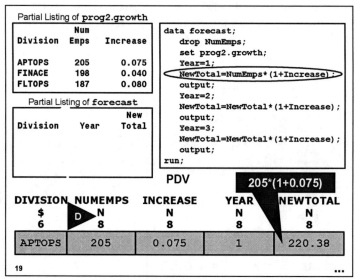

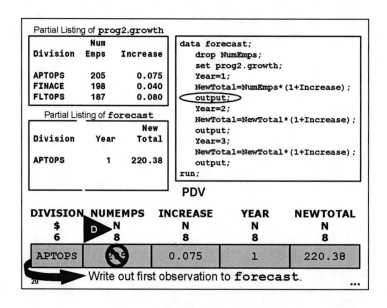

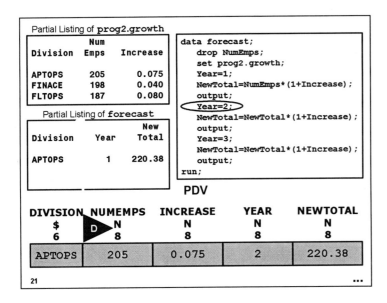

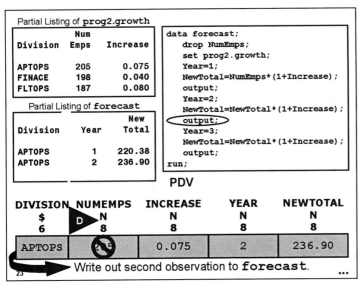

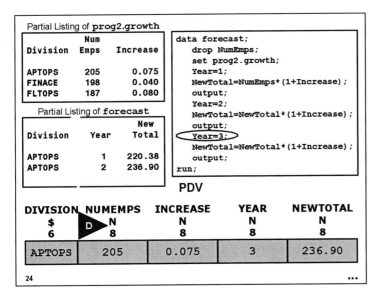

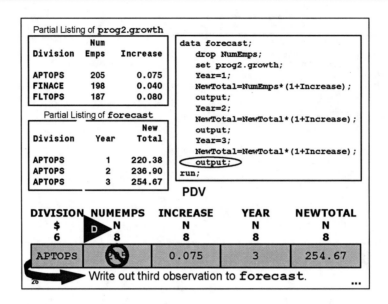

Partial Listing of **prog2.growth**

Division	Num Emps	Increase
APTOPS	205	0.075
FINACE	198	0.040
FLTOPS	187	0.080

Partial Listing of **forecast**

Division	Year	New Total
APTOPS	1	220.38
APTOPS	2	236.90
APTOPS	3	254.67

```
data forecast;
   drop NumEmps;
   set prog2.growth;
   Year=1;
   NewTotal=NumEmps*(1+Increase);
   output;
   Year=2;
   NewTotal=NewTotal*(1+Increase);
   output;
   Year=3;
   NewTotal=NewTotal*(1+Increase);
   output;
run;
```

PDV

DIVISION $ 6	NUMEMPS N 8	INCREASE N 8	YEAR N 8	NEWTOTAL N 8
APTOPS		0.075	3	254.67

Write out third observation to **forecast**.

26 ...

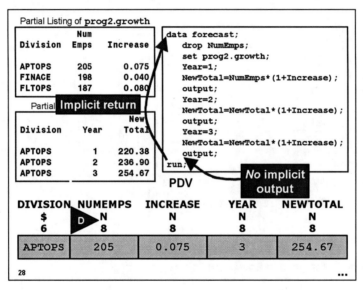

Partial Listing of **prog2.growth**

Division	Num Emps	Increase
APTOPS	205	0.075
FINACE	198	0.040
FLTOPS	187	0.080

Partial Listing of **forecast**

Division	Year	New Total
APTOPS	1	220.38
APTOPS	2	236.90
APTOPS	3	254.67

Implicit return

```
data forecast;
   drop NumEmps;
   set prog2.growth;
   Year=1;
   NewTotal=NumEmps*(1+Increase);
   output;
   Year=2;
   NewTotal=NewTotal*(1+Increase);
   output;
   Year=3;
   NewTotal=NewTotal*(1+Increase);
   output;
run;
```

No implicit output

PDV

DIVISION $ 6	NUMEMPS N 8	INCREASE N 8	YEAR N 8	NEWTOTAL N 8
APTOPS	205	0.075	3	254.67

28 ...

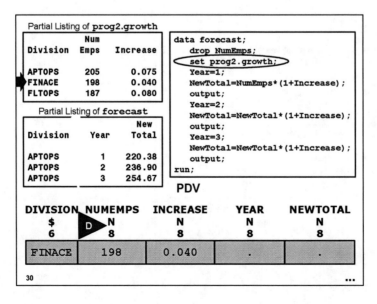

Partial Listing of **prog2.growth**

Division	Num Emps	Increase
APTOPS	205	0.075
FINACE	198	0.040
FLTOPS	187	0.080

Partial Listing of **forecast**

Division	Year	New Total
APTOPS	1	220.38
APTOPS	2	236.90
APTOPS	3	254.67

```
data forecast;
   drop NumEmps;
   set prog2.growth;
   Year=1;
   NewTotal=NumEmps*(1+Increase);
   output;
   Year=2;
   NewTotal=NewTotal*(1+Increase);
   output;
   Year=3;
   NewTotal=NewTotal*(1+Increase);
   output;
run;
```

PDV

DIVISION $ 6	NUMEMPS N 8	INCREASE N 8	YEAR N 8	NEWTOTAL N 8
FINACE	198	0.040	.	.

30 ...

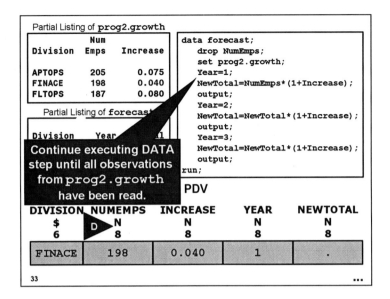

Partial Listing of **prog2.growth**

Division	Num Emps	Increase
APTOPS	205	0.075
FINACE	198	0.040
FLTOPS	187	0.080

```
data forecast;
   drop NumEmps;
   set prog2.growth;
   Year=1;
   NewTotal=NumEmps*(1+Increase);
   output;
   Year=2;
   NewTotal=NewTotal*(1+Increase);
   output;
   Year=3;
   NewTotal=NewTotal*(1+Increase);
   output;
run;
```

Partial Listing of **forecast**

| Division | Year | |

Continue executing DATA step until all observations from prog2.growth have been read.

PDV

DIVISION	NUMEMPS	INCREASE	YEAR	NEWTOTAL
$ 6	D N 8	N 8	N 8	N 8
FINACE	198	0.040	1	.

33   ...

A Forecasting Application

Partial Log

```
NOTE: There were 5 observations read from
the data set PROG2.GROWTH.
NOTE: The data set WORK.FORECAST has 15
observations and 4 variables.
```

34

A Forecasting Application

```
proc print data=forecast noobs;
   format NewTotal 6.;
run;
```

Partial PROC PRINT Output

Division	Increase	Year	New Total
APTOPS	0.075	1	220
APTOPS	0.075	2	237
APTOPS	0.075	3	255
FINACE	0.040	1	206
FINACE	0.040	2	214

35   c02s1d1.sas

Applying the 6. format to **NewTotal** does not change the values stored in the **forecast** data set. A SAS function can be used to change the stored value.

SAS functions are discussed in Chapter 5, "Data Transformations."

 **Exercises**

1. Outputting Multiple Observations

Rotating, or transposing, a SAS data set can be accomplished by using explicit OUTPUT statements in a DATA step. When a data set is rotated, the values of an observation in the input data set become values of a variable in the output data set.

Use explicit OUTPUT statements to rotate `prog2.donate` into a data set called `rotate`. Create four output observations in `rotate` from each input observation in `prog2.donate`.

The `rotate` data set should have three variables: `ID`, `Qtr`, and `Amount`. Print the data set to verify your results.

Partial Listing of `prog2.donate`

ID	Qtr1	Qtr2	Qtr3	Qtr4
E00224	12	33	22	.
E00367	35	48	40	30
E00441	.	63	89	90
E00587	16	19	30	29
E00598	4	8	6	1

Partial Listing of `rotate`

Obs	ID	Qtr	Amount
1	E00224	1	12
2	E00224	2	33
3	E00224	3	22
4	E00224	4	.
5	E00367	1	35
6	E00367	2	48
7	E00367	3	40
8	E00367	4	30
9	E00441	1	.
10	E00441	2	63
11	E00441	3	89
12	E00441	4	90

2.2   Writing to Multiple SAS Data Sets

Objectives

- Create multiple SAS data sets in a single DATA step.
- Use conditional processing to control the data set(s) to which an observation is written.

38

Writing to Multiple SAS Data Sets

The data set `prog2.military` contains information about air facilities maintained by the Army, Navy, Air Force, and Marines.

Create four SAS data sets, `army`, `navy`, `airforce`, and `marines`. Each of the four data sets should contain information about a single branch of the armed forces.

39

 Army air facilities are referred to as air fields, while Naval and Marine air facilities are referred to as air stations. Air Force air facilities are referred to as air bases.

Writing to Multiple SAS Data Sets

```
proc print data=prog2.military noobs;
   var Code Type;
run;
```

Partial PROC PRINT Output

Code	Type
SKF	Air Force
DPG	Army
HIF	Air Force
NFE	Naval
DAA	Army

40

The DATA Statement (Review)

The DATA statement begins a DATA step and provides names for any output SAS data sets.

You can create multiple SAS data sets in a single DATA step by listing the names of the output data sets separated by a space.

> **DATA** *<data-set-name-1> < ...data-set-name-n>*;

41

If you do not specify a SAS data set name or the reserved name _NULL_ in a DATA statement, then by default SAS automatically creates data sets with the names **data1**, **data2**, and so on in the **work** library.

The OUTPUT Statement (Review)

By default, the explicit OUTPUT statement writes the
current observation to every SAS data set listed in the
DATA statement.

You can specify the name(s) of a data set or data sets to
which SAS writes the observation.

OUTPUT <*SAS-data-set-1 ...SAS-data-set-n*>;

42

SAS-data-set-1 through *SAS-data-set-n* must also appear in the DATA statement.

🖉   To specify multiple data sets in a single OUTPUT statement, separate the
data set names with a space.

```
output data1 data2;
```

Writing to Multiple SAS Data Sets

```
data army navy airforce marines;
   drop Type;
   set prog2.military;
   if Type eq 'Army' then
      output army;
   else if Type eq 'Naval' then
      output navy;
   else if Type eq 'Air Force' then
      output airforce;
   else if Type eq 'Marine' then
      output marines;
run;
```

43

An alternate form of conditionally executing statements uses SELECT groups.

```
SELECT <(select-expression)>;
    WHEN-1 (when-expression-1 <...,when-expression-n>)
               statement;
   <...WHEN-n (when-expression-1 <...,when-expression-n>)
               statement;>
    <OTHERWISE statement;>
END;
```

The DATA step shown above could be rewritten to use SELECT groups as follows:

```
data army navy airforce marines;
   drop Type;
   set prog2.military;
   select (Type);
      when ('Army') output army;
      when ('Naval') output navy;
      when ('Air Force') output airforce;
      when ('Marine') output marines;
      otherwise;
   end;
run;
```

See SAS OnlineDoc for Version 8 or *SAS® Language Reference: Dictionary, Version 8,* for more information about using SELECT groups.

Writing to Multiple SAS Data Sets

Partial SAS Log

```
NOTE: There were 137 observations read
from the data set PROG2.MILITARY.
NOTE: The data set WORK.ARMY has 41
observations and 5 variables.
NOTE: The data set WORK.NAVY has 28
observations and 5 variables.
NOTE: The data set WORK.AIRFORCE has 64
observations and 5 variables.
NOTE: The data set WORK.MARINES has 4
observations and 5 variables.
```

44   c02s2d1.sas

 **Exercises**

2. Writing to Multiple SAS Data Sets

The data set **prog2.elements** contains information about the known elements on the periodic table. Each observation contains an element's name, symbol, atomic number, and state. The value of **State** refers to whether the element is a gas, liquid, solid, or synthetic at room temperature.

✎   A *synthetic element* is an element that is not present in nature.

Create four SAS data sets, **gas**, **liquid**, **solid**, and **synthetic**. Each data set will contain information about those elements that have that state at room temperature. Each of these four data sets should contain three variables; they should not contain the **State** variable.

✎   Character values are case-sensitive.

The **gas** data set should contain 10 observations. The **liquid** data set should contain 4 observations. The **solid** data set should contain 78 observations. The **synthetic** data set should contain 23 observations.

Partial Listing of **prog2.elements**

		Atomic	
Name	Symbol	Num	State
Actinium	Ac	89	Solid
Aluminum	Al	13	Solid
Americium	Am	95	Synthetic
Antimony	Sb	51	Solid
Argon	Ar	18	Gas
Arsenic	As	33	Solid
Astatine	At	85	Solid
Barium	Ba	56	Solid
Berkelium	Bk	97	Synthetic
Beryllium	Be	4	Solid
Bismuth	Bi	83	Solid
Bohrium	Bh	107	Solid
Boron	B	5	Solid
Bromine	Br	35	Liquid

Listing of `liquid`

Obs	Name	Symbol	Atomic Num
1	Bromine	Br	35
2	Cesium	Cs	55
3	Francium	Fr	87
4	Mercury	Hg	80

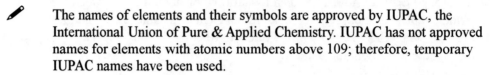

The names of elements and their symbols are approved by IUPAC, the International Union of Pure & Applied Chemistry. IUPAC has not approved names for elements with atomic numbers above 109; therefore, temporary IUPAC names have been used.

Currently, elements 113 (Ununtrium, Uut), 115 (Ununpentium, Uup), and 117 (Ununseptium, Uus) are not known.

2.3   Selecting Variables and Observations

Objectives

- Control which variables are written to an output data set during a DATA step.
- Control which variables are read from an input data set during a DATA step.
- Control how many observations are processed from an input data set during a DATA or PROC step.

47

Controlling Variable Output

By default, the SAS System writes all variables from every input data set to every output data set.

In the DATA step, the DROP and KEEP statements can be used to control which variables are written to output data sets.

48

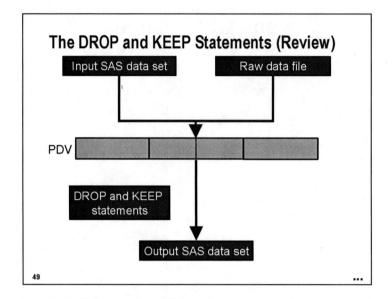

Creating Multiple SAS Data Sets (Review)

```
proc contents data=prog2.military;
run;
```

Partial PROC CONTENTS Output

```
-----Alphabetic List of Variables and Attributes-----

    #     Variable    Type    Len    Pos

    6     Airport     Char     40     37
    3     City        Char     20     12
    2     Code        Char      3      9
    5     Country     Char      3     34
    4     State       Char      2     32
    1     Type        Char      9      0
```

50

Creating Multiple SAS Data Sets (Review)

```
data army navy airforce marines;
   drop Type;
   set prog2.military;
   if Type eq 'Army' then
      output army;
   else if Type eq 'Naval' then
      output navy;
   else if Type eq 'Air Force' then
      output airforce;
   else if Type eq 'Marine' then
      output marines;
run;
```

51

Creating Multiple SAS Data Sets (Review)

Partial Log

```
NOTE: There were 137 observations read
from the data set PROG2.MILITARY.
NOTE: The data set WORK.ARMY has 41
observations and 5 variables.
NOTE: The data set WORK.NAVY has 28
observations and 5 variables.
NOTE: The data set WORK.AIRFORCE has 64
observations and 5 variables.
NOTE: The data set WORK.MARINES has 4
observations and 5 variables.
```

52

Controlling Variable Output

The DROP and KEEP statements apply to all output data sets.

However, when you create multiple output data sets, you can use the DROP= and KEEP= data set options to write different variables to different data sets.

53

The DROP= Data Set Option

The DROP= data set option excludes variables from processing or from output SAS data sets.

When the DROP= data set option is associated with an output data set, SAS does not write the specified variables to the output data set. However, the specified variables are available for processing.

SAS-data-set(DROP=*variable-1 variable-2 ...variable-n*)

54

variable-1 through *variable-n* lists one or more variable names separated by spaces.

✎ If the DROP= data set option is associated with an input data set, the specified variables are not available for processing.

The KEEP= Data Set Option

The KEEP= data set option specifies variables for processing or for writing to output SAS data sets.

When the KEEP= data set option is associated with an output data set, only the specified variables are written to the output data set. However, all variables are available for processing.

SAS-data-set(KEEP=*variable-1 variable-2 ...variable-n*)

55

variable-1 through *variable-n* lists one or more variable names separated by spaces.

✎ If the KEEP= data set option is associated with an input data set, only the specified variables are available for processing.

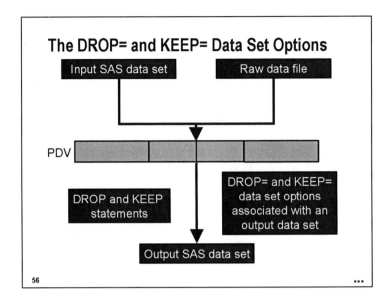

Controlling Variable Output

```
data army(drop=City State Country Type)
     navy(drop=Type)
     airforce(drop=Code Type)
     marines;
   set prog2.military;
   if Type eq 'Army' then
      output army;
   else if Type eq 'Naval' then
        output navy;
   else if Type eq 'Air Force' then
        output airforce;
   else if Type eq 'Marine' then
        output marines;
run;
```

57

✏️   You cannot specify the DROP= data set option in the OUTPUT statement.

Controlling Variable Output

Partial Log

```
NOTE: There were 137 observations read
from the data set PROG2.MILITARY.
NOTE: The data set WORK.ARMY has 41
observations and 2 variables.
NOTE: The data set WORK.NAVY has 28
observations and 5 variables.
NOTE: The data set WORK.AIRFORCE has 64
observations and 4 variables.
NOTE: The data set WORK.MARINES has 4
observations and 6 variables.
```

58

Controlling Variable Output

```
data army(keep=Code Airport)
     navy(keep=Code Airport City State Country)
     airforce(keep=Airport City State Country)
     marines;
  set prog2.military;
  if Type eq 'Army' then
     output army;
  else if Type eq 'Naval' then
     output navy;
  else if Type eq 'Air Force' then
     output airforce;
  else if Type eq 'Marine' then
     output marines;
run;
```

59

You cannot specify the KEEP= data set option in the OUTPUT statement.

Controlling Variable Output

Partial Log

```
NOTE: There were 137 observations read
from the data set PROG2.MILITARY.
NOTE: The data set WORK.ARMY has 41
observations and 2 variables.
NOTE: The data set WORK.NAVY has 28
observations and 5 variables.
NOTE: The data set WORK.AIRFORCE has 64
observations and 4 variables.
NOTE: The data set WORK.MARINES has 4
observations and 6 variables.
```

60

In many cases, you have a choice between using a DROP= data set option (or DROP statement) or a KEEP= data set option (or KEEP statement). Typically, choose the data set option or statement that minimizes the amount of typing.

For example, a combination of DROP= and KEEP= data set options can reduce the amount of typing necessary in the following example:

```
data army(keep=Code Airport)
     navy(drop=Type)
     airforce(drop=Code Type)
     marines;
   set prog2.military;
   if Type eq 'Army' then
      output army;
   else if Type eq 'Naval' then
      output navy;
   else if Type eq 'Air Force' then
      output airforce;
   else if Type eq 'Marine' then
      output marines;
run;
```

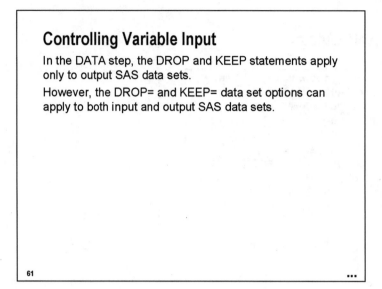

In PROC steps, you can use the DROP= or KEEP= data set options, but not the DROP or KEEP statements.

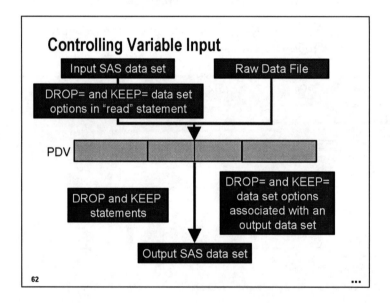

The INPUT statement controls which variables from a raw data file are read into the PDV.

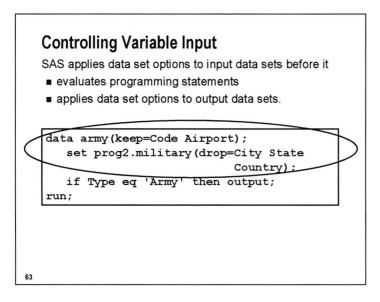

If a DROP or KEEP statement is used at the same time as a data set option, the statement is applied first.

If a DROP statement is used at the same time as a KEEP statement, or a DROP= data set option is used at the same time as a KEEP= data set option, only the KEEP statement or KEEP= data set option is applied.

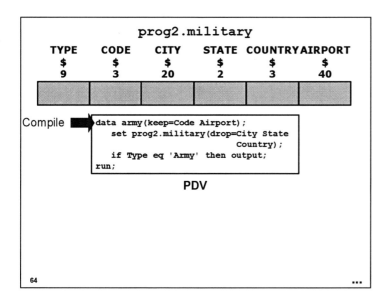

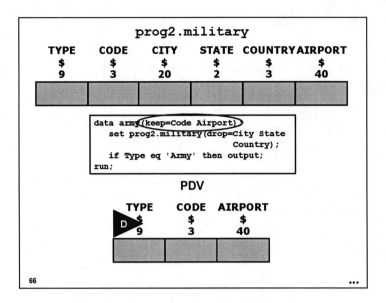

Controlling Which Observations Are Read

By default, SAS begins processing a SAS data set with the first observation and continues processing until the last observation.

The FIRSTOBS= and OBS= data set options can be used to control which observations are processed.

You can use FIRSTOBS= and OBS= with input data sets only. You cannot use either data set option in the DATA statement.

The OBS= Data Set Option

The OBS= data set option specifies an ending point for processing an input data set.

> *SAS-data-set*(OBS=*n*)

This option specifies the number of the last observation to process, not how many observations should be processed.

68

n specifies a positive integer that is less than or equal to the number of observations in the data set or zero.

 The OBS= data set option overrides the OBS= system option for the individual data set.

To guarantee that SAS processes all observation from a data set, you can use the following syntax:

> *SAS-data-set*(OBS=MAX)

Controlling Which Observations Are Read

The OBS= data set option in the SET statement stops reading after observation 25 in the **prog2.military** data set.

```
data army;
   set prog2.military(obs=25);
   if Type eq 'Army' then output;
run;
```

69

Controlling Which Observations Are Read

Partial Log

```
60    data army;
61       set prog2.military(obs=25);
62       if Type eq 'Army' then output;
63    run;

NOTE: There were 25 observations read
from the data set PROG2.MILITARY.
NOTE: The data set WORK.ARMY has 10
observations and 6 variables.
```

70

The FIRSTOBS= Data Set Option

The FIRSTOBS= data set option specifies a starting point
for processing an input data set.

> *SAS-data-set*(FIRSTOBS=*n*)

FIRSTOBS= and OBS= are often used together to define
a range of observations to be processed.

71

n specifies a positive integer that is less than or equal to the number of observations
in the data set.

 The FIRSTOBS= data set option overrides the FIRSTOBS= system option
for the individual data set.

Controlling Which Observations Are Read

The FIRSTOBS= and OBS= data set options in the SET statement read 15 observations from **prog2.military**. Processing begins with observation 11 and ends with observation 25.

```
data army;
    set prog2.military(firstobs=11 obs=25);
    if Type eq 'Army' then
        output;
run;
```

72

Controlling Which Observations Are Read

Partial Log

```
67   data army;
68       set prog2.military(firstobs=11 obs=25);
69       if Type eq 'Army' then output;
70   run;

NOTE: There were 15 observations read from the
data set PROG2.MILITARY.
NOTE: The data set WORK.ARMY has 5 observations
and 6 variables.
```

73

Controlling Which Observations Are Read

The FIRSTOBS= and OBS= data set options can also be used in a PROC step.

The following PROC PRINT step begins processing the **army** data set at observation 2 and stops processing the **army** data set after observation 4.

```
proc print data=army(firstobs=2 obs=4);
   var Code Airport;
run;
```

74

The DROP= and KEEP= data set options can be used to exclude variables from processing during a PROC step.

```
proc print data=army(drop=City State Country Type);
run;
```

However, DROP= and KEEP= do **not** affect the order in which the variables are processed.

Controlling Which Observations Are Read

Partial Log

```
75   proc print data=army(firstobs=2 obs=4);
76      var Code Airport;
77   run;

NOTE: There were 3 observations read from the
data set WORK.ARMY.
```

75

Controlling Which Observations Are Read

Partial Output

Obs	Code	Airport
2	LGF	Laguna Army Air Field
3	SYL	Roberts Army Air Field
4	HGT	Tusi Army Heliport

76   c02s3d1.sas

 **Exercises**

3.   Controlling Input and Output Size

Recall that **prog2.elements** contains information about the known elements on the periodic table. Each observation contains an element's name, symbol, atomic number, and state. The value of **State** refers to whether the element is a gas, liquid, solid, or synthetic at room temperature.

Partial Listing of **prog2.elements**

| | | Atomic | |
Name	Symbol	Num	State
Actinium	Ac	89	Solid
Aluminum	Al	13	Solid
Americium	Am	95	Synthetic
Antimony	Sb	51	Solid
Argon	Ar	18	Gas

Create two SAS data sets, **natural** and **synthetic**.

The **natural** data set will contain information about elements that are solids, liquids, or gases at room temperature. The **natural** data set should contain three variables, **Name**, **AtomicNum**, and **State**, and 92 observations.

The **synthetic** data set should contain two variables, **Name** and **AtomicNum**, and 23 observations.

Partial Listing of **natural**

| | | Atomic | |
Obs	Name	Num	State
1	Actinium	89	Solid
2	Aluminum	13	Solid
3	Antimony	51	Solid
4	Argon	18	Gas
5	Arsenic	33	Solid

Partial Listing of **synthetic**

| | | Atomic |
Obs	Name	Num
1	Americium	95
2	Berkelium	97
3	Californium	98
4	Curium	96
5	Dubnium	105

2.4 Writing to an External File

Objectives

- Write observations from a SAS data set to a comma-delimited external file.
- Use DATA step logic to insert a header record and a footer record into an external file.

79

Introduction

You can use the DATA step to write

- a custom report
- data to an external file to be read by other programming languages or software.

80

You can also use the EXPORT procedure to read data from a SAS data set and write it to an external data source. External data sources can include database tables, PC files, spreadsheets, and delimited external files.

    PROC EXPORT is available on the following operating environments: OS/2, UNIX, OpenVMS, and Windows.

Introduction

READING FROM AN EXTERNAL FILE	WRITING TO AN EXTERNAL FILE
The **DATA** statement begins the DATA step.	The **DATA** statement begins the DATA step.
The **INFILE** statement identifies an external file to read with an INPUT statement.	The **FILE** statement identifies an external file to write with a PUT statement.
The **INPUT** statement describes the arrangement of values in the input data record.	The **PUT** statement describes the arrangement of values in the output data record.

81

...

The DATA Statement

Usually, the DATA statement specifies at least one data set name that the SAS System uses to create an output data set.

Using the keyword _NULL_ as the data set name causes SAS to execute the DATA step without writing observations to a data set.

```
DATA   _NULL_;
```

82

The FILE Statement

The FILE statement can be used to specify the output destination for subsequent PUT statements.

General form of the FILE statement:

> **FILE** *file-specification <options>*;

You can use the FILE statement in conditional processing (IF-THEN/ELSE or SELECT) because it is executable.

83

file-specification identifies an external file that the DATA step uses to write output from a PUT statement. *file-specification* can have these forms:

'external-file' specifies the physical name of an external file, which is enclosed in quotation marks. The physical name is the name by which the operating environment recognizes the file.

fileref specifies the file reference for an external file. You must have previously associated *fileref* with an external file in a FILENAME statement or function, or in an appropriate operating environment command.

LOG is a reserved file reference that directs the output from subsequent PUT statements to the SAS log.

PRINT is a reserved file reference that directs the output from subsequent PUT statements to the same print file as the output that is produced by SAS procedures.

The default for *file-specification* is the SAS log.

You can use multiple FILE statements to write to more than one external file in a single DATA step.

You can use PRINT as your initial *file-specification* to verify the contents of your output file prior to creating an external file.

The FILENAME statement associates a SAS file reference with an external file or an output device.

FILENAME *fileref* *<device-type>* *'external-file'* *<host-options>*;

---

fileref　　　　　　specifies any SAS name.

device-type　　　specifies the type of device or the access method that is used if the fileref points to an input or output device or location that is not a physical file.

'external-file'　　specifies a physical name of an external file. The physical name is the name that is recognized by the operating environment.

host-options　　　specify details, such as file attributes and processing attributes, that are specific to your operating environment.

The PUT Statement

The PUT statement can write lines to the external file that is specified in the most recently executed FILE statement.

General form of the PUT statement:

PUT *variable-1 variable-2 ... variable-n*;

With *simple list output*, you list the names of the variables whose values you want written. The PUT statement writes a variable value, inserts a single blank, and then writes the next value.

84

variable-1 through *variable-n* are the variables whose values are written.

In addition to variable values, you can also use a quoted character string to specify a string of text to write. When a quoted character string is written, SAS does not automatically insert a blank space. The output pointer stops at the column that immediately follows the last character in the string.

The values of character variables are left-aligned in the field; leading and trailing blanks are removed.

A null PUT statement can be used to output a blank line:

```
put;
```

Modified List Output

Modified list output increases the versatility of the PUT statement because you can specify a SAS format to control how the variable values are written.

To use modified list output, use the colon (:) format modifier in the PUT statement between the variable name and the format.

> **PUT** *variable-1 : format-1.*
>   *variable-2 : format-2.*
>   .
>   .
>   .
>   *variable-n : format-n.*;

85

format-1. through *format-n.* specify formats to use when the data values are written. You can specify either SAS formats or user-defined formats.

The colon format modifier enables you to specify a format that the PUT statement uses to write the variable value. All leading and trailing blanks are still deleted, and each value is followed by a single blank.

    See SAS OnlineDoc for Version 8 or *SAS® Language Reference: Dictionary, Version 8* for a complete list of SAS formats and their usage.

Writing to an External File

The **prog2.maysales** data set contains information about houses. Read this data set and write the data to an external file.

prog2.maysales

Description	List Date	Sell Date	SellPrice
Colonial	13803	14001	355182.74
Townhouse	13894	14016	241225.17
Townhouse	14108	14392	238135.98
Ranch	14585	14736	219391.80
Victorian	14805	15106	358186.78

86

Writing to an External File

```
data _null_;
   set prog2.maysales;
   file 'raw-data-file';
   put Description
        ListDate : date9.
        SellDate : date9.
        SellPrice : dollar8.;
run;
```

Why is the $ omitted after **Description** in the PUT
statement?

87

Examples of raw data filenames:

OS/390	*userid*.prog2.rawdata(export)
Windows	c:\prog2\export.dat
UNIX	/prog2/export.dat

🖉   A FILENAME statement can be used to associate the fileref EXTFILE with
the raw data file:

```
filename extfile 'raw-data-file';
```

The FILE statement can be subsequently revised:

```
file extfile;
```

Writing to an External File

Partial SAS Log

```
NOTE: 5 records were written to the file
'export.dat'.
      The minimum record length was 34.
      The maximum record length was 38.
NOTE: There were 5 observations read from
the data set PROG2.MAYSALES.
```

Can you use PROC PRINT to view the raw data file?

88

The FSLIST Procedure

The FSLIST procedure enables you to browse external files that are not SAS data sets within an interactive SAS session.

> **PROC FSLIST** FILEREF=*file-specification <option(s)>*;
> **RUN**;

Remember to close the FSLIST window when you have finished browsing your external file.

89

---

file-specification specifies the external file to browse. *file-specification* must be specified, and it can be one of the following:

'external-file'   is the complete operating environment file specification for the external file. You must enclose the name in quotation marks.

Fileref   specifies the fileref of an external file. You must have previously associated *fileref* with an external file in a FILENAME statement or function, or in an appropriate operating environment command.

 Aliases for FILEREF= include FILE=, DDNAME=, and DD=.

You can use any text editor available for your operating environment to view the external file. For instance, Windows users can use Notepad or Microsoft Word, UNIX users can use emacs or vi, and OS/390 users can use ISPF.

Reading from an External File

```
proc fslist fileref='raw-data-file';
run;
```

```
Colonial 16OCT1997 02MAY1998 $355,183
Townhouse 15JAN1998 17MAY1998 $241,225
Townhouse 17AUG1998 28MAY1999 $238,136
Ranch 07DEC1999 06MAY2000 $219,392
Victorian 14JUL2000 11MAY2001 $358,187
```

How can you add a single row of column headers before the rows of data?

90

The _N_ Automatic Variable (Review)

The _N_ automatic variable is created by every DATA step.

Each time the DATA step loops past the DATA statement, _N_ is incremented by 1. Therefore, the value of _N_ represents the number of times the DATA step has iterated.

_N_ is added to the program data vector but is not output.

91

Writing to an External File

```
data _null_;
   set prog2.maysales;
   file 'raw-data-file';
   if _N_=1 then
      put 'Description ' 'ListDate '
          'SellDate ' 'SellPrice';
   put Description
       ListDate : date9.
       SellDate : date9.
       SellPrice : dollar8.;
run;
```

Why is the second PUT statement not contained in an ELSE statement?

92

The IF-THEN statement shown above can also be written as

```
if _N_=1 then
   put 'Description ListDate SellDate SellPrice';
```

Exercise caution when indenting or breaking lines within a quoted string. The following PUT statement produces unexpected results:

```
if _N_=1 then
   put 'Description ListDate SellDate
       SellPrice';
```

Because of the indention within the quoted string, the following results are produced:

```
Description ListDate SellDate        SellPrice
```

Writing to an External File

```
proc fslist fileref='raw-data-file';
run;
```

```
Description ListDate SellDate SellPrice
Colonial 16OCT1997 02MAY1998 $355,183
Townhouse 15JAN1998 17MAY1998 $241,225
Townhouse 17AUG1998 28MAY1999 $238,136
Ranch 07DEC1999 06MAY2000 $219,392
Victorian 14JUL2000 11MAY2001 $358,187
```

How can you add a footer record after the rows of data?

93

The END= Option in the SET Statement

The END= option in the SET statement creates and names a temporary variable that acts as an end-of-file indicator.

> **SET** *SAS-data-set* END=*variable <options>;*

The temporary variable, which is initialized to 0, is set to 1 when the SET statement reads the last observation of the data set listed.

The variable is not added to any new data set.

94

END= is an option in the SET statement. It is not a data set option; it is not enclosed in parentheses.

```
Writing to an External File
data _null_;
    set prog2.maysales end=IsLast;
    file 'raw-data-file';
    if _N_=1 then
        put 'Description ' 'ListDate '
            'SellDate ' 'SellPrice';
    put Description
        ListDate : date9.
        SellDate : date9.
        SellPrice : dollar8.;
    if IsLast=1 then
        put 'Data: PROG2.MAYSALES';
run;
```

95

```
if IsLast=1 then
    put 'Data: PROG2.MAYSALES';
```

can be replaced with

```
if IsLast then
    put 'Data: PROG2.MAYSALES';
```

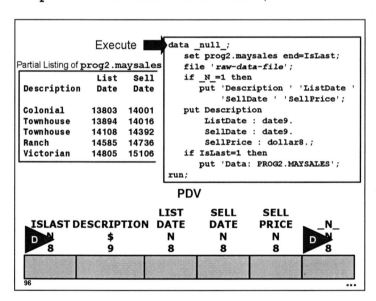

The **prog2.maysales** data set contains four variables: **Description**, **ListDate**, **SellDate**, and **SellPrice**. The **SellPrice** variable is not displayed in the representations of **prog2.maysales**.

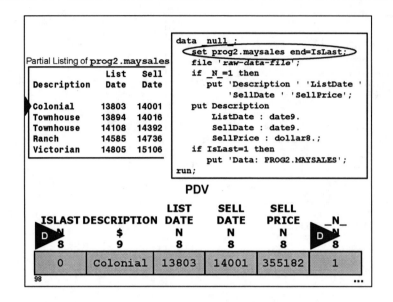

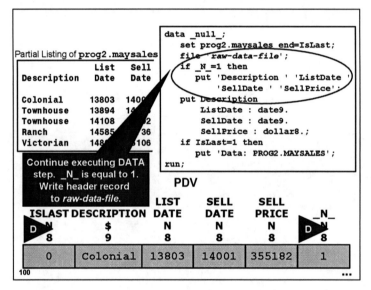

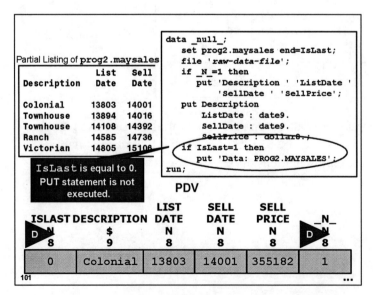

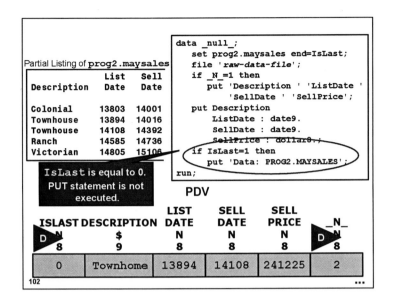

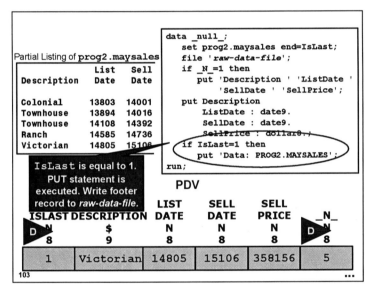

Writing to an External File

```
proc fslist fileref='raw-data-file';
run;
```

```
Description ListDate SellDate SellPrice
Colonial 16OCT1997 02MAY1998 $355,183
Townhouse 15JAN1998 17MAY1998 $241,225
Townhouse 17AUG1998 28MAY1999 $238,136
Ranch 07DEC1999 06MAY2000 $219,392
Victorian 14JUL2000 11MAY2001 $358,187
Data: PROG2.MAYSALES
```

104

Specifying an Alternate Delimiter

Use the DLM= option in the FILE statement to create a file with an alternate delimiter (other than a blank).

> **FILE** *file-specification* DLM='*quoted-string*'
>   *<other-options>*;

You can also specify a character variable whose value contains your delimiter, instead of a quoted string.

105

'*quoted-string*' specifies an alternate delimiter (other than the default, a blank) to be used for simple or modified list output. Although a character string or character variable is accepted, only the first character of the string or variable is used as the output delimiter.

    DLM= is an alias for DELIMITER=.

Writing to an External File

```
data _null_;
   set prog2.maysales end=IsLast;
   file 'raw-data-file' dlm=',';
   if _N_=1 then
      put 'Description,ListDate,'
          'SellDate,SellPrice';
   put Description
       ListDate : date9.
       SellDate : date9.
       SellPrice : dollar8.;
   if IsLast=1 then
      put 'Data: PROG2.MAYSALES';
run;
```

106

The IF-THEN statement shown above can also be written as

```
if _N_=1 then
   put 'Description,ListDate,SellDate,SellPrice';
```

Writing to an External File

```
proc fslist fileref='raw-data-file';
run;
```

```
Description,ListDate,SellDate,SellPrice
Colonial,16OCT1997,02MAY1998,$355,183
Townhouse,15JAN1998,17MAY1998,$241,225
Townhouse,17AUG1998,28MAY1999,$238,136
Ranch,07DEC1999,06MAY2000,$219,392
Victorian,14JUL2000,11MAY2001,$358,187
Data: PROG2.MAYSALES
```

What is the role of each comma in the records containing data?

107

Embedded Delimiters

These commas act as delimiters. The DLM= option in the FILE statement causes their appearance.

Partial Output

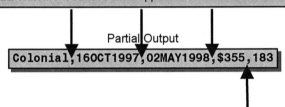

```
Colonial,16OCT1997,02MAY1998,$355,183
```

This comma acts as part of a SAS format. The DOLLAR8. format in the PUT statement causes its appearance.

How many data values are contained in each record?
How many comma-delimited fields are in each record?

108   ...

Accounting for Embedded Delimiters

Use the DSD option in the FILE statement to write data items that contain embedded delimiters.

> **FILE** *file-specification* DLM='*quoted-string*' DSD
> *<other-options>*;

Any data item that contains the specified delimiter is quoted with the double quotation mark (") when the data item is output.

109

Any double quotation marks that are embedded in data items that contain embedded delimiters are promoted. For example, if the FILE statement contains DLM=',' and DSD, the data item, `one of the "100 Best Companies to Work for in America"` is written as `"one of the ""100 Best Companies to Work for in America"""` in simple and modified list output.

 If you specify DSD, the default delimiter is assumed to be a comma.

Writing to an External File

```
data _null_;
   set prog2.maysales;
   file 'raw-data-file' dlm=',' dsd;
   put Description
        ListDate : date9.
        SellDate : date9.
        SellPrice : dollar8.;
run;
```

110

Writing to an External File

```
proc fslist fileref='raw-data-file';
run;
```

```
Colonial,16OCT1997,02MAY1998,"$355,183"
Townhouse,15JAN1998,17MAY1998,"$241,225"
Townhouse,17AUG1998,28MAY1999,"$238,136"
Ranch,07DEC1999,06MAY2000,"$219,392"
Victorian,14JUL2000,11MAY2001,"$358,187"
```

111   c02s4d1.sas

 **Exercises**

4. Writing to an External File

The data set **prog2.visits** contains information about patients who visited a doctor's office. Create a comma-delimited external file that contains the information from **prog2.visits**. The name of your external file is dependent on your operating environment.

The values of **Date** should be output in the form *mmddyyyy*, where *mm* is an integer that represents the month, *dd* is an integer that represents the day of the month, and *yyyy* is a four-digit integer that represents the year.

The values of **Fee** should be output with dollar signs and two decimal places. Be sure to use an appropriate format width.

Ensure that values that contain embedded delimiters are quoted with double quotation marks as they are output.

Use the FSLIST procedure to view your external file. Remember to close the FSVIEW window when you have finished browsing your external file.

Listing of **prog2.visits**

ID	Date	Fee
243-88-4364	22JUL2001	864.10
193-27-9815	22JUL2001	621.00
278-80-5793	23JUL2001	1228.75
926-36-3948	24JUL2001	897.25
618-96-1764	24JUL2001	897.25
679-72-1759	25JUL2001	952.50
618-96-1764	26JUL2001	731.50
679-72-1759	26JUL2001	1781.25
236-76-1574	29JUL2001	897.25
345-10-3912	29JUL2001	1228.75
679-72-1759	30JUL2001	1339.25
278-80-5793	30JUL2001	676.25

The values of **Date** are displayed with a permanently assigned DATE9. format. The values of **Date** should not be output using this format.

Desired Output (External File)

```
243-88-4364,07/22/2001,$864.10
193-27-9815,07/22/2001,$621.00
278-80-5793,07/23/2001,"$1,228.75"
926-36-3948,07/24/2001,$897.25
618-96-1764,07/24/2001,$897.25
679-72-1759,07/25/2001,$952.50
618-96-1764,07/26/2001,$731.50
679-72-1759,07/26/2001,"$1,781.25"
236-76-1574,07/29/2001,$897.25
345-10-3912,07/29/2001,"$1,228.75"
679-72-1759,07/30/2001,"$1,339.25"
278-80-5793,07/30/2001,$676.25
```

2.5 Solutions to Exercises

1. Outputting Multiple Observations

```
data rotate;
   drop Qtr1 Qtr2 Qtr3 Qtr4;
   set prog2.donate;
   Qtr=1;
   Amount=Qtr1;
   output;
   Qtr=2;
   Amount=Qtr2;
   output;
   Qtr=3;
   Amount=Qtr3;
   output;
   Qtr=4;
   Amount=Qtr4;
   output;
run;

proc print data=rotate;
run;
```

2. Writing to Multiple SAS Data Sets

```
data gas liquid solid synthetic;
   drop State;
   set prog2.elements;
   if State eq 'Gas' then
      output gas;
   else if State eq 'Liquid' then
      output liquid;
   else if State eq 'Solid' then
      output solid;
   else if State eq 'Synthetic' then
      output synthetic;
run;

proc print data=liquid;
run;
```

3.   Controlling Input and Output Size

```
data natural(keep=Name AtomicNum State)
     synthetic(keep=Name AtomicNum);
   set prog2.elements;
   if State eq 'Synthetic' then
      output synthetic;
   else
      output natural;
run;

proc print data=natural;
run;

proc print data=synthetic;
run;
```

Alternate Solution

```
data natural(keep=Name AtomicNum State)
     synthetic(keep=Name AtomicNum);
   set prog2.elements;
   if State in ('Solid','Liquid','Gas') then
      output natural;
   else
      output synthetic;
run;

proc print data=natural;
run;

proc print data=synthetic;
run;
```

4. Writing to an External File

```
data _null_;
   set prog2.visits;

   /* The DLM= option in the FILE statement separates
      the data values with commas.  The DSD option in
      the FILE statement accounts for embedded
      delimiters. */

   file 'visits.csv' dlm=',' dsd;
   put ID
       Date : mmddyy10.
       Fee : dollar10.2;
run;

   /* The FILE statement is applicable to the
      Windows and UNIX operating environments.
      OS/390 users should use:

      file '.prog2.rawdata(visits)'; */

proc fslist fileref='visits.csv';
run;

   /* The PROC FSLIST statement is applicable
      to the Windows and UNIX operating
      environments. OS/390 users should use:

      proc print fileref='.prog2.rawdata(visits)';
      run */
```

Chapter 3   Summarizing Data

3.1   Creating an Accumulating Total Variable

Objectives

- Understand how the SAS System initializes the value of a variable in the PDV.
- Prevent reinitialization of a variable in the PDV.
- Create an accumulating variable.

3

Creating an Accumulating Variable

SaleDate	SaleAmt
01APR2001	498.49
02APR2001	946.50
03APR2001	994.97
04APR2001	564.59
05APR2001	783.01
06APR2001	228.82
07APR2001	930.57
08APR2001	211.47
09APR2001	156.23
10APR2001	117.69
11APR2001	374.73
12APR2001	252.73

The SAS data set `prog2.daysales` contains daily sales data for a retail store. There is one observation for each day in April showing the date (`saleDate`) and the total receipts for that day (`SaleAmt`).

4

Creating an Accumulating Variable

The store manager also wants to see a running total of sales for the month as of each day.

Partial Output

SaleDate	Sale Amt	Mth2Dte
01APR2001	498.49	498.49
02APR2001	946.50	1444.99
03APR2001	994.97	2439.96
04APR2001	564.59	3004.55
05APR2001	783.01	3787.56

5

Creating Mth2Dte

By default, variables created with an assignment statement are initialized to missing at the top of the DATA step.

```
Mth2Dte=Mth2Dte+SaleAmt;
```

An accumulating variable must retain its value from one observation to the next.

6

The RETAIN Statement

General form of the RETAIN statement:

```
RETAIN variable-name <initial-value> ... ;
```

The RETAIN statement prevents SAS from re-initializing the values of new variables at the top of the DATA step.

Previous values of retained variables are available for processing across iterations of the DATA step.

7

The RETAIN Statement

The RETAIN statement

- retains the value of the variable in the PDV across iterations of the DATA step
- initializes the retained variable to missing before the first execution of the DATA step if an initial value is not specified
- is a compile-time-only statement.

8

The RETAIN statement has no effect on variables that are read with SET, MERGE, or UPDATE statements; values read from SAS data sets are automatically retained.

A variable referenced in the RETAIN statement appears in the output SAS data set only if it is given an initial value or referenced elsewhere in the DATA step.

Retain Mth2Dte and Set an Initial Value

If you do not supply an initial value, all the values of `Mth2Dte` will be missing.

```
retain Mth2Dte 0;
```

9

Creating an Accumulating Variable

```
data mnthtot;
   set prog2.daysales;
   retain Mth2Dte 0;
   Mth2Dte=Mth2Dte+SaleAmt;
run;
```

10

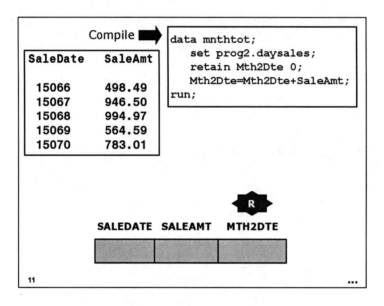

11

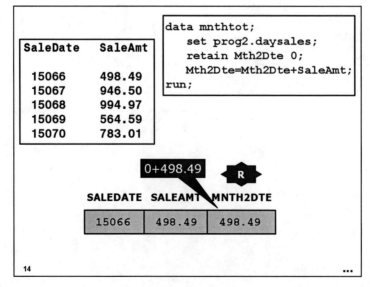

14

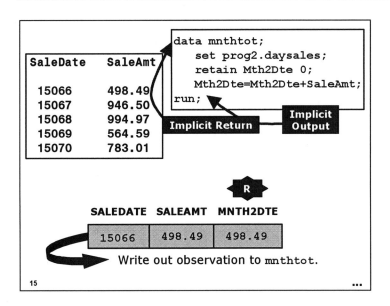

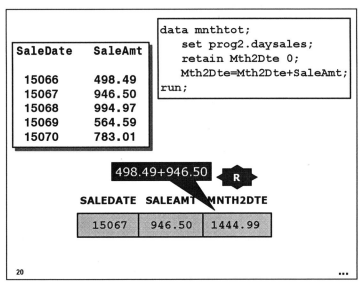

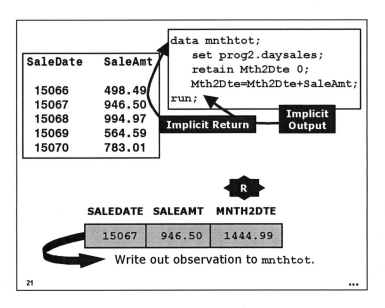

Creating an Accumulating Variable

```
proc print data=mnthtot noobs;
   format SaleDate date9.;
run;
```

Partial PROC PRINT Output

SaleDate	Sale Amt	Mth2Dte
01APR2001	498.49	498.49
02APR2001	946.50	1444.99
03APR2001	994.97	2439.96
04APR2001	564.59	3004.55
05APR2001	783.01	3787.56

31

Accumulating Totals: Missing Values

What happens if there are missing values for SaleAmt?

```
data mnthtot;
   set prog2.daysales;
   retain Mth2Dte 0;
   Mth2dte=Mth2Dte+SaleAmt;
run;
```

32

Undesirable Output

SaleDate	Sale Amt	Mth2Dte
01APR2001	498.49	498.49
02APR2001	.	.
03APR2001	994.97	.
04APR2001	564.59	.
05APR2001	783.01	.

Missing value

Subsequent values of Mth2Dte are missing

33

The result of any mathematical operation on a missing value is missing. With the above code, one missing value for **SaleAmt** causes all subsequent values of **Mth2Dte** to be missing. You can solve this problem by using the SUM function in the assignment statement:

Mth2Dte=sum(Mth2Dte,SaleAmt);

See Chapter 5, "Data Transformations," for details.

However, the sum **statement** is a more efficient solution.

The Sum Statement

When creating an accumulating variable, an alternative to the RETAIN statement is the sum statement.

General form of the sum statement:

> *variable + expression*;

34

 Like the assignment statement, the sum statement does not begin with a keyword.

The Sum Statement

The sum statement
- creates the variable on the left side of the plus sign if it does not already exist
- initializes the variable to zero before the first iteration of the DATA step
- automatically retains the variable
- adds the value of the *expression* to the variable at execution
- ignores missing values.

35

Accumulating Totals: Missing Values

```
data mnthtot2;
   set prog2.daysales2;
   Mth2Dte+SaleAmt;
run;
```

36

Accumulating Totals: Missing Values

```
proc print data=mnthtot2 noobs;
   format SaleDate date9.;
run;
```

Partial PROC PRINT Output

SaleDate	SaleAmt	Mth2Dte
01APR2001	498.49	498.49
02APR2001	.	498.49
03APR2001	994.97	1493.46
04APR2001	564.59	2058.05
05APR2001	783.01	2841.06

37   c03s1d1.sas

 **Exercises**

1. Creating an Accumulating Total Variable

The data set **prog2.states** contains the state name (**State**), the date the state entered the United States (**EnterDate**), and the size of the state in square miles (**Size**) for all 50 U.S. states. The data set is sorted by **EnterDate**.

Partial Listing of **prog2.states**

State	Size	EnterDate
Delaware	1955	07DEC1787
Pennsylvania	44820	12DEC1787
New Jersey	7418	18DEC1787
Georgia	57918	02JAN1788
Connecticut	4845	09JAN1788
Massachusetts	7838	06FEB1788
Maryland	9775	28APR1788
South Carolina	30111	23MAY1788

✎   The variable **EnterDate** has the permanent format DATE9.

Create the SAS data set **work.usarea** that contains the new variable **TotArea**, which is a running total of the size of the United States as each state was added, and the new variable **NumStates**, which shows how many states were in the union at that point.

Partial Listing of **work.usarea**

Obs	State	EnterDate	Size	TotArea	Num States
1	Delaware	07DEC1787	1955	1955	1
2	Pennsylvania	12DEC1787	44820	46775	2
3	New Jersey	18DEC1787	7418	54193	3
4	Georgia	02JAN1788	57918	112111	4
5	Connecticut	09JAN1788	4845	116956	5
6	Massachusetts	06FEB1788	7838	124794	6
7	Maryland	28APR1788	9775	134569	7
8	South Carolina	23MAY1788	30111	164680	8

3.2 Accumulating Totals for a Group of Data

Objectives

- Define First. and Last. processing.
- Calculate an accumulating total for groups of data.
- Use a subsetting IF statement to output selected observations.

40

Accumulating Totals for Groups

EmpID	Salary	Div
E00004	42000	HUMRES
E00009	34000	FINACE
E00011	27000	FLTOPS
E00036	20000	FINACE
E00037	19000	FINACE
E00048	19000	FLTOPS
E00077	27000	APTOPS
E00097	20000	APTOPS
E00107	31000	FINACE
E00123	20000	APTOPS
E00155	27000	APTOPS
E00171	44000	SALES

The SAS data set `prog2.empsals` contains each employee's identification number (`EmpID`), salary (`Salary`), and division (`Div`). There is one observation for each employee.

41

Desired Output

Human resources wants a new data set that shows total salary paid for each division.

Div	DivSal
APTOPS	410000
FINACE	163000
FLTOPS	318000
HUMRES	181000
SALES	373000

42

Grouping the Data

You must group the data in the SAS data set before you can perform processing.

43

Review of the SORT Procedure

You can rearrange the observations into groups using the SORT procedure.

General form of a PROC SORT step:

```
PROC SORT DATA=input-SAS-data-set
          <OUT=output-SAS-data-set>;
     BY <DESCENDING> BY-variable ...;
RUN;
```

44

The SORT Procedure

The SORT procedure

- rearranges the observations in a DATA set
- can sort on multiple variables
- creates a SAS data set that is a sorted copy of the input SAS data set
- replaces the input data set by default.

45

Sorting by Div

```
proc sort data=prog2.empsals out=salsort;
   by Div;
run;
```

46

Processing Data in Groups

Div	Salary		DivSal
APTOPS	20000		
APTOPS	100000		170000
APTOPS	50000		
FINACE	25000		
FINACE	20000		95000
FINACE	23000		
FINACE	27000		
SALES	10000		22000
SALES	12000		

47

BY-Group Processing

General form of a BY statement used with the SET statement:

```
DATA output-SAS-data-set;
    SET input-SAS-data-set;
    BY BY-variable ... ;
    <additional SAS statements>
RUN;
```

The BY statement in the DATA step enables you to process your data in groups.

48

When a BY statement is used with a SET statement, the data must

- be sorted or grouped in order by the BY variable(s)

- have an index based on the BY variable(s)

- reside in a DBMS table.

BY-Group Processing

A BY statement in a DATA step creates temporary variables for each variable listed in the BY statement.

General form of the names of BY variables in a DATA step:

```
First.BY-variable
Last.BY-variable
```

50

First. and Last. Values

- The **First.** variable has a value of 1 for the first observation in a BY group; otherwise, it equals 0.
- The **Last.** variable has a value of 1 for the last observation in a BY group; otherwise, it equals 0.

Use these temporary variables to conditionally process sorted, grouped, or indexed data.

51

First. / Last. Example

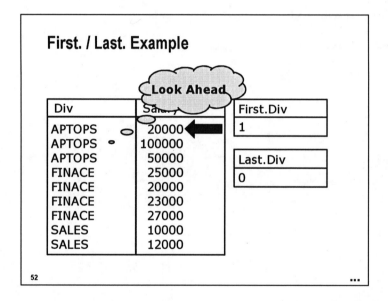

52 ...

First. / Last. Example

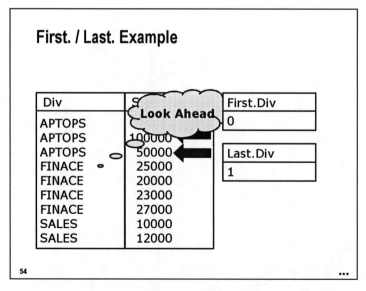

54 ...

What Must Happen When?

There is a three-step process for accumulating totals:

1. Set the accumulating variable to 0 at the start of each BY group.

2. Increment the accumulating variable with a sum statement (automatically retains).

3. Output only the last observation of each BY group.

57

Accumulating Totals for Groups

1. Set the accumulating variable to 0 at the start of each BY group.

```
data divsals(keep=Div DivSal);
   set salsort;
   by Div;
   if First.Div then DivSal=0;
   additional SAS statements
run;
```

58

Accumulating Totals for Groups

2. Increment the accumulating variable with a sum statement (automatically retains).

```
data divsals(keep=Div DivSal);
   set salsort;
   by Div;
   if First.Div then DivSal=0;
   DivSal+Salary;
   additional SAS statements
run;
```

59

First. / Last. Example

Div	Salary	DivSal
APTOPS	20000	20000
APTOPS	100000	120000
APTOPS	50000	170000
FINACE	25000	25000
FINACE	20000	45000
FINACE	23000	68000
FINACE	27000	91000
SALES	10000	10000
SALES	12000	22000

60

Subsetting IF Statement

The subsetting IF defines a condition that the observation must meet to be further processed by the DATA step.

General form of the subsetting IF statement:

IF *expression*;

- If the expression is true, the DATA step continues processing the current observation.
- If the expression is false, SAS returns to the top of the DATA step.

61

Accumulating Totals for Groups

3. Output only the last observation of each BY group.

```
data divsals(keep=Div DivSal);
   set salsort;
   by Div;
   if First.Div then DivSal=0;
   DivSal+Salary;
   if Last.Div;
run;
```

62

✎   The statement `if Last.BY-variable;` means if Last.*BY-variable* is
true. A numeric value is considered true if it is not equal to 0 and not
missing.

Subsetting IF Statement (Review)

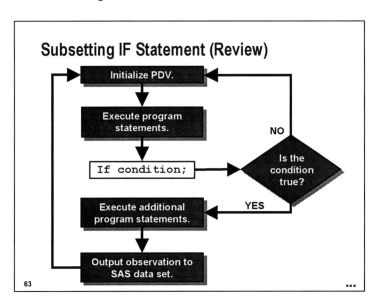

63

Accumulating Totals for Groups

Partial Log

```
NOTE: There were 39 observations read
      from the data set WORK.SALSORT.
NOTE: The data set WORK.DIVSALS has 5
      observations and 2 variables.
NOTE: DATA statement used:
      real time             0.74 seconds
      cpu time              0.33 seconds
```

64

Accumulating Totals for Groups

```
proc print data=divsals noobs;
run;
```

PROC PRINT Output

Div	DivSal
APTOPS	410000
FINACE	163000
FLTOPS	318000
HUMRES	181000
SALES	373000

65

c03s2d1.sas

Input Data

EmpID	Salary	Region	Div
E00004	42000	E	HUMRES
E00009	34000	W	FINACE
E00011	27000	W	FLTOPS
E00036	20000	W	FINACE
E00037	19000	E	FINACE
E00077	27000	C	APTOPS
E00097	20000	E	APTOPS
E00107	31000	E	FINACE
E00123	20000	NC	APTOPS
E00155	27000	W	APTOPS
E00171	44000	W	SALES
E00188	37000	W	HUMRES
E00196	43000	C	APTOPS
E00210	31000	E	APTOPS
E00222	250000	NC	SALES
E00236	41000	W	APTOPS

The SAS data set prog2.regsals contains each employee's ID number (EmpID), salary (Salary), region (Region), and division (Div). There is one observation for each employee.

66

Desired Output

Human resources wants a new data set that shows the total salary paid and the total number of employees for each division in each region.

Partial Output

Region	Div	DivSal	Num Emps
C	APTOPS	70000	2
E	APTOPS	83000	3
E	FINACE	109000	4
E	FLTOPS	122000	3
E	HUMRES	178000	5
NC	APTOPS	37000	2
NC	FLTOPS	28000	1

67

Sorting by Region and Div

The data must be sorted by **Region** and **Div**. **Region** is the primary sort variable. **Div** is the secondary sort variable.

```
proc sort data=prog2.regsals out=regsort;
   by Region Div;
run;
```

68

Sorting by Region and Div

```
proc print data=regsort noobs;
run;
```

Partial PROC PRINT Output

Region	Div	Salary
C	APTOPS	27000
C	APTOPS	43000
E	APTOPS	20000
E	APTOPS	31000
E	APTOPS	32000
E	FINACE	19000
E	FINACE	31000

69

Multiple BY Variables

```
data regdivsals;
   set regsort;
   by Region Div;
   additional SAS statements
run;
```

70

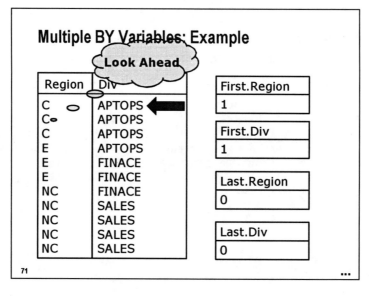

Multiple BY Variables: Example

71   ...

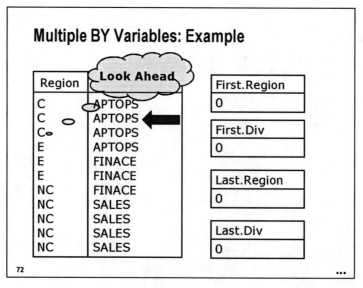

Multiple BY Variables: Example

72   ...

Multiple BY Variables: Example

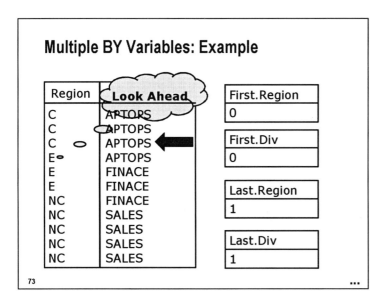

73   ...

Multiple BY Variables: Example

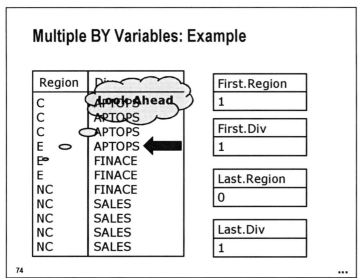

74   ...

Multiple BY Variables

When you use more than one variable in the BY statement, a change in the primary variable forces **Last.** *BY-variable*=1 for the secondary variable.

Region	Div	First. Region	Last. Region	First. Div	Last.Div
C	APTOPS	1	0	1	0
C	APTOPS	0	1	0	1
E	APTOPS	1	0	1	0
E	APTOPS	0	0	0	0
E	APTOPS	0	0	0	1
E	FINACE	0	0	1	0

76

Multiple BY Variables

```
    /*Summarize salaries by division*/
data regdivsals(keep=Region Div
                    DivSal NumEmps);
   set regsort;
   by Region Div;
   if First.Div then do;
      DivSal=0;
      NumEmps=0;
   end;
      DivSal+Salary;
      NumEmps+1;
   if Last.Div;
run;
```

77

Multiple BY Variables

Partial Log

```
NOTE: There were 39 observations read
      from the data set WORK.REGSORT.
NOTE: The data set WORK.REGDIVSALS has
      14 observations and 4 variables.
NOTE: DATA statement used:
      real time          0.07 seconds
      cpu time           0.07 seconds
```

78

Multiple BY Variables

```
proc print data=regdivsals noobs;
run;
```

Partial PROC PRINT Output

Region	Div	DivSal
C	APTOPS	70000
E	APTOPS	83000
E	FINACE	109000
E	FLTOPS	122000

79

c03s2d2.sas

 **Exercises**

2.   Accumulating Totals for a Group of Data

The data set `prog2.flymiles` has one observation for each trip a frequent flier has made with an airline. It shows the frequent flier number (`ID`) and the number of miles earned for that trip (`Miles`).

Partial Listing of `prog2.flymiles`

ID	Miles
F212	763
F161	272
F31351	800
F25122	733
F25122	859
F31351	437
F31351	1553
F31351	312
F161	224

✎   The data set is not sorted by `ID`.

Create a data set named `work.freqmiles` that has one observation for each frequent flyer as well as a new variable named `TotMiles`, which shows the total number of frequent flier miles the person has earned.

Listing of `work.freqmiles`

Obs	ID	Tot Miles
1	F161	5813
2	F212	6454
3	F25122	10208
4	F31351	5090

3.   Accumulating Totals for Groups of Data Using More than One BY Variable

The data set `prog2.flydays` has one observation for each trip a frequent flier has made with an airline. It contains the frequent flier number (`ID`), the number of miles earned for that trip (`Miles`), and a variable that indicates whether the miles were earned on a weekday flight (`Code='MF'`) or a weekend flight (`Code='SS'`).

Partial Listing of `prog2.flydays`

ID	Code	Miles
F212	SS	763
F161	MF	272
F31351	SS	800
F25122	SS	733
F25122	MF	859
F31351	SS	437
F31351	SS	1553
F31351	MF	312
F161	SS	2245

Create a SAS data set named `work.daymiles` that shows how many total miles each frequent flier earned for each type of flight.

Listing of `work.daymiles`

Obs	ID	Code	Tot Miles
1	F161	MF	2633
2	F161	SS	3180
3	F212	MF	976
4	F212	SS	5478
5	F25122	MF	7007
6	F25122	SS	3201
7	F31351	MF	2100
8	F31351	SS	2990

4. Detecting Duplicate Observations Using BY-Group Processing (Optional)

The data set `prog2.dupsals` has the variables `EmpID` and `Salary`.

Partial Listing of `prog2.dupsals`

EmpID	Salary
E00290	37000
E00379	25000
E00037	19000
E00037	27526
E00236	41000
E00236	59978
E00372	36000
E00372	41011
E00421	31000
E00424	17000

The data set should contain only one observation per employee (that is, all employee ID numbers should be unique). However, a SAS programmer has discovered some duplicate observations. Write a DATA step that sends duplicate observations to a data set named `work.baddata` and nonduplicate observations to a data set named `work.gooddata`.

Listing of `work.gooddata`

Obs	EmpID	Salary
1	E00048	19000
2	E00077	27000
3	E00107	31000
4	E00123	20000
5	E00155	27000
6	E00188	37000
7	E00196	43000
8	E00210	31000
9	E00259	32000
10	E00272	22000
11	E00290	37000
12	E00379	25000
13	E00388	25000
14	E00421	31000
15	E00424	17000
16	E00427	27000

Partial Listing of `work.baddata`

Obs	EmpID	Salary
1	E00004	42000
2	E00004	62902
3	E00009	34000
4	E00009	49761
5	E00011	27000
6	E00011	38193
7	E00036	20000
8	E00036	27057
9	E00037	19000
10	E00037	27526
11	E00097	20000

Hint 1: To create two data sets, list them both in the DATA statement. To control which data set an observation is written to, use the OUTPUT statement. (Refer to Chapter 2, "Controlling Input and Output.")

Hint 2: The variable `EmpID` is a unique identifier for each employee. If there is only one observation for an employee, then `First.EmpID` =1 and `Last.EmpID`=1. If that is not the case, the observation is a duplicate. Remember that in order to use BY-group processing, you must sort by the BY variable and use a BY statement in your DATA step.

3.3 Solutions to Exercises

1. Creating an Accumulating Total Variable

```
data usarea;
   set prog2.states;
   TotArea+Size;
   NumStates+1;
    /*Sum statements create TotArea and NumStates,
       retain, set  initial values to 0, and ignore
       missing values of size*/
run;

proc print data=usarea;
run;
```

2. Accumulating Totals for a Group of Data

```
   /*Data must be sorted or indexed for
     BY-group processing*/
proc sort data=prog2.flymiles out=milesort;
   by ID;
run;

data freqmiles(drop=miles);
   set milesort;
   by ID;
    /*BY statement create First.ID and Last.ID*/
   if First.ID then TotMiles=0;
    /*Set TotMiles to 0 when ID changes*/
   TotMiles+Miles;
      /*Sum statement creates TotArea, retains it,
        sets initial value to 0, and ignores missing
        values of size*/
   if Last.ID;  /*Output only the last of
                              each BY group*/
run;

   /*Create a list report of the data set to verify
     the output*/

proc print data=freqmiles;
run;
```

3. Accumulating Totals for a Group of Data Using More than One BY Variable

```
    /*Data must be sorted or indexed for
     BY-group processing*/
proc sort data=prog2.flydays out=daysort;
   by ID Code;
run;

data daymiles(drop=Miles);
   set daysort;
   by ID Code;
     /*BY statement creates First.ID, Last.ID
                            First.Code, and Last.Code*/
   if First.Code then TotMiles=0;
   /*Set TotMiles to 0 when subgroup changes*/
   TotMiles+Miles;
      /*Sum statement creates TotArea, retains it,
        sets initial value to 0, and ignores missing
        values of size*/
   if Last.Code then output;/*Output only the last of
                            each BY group*/
run;

   /*Create a list report of the data set to verify
     the output*/

proc print data=daymiles;
run;
```

4. Detecting Duplicate Observations Using BY-Group Processing (Optional)

```
/*Data must be sorted or indexed for
    BY-group processing*/
proc sort data=prog2.dupsals out=dupsort;
   by EmpID;
run;

data gooddata baddata;
    /*Both new data sets must be listed
      on the DATA statement*/
   set dupsort;
   by EmpID;
      /*BY statement creates First.EmpID and
        Last.EmpID*/
   if First.EmpID and Last.EmpID
       /*first and last of this ID means it's unique*/
       then output gooddata;
       else output baddata;
run;

/*Create list reports to verify results*/

proc print data=gooddata;
   title 'Non-Duplicate EmpIDs';
run;

proc print data=baddata;
   title 'Duplicate EmpIDs';
run;
```

Chapter 4   Reading and Writing Different Types of Data

4.1 Reading Delimited Raw Data Files

Objectives

- Read a space-delimited raw data file.
- Read a comma-delimited raw data file.
- Read a raw data file with missing data at the end of a row.
- Read a raw data file with missing data represented by consecutive delimiters.

3

List Input with the Default Delimiter

```
50001 4feb1989 132 530
50002 11nov1989 152 540
50003 22oct1991 90 530
50004 4feb1993 172 550
50005 24jun1993 170 510
50006 20dec1994 180 520
```

- The data is not in fixed columns.
- The fields are separated by spaces.
- There is one nonstandard field.

4

List Input

Raw data with fields not in fixed columns is called *free format*. Use list input to read free-format data.

The list input style signals to the SAS System that fields are separated by delimiters.

SAS then reads from delimiter to delimiter instead of from a specific location on the raw data record.

5

Delimiters

Common delimiters are

blanks

commas

tab characters

A space (blank) is the default delimiter.

6

List Input

General form of the INPUT statement for list input:

INPUT *var-1* $ *var-2* . . .*var-n*;

You must specify the variables in the order that they appear in the raw data file.

For standard data, specify a $ after the variable name if it is character. No symbol after the variable name indicates a numeric variable.

7

Input Data

This second field is a date. How does SAS store dates?

```
50001 4feb1989 132 530
50002 11nov1989 152 540
50003 22oct1991 90 530
50004 4feb1993 172 550
50005 24jun1993 170 510
50006 20dec1994 180 520
```

8

Standard Data

The term *standard data* refers to character and numeric data that SAS recognizes automatically.

Some examples of standard **numeric** data include

- 35469.93
- 3E5 (exponential notation)
- -46859

Standard **character** data is any character you can type on your keyboard. Standard character values are always left-justified by SAS.

9

The following are the only acceptable characters in a standard numeric field:

0 1 2 3 4 5 6 7 8 9 . E e - +

Nonstandard Data

The term *nonstandard data* refers to character and numeric data that SAS does not recognize automatically.

Examples of nonstandard numeric data include

- 12/12/2012
- 29FEB2000
- 4,242
- $89,000

10

Informats

To read in nonstandard data, you must apply an informat.

General form of an informat:

<$>INFORMAT-NAMEw.<d>

Informats are instructions that specify how SAS reads raw data.

11

$	indicates a character informat.
INFORMAT-NAME	is the name of the informat.
w	is an optional field width.
.	is the **required** delimiter.
d	is an optional decimal specification for numeric informats.

Informats

Examples of informats are

COMMA6.	reads numeric data ($4,242) and strips out selected nonnumeric characters, such as dollar signs and commas.
MMDDYY10.	reads dates in the form 12/31/2012.
DATE9.	reads dates in the form 29Feb2000.

12

Specifying an Informat

To specify an informat, use the colon (:) format modifier in the INPUT statement between the variable name and the informat.

General form of a format modifier in an INPUT statement:

> **INPUT** *variable : informat*;

13

Without the Colon

The colon signals that SAS should read from delimiter to delimiter.

If the colon is omitted, SAS reads the length of the **informat**, which may cause it to read past the end of the field.

- No error message is printed.
- You may see invalid data messages or unexpected data values.

14

Reading a Delimited Raw Data File

How does SAS determine the lengths of these variables?

```
data airplanes;
   infile 'raw-data-file';
   input ID $
         InService : date9.
         PassCap CargoCap;
run;
```

15

Lengths of Variables

When you use list input, the default length for character and numeric variables is 8 bytes.

You can set the length of character variables with a LENGTH statement or with an informat.

General form of a LENGTH statement:

LENGTH *variable-name <$> length-specification ...;*

16

Setting the Length of a Variable

```
data airplanes;
   length ID $ 5;
   infile 'raw-data-file';
   input ID $
         InService : date9.
         PassCap CargoCap;
run;
```

17

An informat also sets the length of a character variable. The following code produces the same result as the code used in the example:

```
data airplanes;
   infile 'raw-data-file';
   input ID : $5.
         InService : date9.
         PassCap CargoCap;
run;
```

✎   If you use this method to set the lengths of character variables, make sure to use the colon modifier.

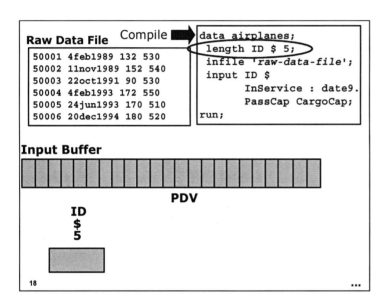

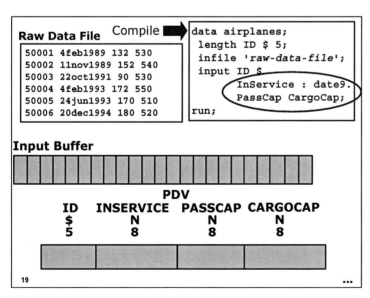

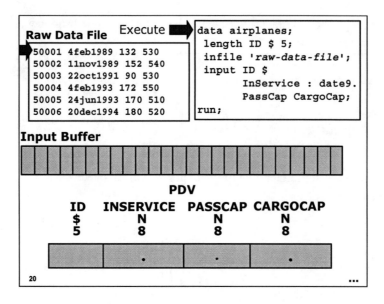

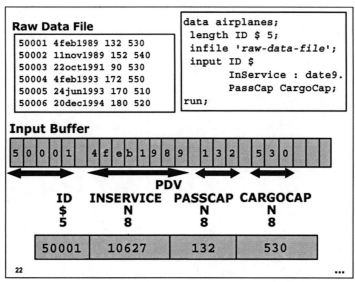

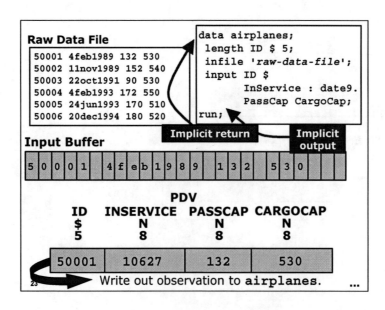

Reading a Raw Data File with List Input

```
proc print data=airplanes noobs;
run;
```

PROC PRINT Output

ID	In Service	Pass Cap	Cargo Cap
50001	10627	132	530
50002	10907	152	540
50003	11617	168	530
50004	12088	172	550
50005	12228	170	510
50006	12772	180	520

33

🖊 **InService** appears as a SAS date, the number of days since January 1, 1960. To change the date's appearance, apply a SAS date format with a FORMAT statement in the PRINT procedure. You can also use a FORMAT statement in the DATA step to permanently associate a format with a variable.

Non-Default Delimiter

The fields are separated by commas.

```
50001, 5feb1989, 132, 530
50002, 11nov1989,152, 540
50003, 22oct1991,168, 530
50004, 4feb1993,172, 550
50005, 24jun1993, 170, 510
50006, 20dec1994, 180,520
```

34

Using the DLM= Option

The DLM= option sets a character or characters that SAS recognizes as a delimiter in the raw data file.

General form of the INFILE statement with the DLM= option:

> **INFILE** *'raw-data-file' DLM='delimiter(s)'*;

Any character you can type on your keyboard can be a delimiter. You can also use hexadecimal characters.

35

If you specify more than one delimiter in the DLM= option, **any** of those characters is recognized as a delimiter. For example, DLM = ',!' indicates that either a comma or an exclamation point acts as a delimiter. By default, two or more consecutive delimiters are treated as one. The DSD option changes this behavior.

One example of a hexadecimal character is a tab character. To specify a tab character on a PC or on UNIX, type **dlm='09'x**. To specify a tab character on OS/390, type **dlm='05'x**.

Specifying a Delimiter

```
data airplanes2;
   length ID $ 5;
   infile 'raw-data-file' dlm=',';
   input ID $
         InService : date9.
         PassCap CargoCap;
run;
```

36

Missing Data at the End of a Row

```
50001 ,25feb1989,132, 530
50002, 11nov1989,152
50003, 22oct1991,168, 530
50004, 4feb1993,172
50005, 24jun1993, 170, 510
50006, 20dec1994, 180, 520
```

37

Missing Data at the End of a Row

By default, when there is missing data at the end of a row,

1. SAS loads the next record to finish the observation
2. a note is written to the log
3. SAS loads a new record at the top of the DATA step and continues processing.

38

Raw Data File

```
50001 ,25feb1989,132, 530
50002, 11nov1989,152
50003, 22oct1991,168, 530
50004, 4feb1993,172
50005, 24jun1993, 170, 510
50006, 20dec1994, 180, 520
```

```
data airplanes3;
   length ID $ 5;
   infile 'raw-data-file'
          dlm=',';
   input ID $
         InService : date9.
         PassCap CargoCap;
run;
```

Input Buffer

| 5 | 0 | 0 | 0 | 1 | | , | 2 | 5 | f | e | b | 1 | 9 | 8 | 9 | , | 1 | 3 | 2 | , | | 5 | 3 | 0 |

PDV

ID	INSERVICE	PASSCAP	CARGOCAP
$	N	N	N
5	8	8	8

| | . | . | . |

45   ...

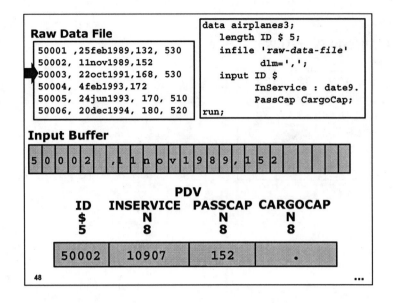

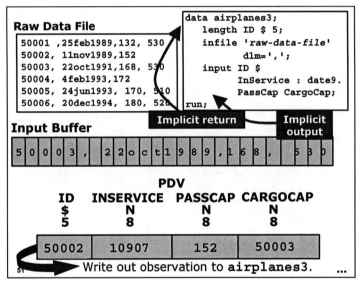

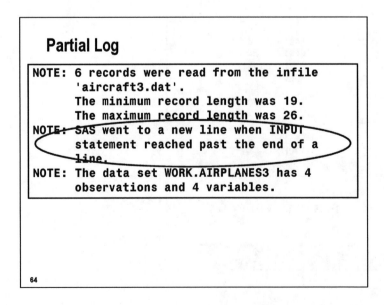

The number of records read **does not** match the number of observations in the SAS data set.

Missing Data at the End of the Row

```
proc print data=airplanes3 noobs;
run;
```

PROC PRINT Output

ID	In Service	Pass Cap	Cargo Cap
50001	10648	132	530
50002	10907	152	50003
50004	12088	172	50005
50006	12772	180	520

65

The MISSOVER Option

The MISSOVER option prevents SAS from loading a new record when the end of the current record is reached.

General form of the INFILE statement with the MISSOVER option:

> **INFILE** *'raw-data-file'* MISSOVER;

If SAS reaches the end of the row without finding values for all fields, variables without values are set to missing.

66

Using the MISSOVER Option

```
data airplanes3;
   length ID $ 5;
   infile 'raw-data-file' dlm=',' missover;
   input ID $
         InService : date9.
         PassCap CargoCap;
run;
```

67

Using the MISSOVER Option

Partial SAS Log

```
NOTE: 6 records were read from the infile
      'aircraft3.dat'.
      The minimum record length was 19.
      The maximum record length was 26.
NOTE: The data set WORK.AIRPLANES3 has 6 observations
      and 4 variables.
NOTE: DATA statement used:
      real time           0.42 seconds
      cpu time            0.07 seconds
```

68

Using the MISSOVER Option

```
proc print data=airplanes3 noobs;
run;
```

PROC PRINT Output

	In	Pass	Cargo
ID	Service	Cap	Cap
50001	10648	132	530
50002	10907	152	.
50003	11617	168	530
50004	12088	172	.
50005	12228	170	510
50006	12772	180	520

69

The MISSOVER option is also valid in formatted and column input and can be used when you want to ensure that incomplete fields are set to missing. Suppose there is a raw data file with the following values:

```
1
22
333
```

If the shorter records are not padded with blanks, reading the file with the following code produces all missing values:

```
data nums;
   infile 'file-name' missover;
   input num 4.;
run;
```

Notice the informat. This specifies that SAS is to look for exactly 4 bytes of data. In this case, the MISSOVER option indicates the variable is to be set to missing if the field is 3 bytes or less.

The **TRUNCOVER** option prevents SAS from loading a new record without setting incomplete fields to missing. If the same raw data file is read with the code

```
data nums;
   infile 'file-name' truncover;
   input num 4.;
run;
```

the resulting values are 1, 22, 333.

When used with list input and without informats, MISSOVER and TRUNCOVER produce the same results.

Another INFILE statement option used to deal with variable length records is the **PAD** option. The PAD option instructs SAS to make all records the same length by adding spaces to the end of shorter records. All records are padded to either the default record length or the record length specified by the LRECL= option. It is often used in the Windows operating environment with column or formatted input to keep carriage returns from affecting how raw data is read.

The PAD option is **not appropriate** for reading delimited files with list input because it can cause unexpected results. This is especially true if the data is delimited with spaces or if there is potentially more than one missing field at the end of some rows.

Missing Values without Placeholders

There is missing data represented by two consecutive delimiters.

```
50001 ,25feb1989,, 540
50002, 11nov1989,132, 530
50003, 22oct1991,168, 530
50004, 4feb1993,172, 550
50005, 24jun1993,, 510
50006, 20dec1994, 180,520
```

70

Missing Values without Placeholders

By default, SAS treats two consecutive delimiters as one. Missing data should be represented by a placeholder.

```
5 0 0 0 1 ,25feb1989,.,   5 3 0
```

71

Missing Values without Placeholders

```
data airplanes4;
   length ID $ 5;
   infile 'raw-data-file' dlm=',';
   input ID $
         InService : date9.
         PassCap CargoCap;
run;
```

72

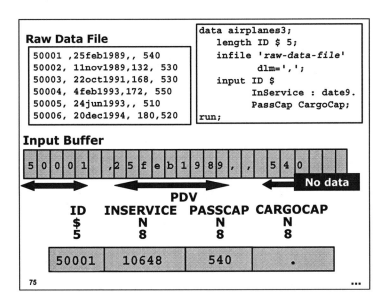

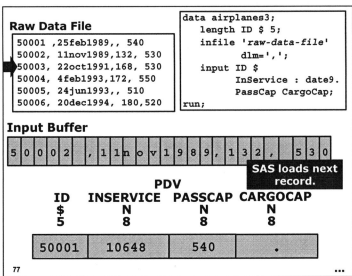

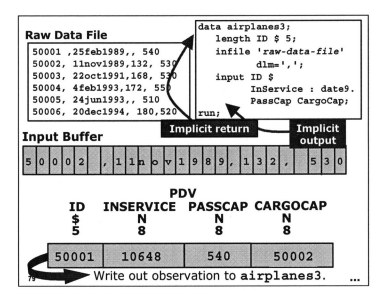

Missing Values without Placeholders

Partial Log

```
NOTE: 6 records were read from the infile
      'aircraft4.dat'.
      The minimum record length was 22.
      The maximum record length was 25.
NOTE: SAS went to a new line when INPUT
      statement reached past the end of a
      line.
NOTE: The data set WORK.AIRPLANES4 has 4
      observations and 4 variables.
```

83

Missing Values without Placeholders

```
proc print data=airplanes4 noobs;
run;
```

PROC PRINT Output

ID	In Service	Pass Cap	Cargo Cap
50001	10907	540	50002
50003	11617	168	530
50004	12088	172	550
50005	12228	510	50006

84

Missing Values without Placeholders

If your data does not have placeholders, use the DSD option.

```
5 0 0 0 1 ,25feb1989 ,, 5 3 0
```

85

The DSD Option

General form of the DSD option in the INFILE statement:

> **INFILE** *'file-name'* DSD;

86

The DSD Option

The DSD option

- sets the default delimiter to a comma
- treats consecutive delimiters as missing values
- enables SAS to read values with embedded delimiters
  if the value is surrounded by double quotes.

87

Using the DSD Option

```
data airplanes4;
   length ID $ 5;
   infile 'raw-data-file' dsd;
   input ID $
         InService : date9.
         PassCap CargoCap;
run;
```

88

Using the DSD Option

```
proc print data=airplanes4 noobs;
run;
```

PROC PRINT Output

ID	In Service	Pass Cap	Cargo Cap
50001	10907	.	540
50002	10648	132	530
50003	11617	168	530
50004	12088	172	550
50005	12228	.	510
50006	12772	180	520

90

INFILE Statement Options

Problem	Option
Non-blank delimiters	DLM='*delimiter(s)*'
Missing data at end of row	MISSOVER
Missing data represented by consecutive delimiters **or** Embedded delimiters where values are surrounded by double quotes	DSD

These options can be used separately or together in the INFILE statement.

Exercises

1. Reading Nonstandard Data

The STATES raw data file contains information on state size, population, and when each state entered the union.

The order and layout of the fields is as follows:

Order	Field	Notes
1	State Name	Longest value is 16 characters
2	State Population	Written in COMMA9.
3	State Size	Square miles (numeric field)
4	Date of Statehood	Written in DATE9.

Sample Records

```
Alabama! 4,447,100! 50750! 14DEC1819
Alaska! 626,932! 570374! 03JAN1959
Arizona! 5,130,632! 113642! 14FEB1912
Arkansas! 2,673,400! 52075! 15JUN1836
California! 33,871,648! 155973! 09SEP1850
Colorado! 4,301,261! 103729! 01AUG1876
Connecticut! 3,405,565! 4845! 09JAN1788
```

Use the STATES raw data file to create the **work.states** data set listed below.

Partial Listing of **work.states**

```
                                       Enter
   Obs    State        Population   Size    Date

    1    Alabama        4447100    50750   -51152
    2    Alaska          626932   570374     -363
    3    Arizona        5130632   113642   -17488
    4    Arkansas       2673400    52075   -45124
    5    California    33871648   155973   -39925
    6    Colorado       4301261   103729   -30467
    7    Connecticut    3405565     4845   -62813
    8    Delaware        783600     1955   -62846
    9    Florida       15982378    53997   -41941
   10    Georgia        8186453    57918   -62820
```

 The variable **EnterDate** is a SAS date, and it is displayed as the number of days since January 1, 1960 by default. To view the values as calendar dates, apply a SAS date format such as DATE9. or MMDDYY10. (See Section 1.4, "Review of Displaying SAS Data Sets.") You can apply the format with a FORMAT statement in either the DATA step or the PROC PRINT step. If you do not use a format, your dates appear as a numeric value representing the number of days since January 1, 1960.

2. Using INFILE Statement Options to Change Defaults

The AROMAS raw data file contains information on different conditions and possible aromatherapy cures. For each record, the condition is listed first followed by up to three possible cures.

Order	Field	Notes
1	Condition	Longest value is 11 characters
2	Possible Cure	Longest value is 11 characters
3	Possible Cure	Longest value is 11 characters
4	Possible Cure	Longest value is 11 characters

Sample Records

```
ANGER "Ylang Ylang"
ANXIETY Bergamot Petitgrain
BOREDOM Lemongrass
DEPRESSION Basil Bergamot Immortelle
DULLNESS Grapefruit Lemongrass Lime
GRIEF Melissa
HEADACHE Chamomile Lavender
FATIGUE Basil Peppermint Rosemary
INSOMNIA Chamomile Lavender Marjoram
```

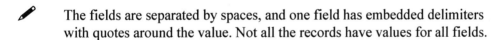 The fields are separated by spaces, and one field has embedded delimiters with quotes around the value. Not all the records have values for all fields.

Use the AROMAS raw data file to create the **work.aromas** data set listed below.

```
                    Aromatherapy Data Set

    Obs    Condition    Cure1         Cure2        Cure3

     1     ANGER        Ylang Ylang
     2     ANXIETY      Bergamot      Petitgrain
     3     BOREDOM      Lemongrass
     4     DEPRESSION   Basil         Bergamot     Immortelle
     5     DULLNESS     Grapefruit    Lemongrass   Lime
     6     GRIEF        Melissa
     7     HEADACHE     Chamomile     Lavender
     8     FATIGUE      Basil         Peppermint   Rosemary
     9     INSOMNIA     Chamomile     Lavender     Marjoram
    10     MIGRAINE     Lavender
    11     STRESS       Benzoin       Bergamot     Chamomile
    12     VERTIGO      Lavender      Peppermint
    13     SHOCK        Peppermint    Petitgrain
```

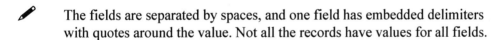 This data set is not intended as medical advice or a guide to aromatherapy.

4.2 Controlling When a Record Loads

Objectives

- Read a raw data file with multiple records per observation.
- Read a raw data file with mixed record types.
- Subset from a raw data file.
- Read a raw data file with multiple observations per record.

94

Multiple Records Per Observation

```
Farr, Sue
Anaheim, CA
869-7008
Anderson, Kay B.
Chicago, IL
483-3321
Tennenbaum, Mary Ann
Jefferson, MO
589-9030
```

A raw data file has three records per employee. Record 1 contains the first and last names, record 2 contains the city and state of residence, and record 3 contains the employee's phone number.

95

Desired Output

The SAS data set should have one observation per employee.

```
LName          FName        City       State    Phone

Farr           Sue          Anaheim    CA       869-7008
Anderson       Kay B.       Chicago    IL       483-3321
Tennenbaum     Mary Ann     Jefferson  MO       589-9030
```

96

The INPUT Statement

The SAS System loads a new record into the input buffer when it encounters an INPUT statement.

You can have multiple INPUT statements in one DATA step.

```
DATA SAS-data-set;
    INPUT var-1 var-2 var-3;
    INPUT var-4 var-5;
    additional SAS statements
```

Each INPUT statement ends with a semicolon.

97

Multiple INPUT Statements

```
data address;
   length  LName FName $ 20
           City $ 25 State $ 2
           Phone $ 8;
   infile 'raw-data-file' dlm=',';
   input LName $ FName $;
   input City $ State $;
   input Phone $;
run;
```

Load Record
Load Record
Load Record

98   ...

Line Pointer Controls

You can also use line pointer controls to control when SAS loads a new record.

> **DATA** *SAS-data-set*;
>   **INPUT** *var-1 var-2 var-3 / var-4 var-5*;
>   *additional SAS statements*

SAS loads the next record when it encounters a forward slash.

99

Reading Multiple Records Per Observation

```
data address;
   length LName FName $ 20
          City $ 25 State $ 2
          Phone $ 8;
   infile 'raw-data-file' dlm=',';
   input LName $ FName $ /
         City $ State $ /
         Phone $;
run;
```

Load Record

Load Record

Load Record

100 · · ·

The forward slash is known as a *relative* line pointer control because it moves the pointer relative to the line it is currently on. There is also an *absolute* line pointer control that moves the pointer to a specific line.

#n moves the pointer to line *n*.

Example:

```
data example;
   infile 'raw-data-file';
   input #1 Name $ Address
         #2 City $ State $
         #3 Phone $;
run;
```

This code would read **Name** and **Address** from record 1, **City** and **State** from record 2, and **Phone** from record 3.

Reading Multiple Records Per Observation

Partial Log

```
NOTE: 9 records were read from
      the infile 'addresses.dat'.
      The minimum record length was 8.
      The maximum record length was 20.
NOTE: The data set WORK.ADDRESS has
      3 observations and 5 variables.
```

101

Reading Multiple Records Per Observation

```
proc print data=address noobs;
run;
```

PROC PRINT Output

LName	FName	City	State	Phone
Farr	Sue	Anaheim	CA	869-7008
Anderson	Kay B.	Chicago	IL	483-3321
Tennenbaum	Mary Ann	Jefferson	MO	589-9030

102   c04s2d1.sas

Mixed Record Types

Not all records have the same format.

```
101 USA 1-20-1999 3295.50
3034 EUR 30JAN1999 1876,30
101 USA 1-30-1999 2938.00
128 USA 2-5-1999 2908.74
1345 EUR 6FEB1999 3145,60
109 USA 3-17-1999 2789.10
```

104   ...

The European sales figures are written with a comma in place of the decimal point. The COMMAX*w.d* informat reads values of this type.

Desired Output

Sales ID	Location	Sale Date	Amount
101	USA	14264	3295.50
3034	EUR	14274	1876.30
101	USA	14274	2938.00
128	USA	14280	2908.74
1345	EUR	14281	3145.60
109	USA	14320	2789.10

105

The INPUT Statement

Two INPUT statements are needed.

```
input  SalesID $ Location $;
if Location='USA' then
   input SaleDate : mmddyy10.
            Amount;
 else if location='EUR' then
      input SaleDate : date9.
            Amount : commax8.;
```

106

Raw Data File

```
101 USA 1-20-1999 3295.50
3034 EUR 30JAN1999 1876,30
101 USA 1-30-1999 2938.00
128 USA 2-5-1999 2908.74
1345 EUR 6FEB1999 3145,60
109 USA 3-17-1999 2789.10
```

```
data sales;
   length SalesID $ 4
          Location $ 3;
   infile 'raw-data-file';
   input SalesID $ Location $;
   if Location='USA' then
      input SaleDate : mmddyy10.
            Amount ;
   else if Location='EUR' then
         input SaleDate : date9.
         Amount : commax8.;
run;
```

Input Buffer

| 1 | 0 | 1 | | U | S | A | | 1 | - | 2 | 0 | - | 1 | 9 | 9 | 9 | | 3 | 2 | 9 | 5 | . | 0 | 0 | | | |

PDV

SALESID	LOCATION	SALEDATE	AMOUNT
		.	.

109   ...

Raw Data File

```
101 USA 1-20-1999 3295.50
3034 EUR 30JAN1999 1876,30
101 USA 1-30-1999 2938.00
128 USA 2-5-1999 2908.7
1345 EUR 6FEB1999 3145,60
109 USA 3-17-1999 2789.10
```

```
data sales;
   length SalesID $ 4
          Location $ 3;
   infile 'raw-data-file';
   input SalesID $ Location $;
   if Location='USA' then
      input SaleDate : mmddyy10.
            Amount ;
   else if Location='EUR' then
         input SaleDate : date9.
         Amount : commax8.;
run;
```

True

Input Buffer

| 1 | 0 | 1 | | U | S | A | | 1 | - | 2 | 0 | - | 1 | 9 | 9 | 9 | | 3 | 2 | 9 | 5 | . | 0 | 0 | | |

PDV

SALESID	LOCATION	SALEDATE	AMOUNT
101	USA	.	.

110   ...

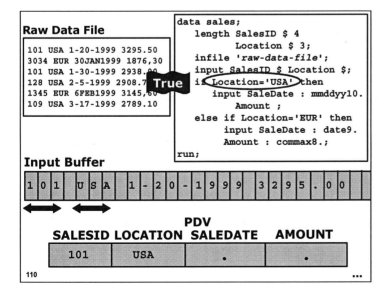

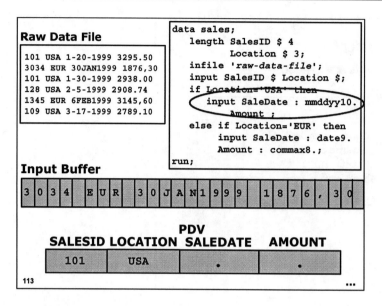

SAS loads a new record into the input buffer each time an INPUT statement is encountered.

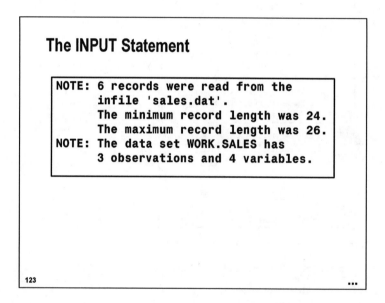

Undesirable Output

Sales ID	Location	Sale Date	Amount
101	USA	.	.
101	USA	.	.
1345	EUR	.	.

124 •••

The Single Trailing @

The single trailing @ option holds a raw data record in the input buffer until SAS

- executes an INPUT statement with no trailing @
- reaches the bottom of the DATA step.

General form of an INPUT statement with the single trailing @:

INPUT *var1 var2 var3 ... @*;

125

Processing the Trailing @

Hold record for next
INPUT statement.

Load next record.

```
input SalesID $ Location $  @;
if location='USA' then
    input SaleDate : mmddyy10.
             Amount;
  else if Location='EUR' then
      input SaleDate : date9.
             Amount : commax8.;
```

126 •••

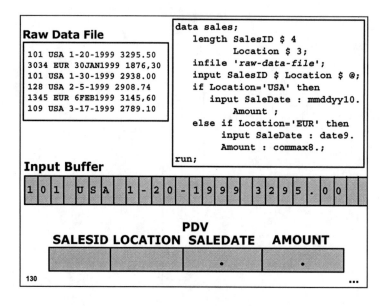

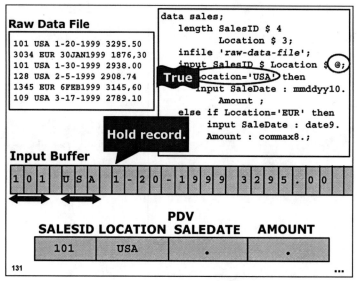

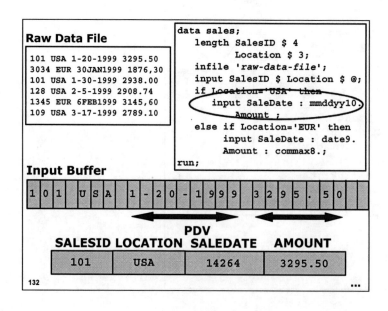

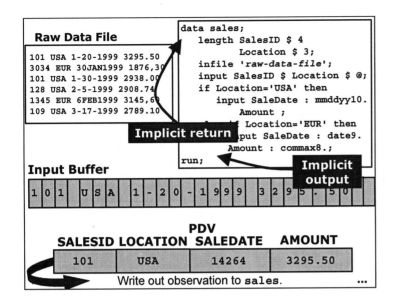

Raw Data File

```
101 USA 1-20-1999 3295.50
3034 EUR 30JAN1999 1876,30
101 USA 1-30-1999 2938.00
128 USA 2-5-1999 2908.74
1345 EUR 6FEB1999 3145,60
109 USA 3-17-1999 2789.10
```

```
data sales;
   length SalesID $ 4
          Location $ 3;
   infile 'raw-data-file';
   input SalesID $ Location $ @;
   if Location='USA' then
      input SaleDate : mmddyy10.
          Amount ;
   else if Location='EUR' then
      input SaleDate : date9.
          Amount : commax8.;
run;
```

Implicit return

Implicit output

Input Buffer

| 1 | 0 | 1 | | U | S | A | | 1 | - | 2 | 0 | - | 1 | 9 | 9 | 9 | | 3 | 2 | 9 | 5 | . | 5 | 0 | |

PDV

SALESID	LOCATION	SALEDATE	AMOUNT
101	USA	14264	3295.50

Write out observation to `sales`.   ...

Mixed Record Types

Partial Log

```
NOTE: 6 records were read from the
      infile 'sales.dat'.
      The minimum record length was 25.
      The maximum record length was 26.
NOTE: The data set WORK.SALES has
      6 observations and 4 variables.
```

137

Mixed Record Types

```
proc print data=sales noobs;
run;
```

PROC PRINT Output

Sales ID	Location	Sale Date	Amount
101	USA	14264	3295.50
3034	EUR	14274	1876.30
101	USA	14274	2938.00
128	USA	14280	2908.74
1345	EUR	14281	3145.60
109	USA	14320	2789.10

138   c04s2d2.sas

Subsetting from a Raw Data File

This scenario uses the raw data file from the previous example.

```
101 USA 1-20-1999 3295.50
3034 EUR 30JAN1999 1876,30
101 USA 1-30-1999 2938.00
128 USA 2-5-1999 2908.74
1345 EUR 6FEB1999 3145,60
109 USA 3-17-1999 2789.10
```

140

Desired Output

The sales manager wants to see sales for the European branch only.

Sales ID	Location	Sale Date	Amount
3034	EUR	14274	1876.30
1345	EUR	14281	3145.60

141

The Subsetting IF

```
data sales;
   length SalesID $ 4
          Location $ 3;
   infile 'raw-data-file';
   input SalesID $ Location $ @;
   if Location='USA' then
      input SaleDate : mmddyy10.
         Amount ;
   else if Location='EUR' then
         input SaleDate : date9.
         Amount : commax8.;
   if Location='EUR';
run;
```

142

The Subsetting IF Statement

The subsetting IF should appear as early in the program as possible but after the variables used in the condition have been created.

143

The Subsetting IF Statement

```
data sales;
   length SalesID $ 4
          Location $ 3;
   infile 'raw-data-file';
   input SalesID $ Location $ @;
   if Location='EUR';
      input SaleDate : date9.
            Amount : commax8.;
run;
```

Because the program reads only European sales, the INPUT statement for USA sales is not needed.

144

In many cases, there is a significant efficiency savings when you read only part of the record, check the subsetting condition, and then read the rest of the record if the condition is met, as opposed to reading the entire record and then checking the subsetting criteria.

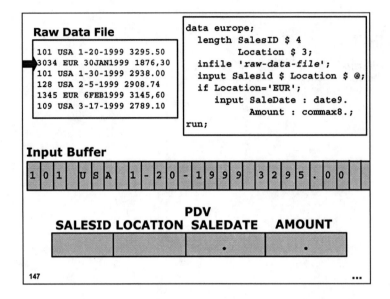

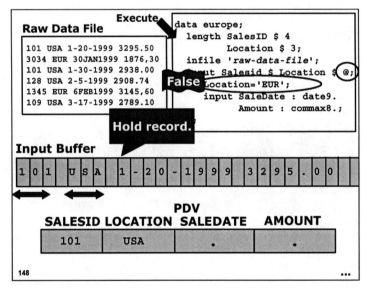

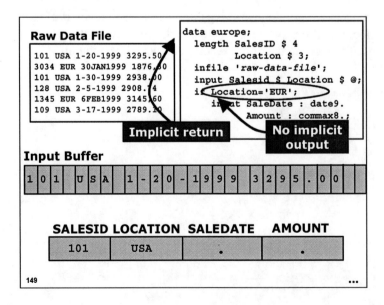

If an observation does not meet the subsetting IF,

- control returns to the top of the DATA step
- the PDV is reset
- a new record is read.

The observation never reaches the bottom of the DATA step and is therefore never output.

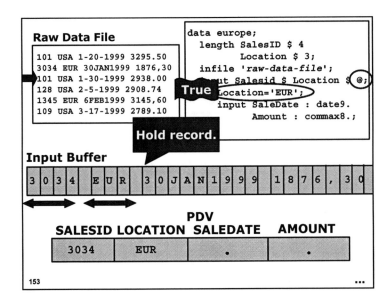

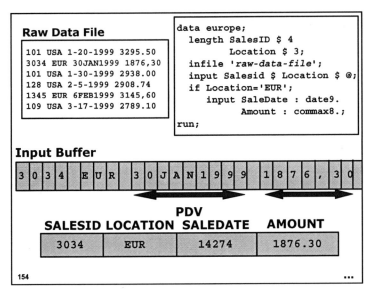

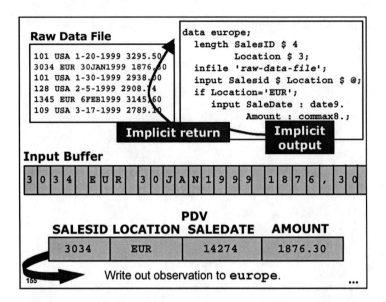

Raw Data File

```
101 USA 1-20-1999 3295.50
3034 EUR 30JAN1999 1876.30
101 USA 1-30-1999 2938.00
128 USA 2-5-1999 2908.74
1345 EUR 6FEB1999 3145.60
109 USA 3-17-1999 2789.10
```

```
data europe;
  length SalesID $ 4
         Location $ 3;
  infile 'raw-data-file';
  input Salesid $ Location $ @;
  if Location='EUR';
    input SaleDate : date9.
          Amount : commax8.;
```

Implicit return → **Implicit output**

Input Buffer

| 3 | 0 | 3 | 4 | | E | U | R | | 3 | 0 | J | A | N | 1 | 9 | 9 | 9 | | 1 | 8 | 7 | 6 | , | 3 | 0 | |

PDV

SALESID	LOCATION	SALEDATE	AMOUNT
3034	EUR	14274	1876.30

Write out observation to **europe**.

155

...

If the subsetting IF condition is true, SAS continues processing the current observtion until it reaches the bottom of the DATA step and the implicit output.

Multiple Observations Per Record

The raw data file RETIRE contains each employee's identification number and this year's contribution to his or her retirement plan. Each record contains information for three employees.

```
E00973 1400 E09872 2003 E73150 2400
E45671 4500 E34805 1980 E47200 4371
```

159

Desired Output

The output SAS data set should have one observation per employee.

EmpID	Contrib
E00973	1400
E09872	2003
E73150	2400
E45671	4500
E34805	1980
E47200	4371

160

Processing: What Is Required?

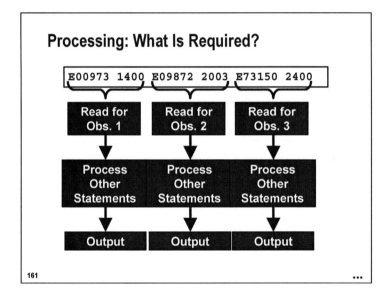

161   ...

The Double Trailing @

The double trailing @ holds the raw data record across iterations of the DATA step until the line pointer moves past the end of the line.

> **INPUT** *var1 var2 var3 ... @@;*

162

The double trailing @ should only be used with list input. If used with column or formatted input, an infinite loop can result.

The Double Trailing @

```
data work.retire;
    length EmpID $ 6;
    infile 'raw-data-file';
    input EmpID $ Contrib @@;
run;
```

Hold until end of record.

163   •••

Creating Multiple Observations Per Record

Partial Log

```
NOTE: 2 records were read from the
      infile 'retire.dat'.
      The minimum record length was 35.
      The maximum record length was 36.
NOTE: SAS went to a new line when INPUT
      statement reached past the end of
      a line.
NOTE: The data set WORK.RETIRE has
      6 observations and 2 variables.
```

The "SAS went to a new line" message is expected because the @@ option indicates that SAS should read until the end of each record.

164

Creating Multiple Observations Per Record

```
proc print data=retire noobs;
run;
```

PROC PRINT Output

EmpID	Contrib
E00973	1400
E09872	2003
E73150	2400
E45671	4500
E34805	1980
E47200	4371

165   c04s2d4.sas

Trailing @ Versus Double Trailing @

Option	Effect
Trailing @ **INPUT** *var-1*... @;	Holds raw data record until 1) an INPUT statement with no trailing @ 2) the bottom of the DATA step.
Double trailing @ **INPUT** *var-1* ... @@;	Holds raw data records in input buffer until SAS reads past end of line.

166

The single trailing @ and the double trailing @ are mutually exclusive; they cannot and should not be used together. If they both appear in the same INPUT statement, the last option specified is used.

 **Exercises**

3. Reading Multiple Records per Observation

Medical data is stored in the raw data file BLOODTYP. The first record contains the patient's identification number and the patient's first and last names. The second record contains a code specifying the medical plan, the patient's blood type, a code indicating whether the patient has any allergies, and the number of dependants covered by the family's health plan.

First Record

Order	Field	Notes
1	ID Number	5-character code
2	Last Name	Longest value is 9 characters
3	First Name	Longest value is 11 characters

Second Record

Order	Field	Notes
1	Plan Type	1-character code
2	Blood Type	Longest value is 3 characters
3	Allergy Code	1-character code: Y=Yes, N=No
4	Number of Dependants	Numeric field

Sample Records

```
E1009 MORGAN GEORGE
F O+ Y 1
E1017 WELCH DARIUS
F AB+ N 2
E1036 MOORE LESLIE
S AB+ Y 1
E1037 EDWARDS JENNIFER
F B- Y 1
E1038 WASHBURN GAYLE
N B+ Y 1
```

Create a SAS data set named **work.medical** that contains the patient's identification number, first name, last name, and blood type.

Partial Listing of **`work.medical`**

```
                Patient Names and Blood Types

    Obs    ID      FName        LName        Blood

     1    E1009   GEORGE       MORGAN        O+
     2    E1017   DARIUS       WELCH         AB+
     3    E1036   LESLIE       MOORE         AB+
     4    E1037   JENNIFER     EDWARDS       B-
     5    E1038   GAYLE        WASHBURN      B+
```

4.   Reading Mixed Record Types

Medical data is stored in the raw data file ALLERGY. The first six fields are always as follows:

First Part of Record

Order	Field	Notes
1	ID Number	5-character code
2	Last Name	Longest value is 9 characters
3	First Name	Longest value is 11 characters
3	Plan Type	1-character code
4	Blood Type	Longest value is 3 characters
5	Allergy Code	1-character code: Y=Yes, N=No

If the patient has an allergy (**`Allergy Code = Y`**), then the rest of the record is as follows:

6	Allergy Type	2-character code indicating type of allergy
7	Number of Dependants	Numeric field

If the patient does not have an allergy (**`Allergy Code = N`**), then the rest of the record is as follows:

6	Number of Dependants	Numeric field

Sample Records

```
E1009 MORGAN GEORGE F O+ Y DY 1
E1017 WELCH DARIUS F AB+ N 2
E1036 MOORE LESLIE S AB+ Y SM 1
E1037 EDWARDS JENNIFER F B- Y HF 1
E1038 WASHBURN GAYLE N B+ Y PA 1
E1050 TUTTLE THOMAS S A+ N 2
E1065 CHAPMAN NEIL F O+ N 2
```

Use conditional input to create the SAS data set named **work.allergies**.

Partial Listing of **work.allergies**

Obs	ID	LName	FName	Plan	Blood	Allergy	Algy Type	Dependents
1	E1009	MORGAN	GEORGE	F	O+	Y	DY	1
2	E1017	WELCH	DARIUS	F	AB+	N		2
3	E1036	MOORE	LESLIE	S	AB+	Y	SM	1
4	E1037	EDWARDS	JENNIFER	F	B-	Y	HF	1
5	E1038	WASHBURN	GAYLE	N	B+	Y	PA	1
6	E1050	TUTTLE	THOMAS	S	A+	N		2
7	E1065	CHAPMAN	NEIL	F	O+	N		2
8	E1076	VENTER	RANDALL	N	A+	N		1
9	E1094	STARR	ALTON	N	B+	Y	SF	1

5. Subsetting from a Raw Data File (Optional)

Modify the DATA step you wrote in the previous problem to create a SAS data set named **work.allergies2** that contains only patients with allergies.

Partial Listing of **work.allergies2**

Obs	ID	LName	FName	Plan	Blood	Allergy	Algy Type	Dependents
1	E1009	MORGAN	GEORGE	F	O+	Y	DY	1
2	E1036	MOORE	LESLIE	S	AB+	Y	SM	1
3	E1037	EDWARDS	JENNIFER	F	B-	Y	HF	1
4	E1038	WASHBURN	GAYLE	N	B+	Y	PA	1

6. Reading Raw Data with Multiple Observations per Record

The raw data file TRANSACT contains daily bank transactions for a given account. For each transaction, the following information is stored:

Order	Field	Notes
1	Date of Transaction	Written in DATE9.
2	Type of Transaction	C=deposit (credit), D=withdrawal (debit)
3	Amount of Transaction	Written in COMMA9.

Sample Records

```
03JAN2001 C 9,253 04JAN2001 D 12,135 06JAN2001 C 10,562
10JAN2001 D 35,950 15JAN2001 C 951 21JAN2001 C 1,226
25JAN2001 C 86 28JAN2001 C 27,500 31JAN2001 D 75,900
```

Create a SAS data set named **work.transactions** that contains all transactions made.

Listing of **work.transactions**

```
        Obs    Date    Type    Amount

         1    14978     C       9253
         2    14979     D      12135
         3    14981     C      10562
         4    14985     D      35950
         5    14990     C        951
         6    14996     C       1226
         7    15000     C         86
         8    15003     C      27500
         9    15006     D      75900
```

7. Creating Multiple SAS Data Sets from a Single Raw Data File (Optional)

Modify the DATA step you wrote in exercise 6 to create two SAS data sets. Name the first **work.credits**; it should contain all the deposit information. Name the second **work.debits**; it should contain all the withdrawal information.

✎ Hint: Create both data sets in one DATA step by listing them both in the DATA statement and using conditional logic with an OUTPUT statement (shown in Section 2.2, "Writing to Multiple Data Sets").

Listing of **work.credits**

Obs	Date	Type	Amount
1	14978	C	9253
2	14981	C	10562
3	14990	C	951
4	14996	C	1226
5	15000	C	86
6	15003	C	27500

Listing of **work.debits**

Obs	Date	Type	Amount
1	14979	D	12135
2	14985	D	35950
3	15006	D	75900

4.3 Reading Hierarchical Raw Data Files

Objectives

- Read a hierarchical file and create one observation per detail record.
- Read a hierarchical file and create one observation per header record.

168

Processing Hierarchical Files

Many files are hierarchical in structure, consisting of

- a header record
- one or more related detail records.

Typically, each record contains a field that identifies whether it is a header record or a detail record.

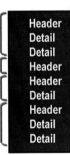

169

Processing Hierarchical Files

You can read a hierarchical file into a SAS data set by creating one observation per detail record and storing the header information as part of each observation.

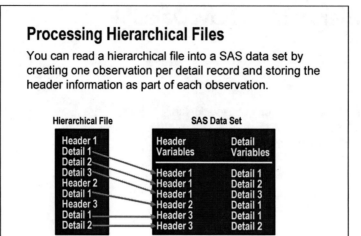

170

Processing Hierarchical Files

You can also create one observation per header record and store the information from detail records in summary variables.

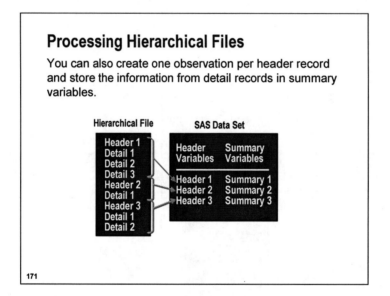

171

Creating One Observation Per Detail

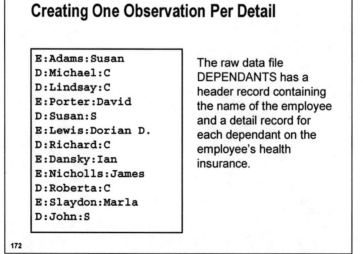

```
E:Adams:Susan
D:Michael:C
D:Lindsay:C
E:Porter:David
D:Susan:S
E:Lewis:Dorian D.
D:Richard:C
E:Dansky:Ian
E:Nicholls:James
D:Roberta:C
E:Slaydon:Marla
D:John:S
```

The raw data file DEPENDANTS has a header record containing the name of the employee and a detail record for each dependant on the employee's health insurance.

172

Desired Output

Personnel would like a list of all the dependants and the name of the associated employee.

EmpLName	EmpFName	DepName	Relation
Adams	Susan	Michael	C
Adams	Susan	Lindsay	C
Porter	David	Susan	S
Lewis	Dorian D.	Richard	C
Nicholls	James	Roberta	C
Slaydon	Marla	John	S

173

Because Personnel is interested only in the dependants, Ian Dansky, who has no dependants, will not appear in the output data set.

A Hierarchical File

```
E:Adams:Susan
D:Michael:C
D:Lindsay:C
E:Porter:David
D:Susan:S
E:Lewis:Dorian D.
D:Richard:C
E:Dansky:Ian
E:Nicholls:James
D:Roberta:C
E:Slaydon:Marla
D:John:S
```

- Not all the records are the same.
- The fields are separated by colons.
- There is a field indicating whether the record is a header or a detail record.

174

How to Read the Raw Data

```
input Type $  @;
   if Type='E' then
      input EmpFName $ EmpLName $;
   else
      input DepName $ Relation $;
```

175

How to Output Only the Dependants

```
input Type $ @;
   if Type='E' then
      input EmpFName $ EmpLName $;
   else do;
      input DepName $ Relation $;
      output;
   end;
```

176

Compile ►

```
E:Adams:Susan
D:Michael:C
D:Lindsay:C
E:Porter:David
D:Susan:S
E:Lewis:Dorian D.
D:Richard:C
E:Dansky:Ian
E:Nicholls:James
D:Roberta:C
E:Slaydon:Marla
D:John:S
```

```
data dependants(drop=Type);
   length EmpLName EmpFName
          DepName $ 20 Relation $ 1;
   infile 'raw-data-file' dlm= ':';
   input Type $ @;
      if Type='E' then
         input EmpLName $ EmpFName $;
      else do;
         input DepName $ Relation $;
         output;
      end;
run;
```

Input Buffer

▶ D

TYPE   EMPLNAME   EMPFNAME   DEPNAME   RELATION

177   •••

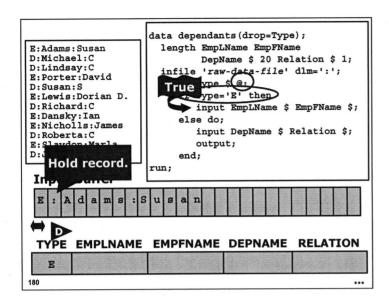

```
E:Adams:Susan
D:Michael:C
D:Lindsay:C
E:Porter:David
D:Susan:S
E:Lewis:Dorian D.
D:Richard:C
E:Dansky:Ian
E:Nicholls:James
D:Roberta:C
E:Slaydon:Marla
D:John:S
```

```
data dependants(drop=Type);
   length EmpLName EmpFName
          DepName $ 20 Relation $ 1;
   infile 'raw-data-file' dlm=':';
   input Type $ @;
      if Type='E' then
          input EmpLName $ EmpFName $;
      else do;
          input DepName $ Relation $;
          output;
      end;
run;
```

True

Hold record.

Input Buffer

| E | : | A | d | a | m | s | : | S | u | s | a | n | | | | | | | |

▶**D**

TYPE	EMPLNAME	EMPFNAME	DEPNAME	RELATION
E				

180   ...

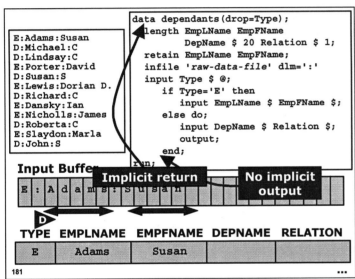

```
E:Adams:Susan
D:Michael:C
D:Lindsay:C
E:Porter:David
D:Susan:S
E:Lewis:Dorian D.
D:Richard:C
E:Dansky:Ian
E:Nicholls:James
D:Roberta:C
E:Slaydon:Marla
D:John:S
```

```
data dependants(drop=Type);
   length EmpLName EmpFName
          DepName $ 20 Relation $ 1;
   retain EmpLName EmpFName;
   infile 'raw-data-file' dlm=':'
   input Type $ @;
      if Type='E' then
          input EmpLName $ EmpFName $;
      else do;
          input DepName $ Relation $;
          output;
      end;
   run;
```

Input Buffer

Implicit return   **No implicit output**

| E | : | A | d | a | m | s | : | S | u | s | a | n | | | | | | | |

▶**D**

TYPE	EMPLNAME	EMPFNAME	DEPNAME	RELATION
E	Adams	Susan		

181   ...

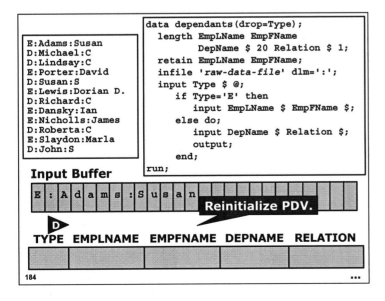

```
E:Adams:Susan
D:Michael:C
D:Lindsay:C
E:Porter:David
D:Susan:S
E:Lewis:Dorian D.
D:Richard:C
E:Dansky:Ian
E:Nicholls:James
D:Roberta:C
E:Slaydon:Marla
D:John:S
```

```
data dependants(drop=Type);
   length EmpLName EmpFName
          DepName $ 20 Relation $ 1;
   retain EmpLName EmpFName;
   infile 'raw-data-file' dlm=':';
   input Type $ @;
      if Type='E' then
          input EmpLName $ EmpFName $;
      else do;
          input DepName $ Relation $;
          output;
      end;
   run;
```

Input Buffer

| E | : | A | d | a | m | s | : | S | u | s | a | n | | | | | | | |

▶**D**

Reinitialize PDV.

TYPE	EMPLNAME	EMPFNAME	DEPNAME	RELATION

184   ...

EmpFName and **EmpLName** are reinitialized at the top of the DATA step. In this case, that is not desirable.

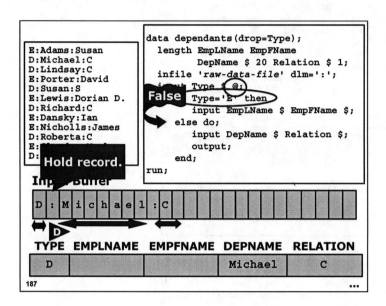

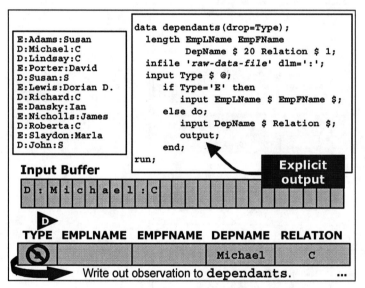

```
Undesirable Output

   Emp      Emp
  LName    FName     DepName     Relation

                     Michael        C
                     Lindsay        C
                     Susan          S
                     Richard        C
                     Roberta        C
                     John           S



190
```

Because SAS only outputs when it reads a detail record, the values of **EmpFName**
and **EmpLName** are missing.

```
The RETAIN Statement
General form of the RETAIN statement:

   RETAIN variable-name <initial-value>;


The RETAIN statement prevents SAS from reinitializing
the values of new variables at the top of the DATA step.
This means that values from previous records are
available for processing.



191
```

By default, variables referenced in the RETAIN statement are set to missing before
the first iteration of the DATA step. To change this, you can specify an initial value
after the variable's name. For more information, see Chapter 3, "Summarizing
Data," or *SAS Language Reference: Dictionary*.

Variables referenced with the RETAIN statement will be in the output data set only if
they are referenced elsewhere in the DATA step or assigned initial values.

Hold EmpLName and EmpFName

```
data dependants(drop=Type);
   length EmpLName EmpFName
          DepName $ 20 Relation $ 1;
   retain EmpLName EmpFName;
   infile 'raw-data-file' dlm=':';
   input Type $ @;
      if Type='E' then
         input EmpLName $ EmpFName $;
      else do;
         input DepName $ Relation $;
         output;
      end;
run;
```

192

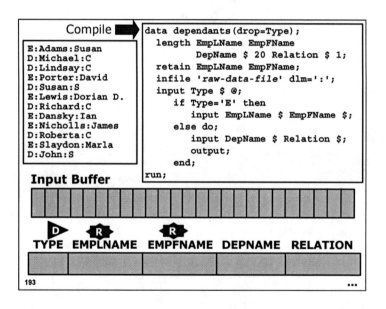

193

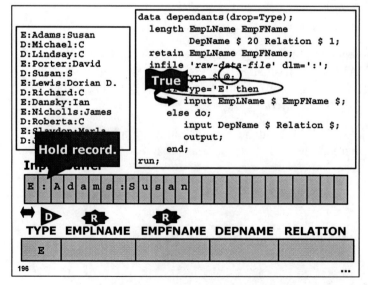

196

As with the conditional input example in the previous section, the trailing @ holds
the record while SAS checks the condition.

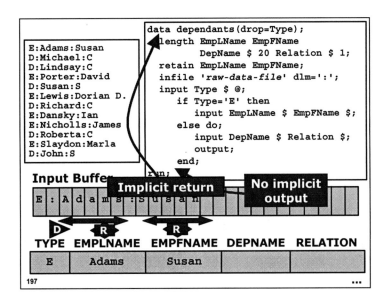

Because of the explicit output in the second DO group, SAS outputs an observation
only when it encounters a detail record.

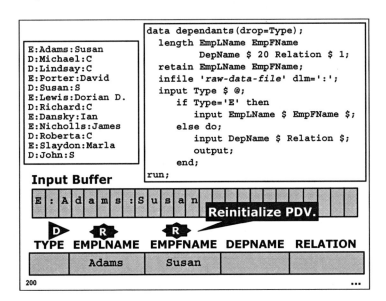

Because of the RETAIN statement, **EmpFName** and **EmpLName** are not reinitialized.

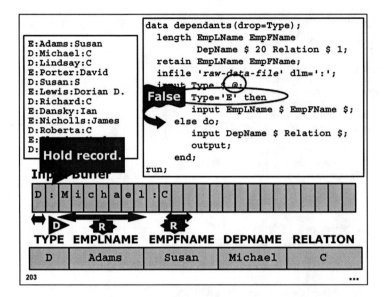

This is a detail record; SAS executes the second of the two DO groups.

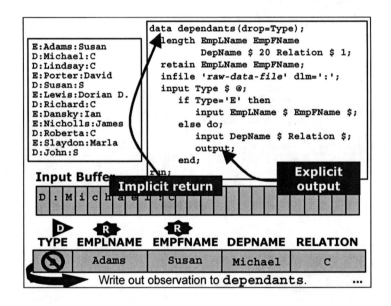

Creating One Observation Per Detail

```
proc print data=work.dependants noobs;
run;
```

PROC PRINT Output

EmpLName	EmpFName	DepName	Relation
Adams	Susan	Michael	C
Adams	Susan	Lindsay	C
Porter	David	Susan	S
Lewis	Dorian D.	Richard	C
Nicholls	James	Roberta	C
Slaydon	Marla	John	S

208

`c04s3d1.sas`

Create One Observation Per Header Record

```
E:E01442
D:Michael:C
D:Lindsay:C
E:E00705
D:Susan:S
E:E01577
D:Richard:C
E:E00997
E:E00955
D:Roberta:C
E:E00224
D:John:S
```

- Employee insurance is free for the employees.
- Each employee pays $50 per month for a spouse's insurance.
- Each employee pays $25 per month for a child's insurance.

209

Desired Output

Personnel wants a list of all employees and their monthly payroll deductions for insurance.

ID	Deduct
E01442	50
E00705	50
E01577	25
E00997	0
E00955	25
E00224	50

210

Calculating the Value of Deduct

```
E:E01442
D:Michael:C
D:Lindsay:C
E:E00705
D:Susan:S
E:E01577
D:Richard:C
E:E00997
E:E00955
D:Roberta:C
E:E00224
D:John:S
```

The values of **Deduct** will change according to the

- type of record read
- value of **Relation** when **Type='D'**.

211

Retaining ID

Values of **ID** and **Deduct** need to be held across iterations of the DATA step.

```
retain ID;
```

- **ID** must be retained with a RETAIN statement.
- **Deduct** will be created with a sum statement, which automatically retains.

212

When to Output ?

```
E:E01442
D:Michael:C
D:Lindsay:C
E:E00705          ◄──── End Observation 1
D:Susan:S
E:E01577          ◄──── End Observation 2
D:Richard:C
E:E00997          ◄──── End Observation 3
E:E00955          ◄──── End Observation 4
D:Roberta:C
E:E00224          ◄──── End Observation 5
D:John:S          ◄──── End Observation 6
```

213

When SAS Loads a Type E Record

1. Output what is currently in the PDV (unless this is the first time through the DATA step).
2. Read the next employee's identification number.
3. Reset `Deduct` to 0.

```
if Type='E' then do;
   if _N_ ne 1 then output;
   input ID $;
   Deduct=0;
end;
```

214

When SAS Loads a Type D Record

1. Read the dependant's name and relationship.
2. Check the relationship.
3. Increment `Deduct` appropriately.

```
else do;
   input DepName $ Relation $;
   if Relation='S' then Deduct+50;
      else if Relation='C' then
      Deduct+25;
   end;
```

215

```
data work.insurance(drop=Type DepName Relation);
   length ID $ 6 DepName $ 20 Relation $ 1;
   retain ID;
   infile 'raw-data-file' dlm=':';
   input Type $ @;
      if Type='E' then do;
      if _N_>1 then output;
         input ID $;
         Deduct=0;
      end;
      else do;
      input DepName $ Relation $;
      if Relation='S' then Deduct+50;
         else if Relation='C' then Deduct+25;
      end;
run;
```

216

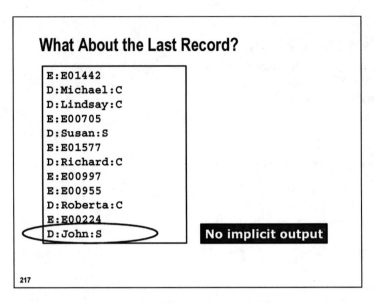

In the current DATA step, SAS only produces an observation when it reads a record with **Type='E'**. There is no employee record after the last record to signal an output.

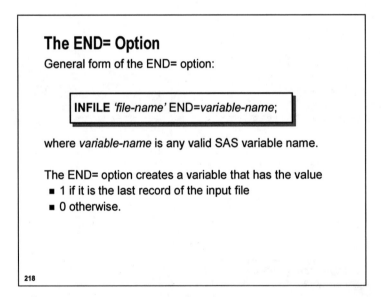

```
data work.insurance(drop=Type DepName Relation);
   length ID $ 6 DepName $ 20 Relation $ 1;
   retain ID;
   infile 'raw-data-file'
          dlm=':' end=LastRec;
   input Type $ @;
      if Type='E' then do;
      if _N_>1 then output;
         input ID $;
         Deduct=0;
      end;
      else do;
      input DepName $ Relation $;
      if Relation='S' then Deduct+50;
         else if Relation='C' then Deduct+25;
      end;
      if LastRec then output;
run;
```

219

SAS outputs only when it encounters

- a header record that is not the first in the raw data file
- the last record in the raw data file.

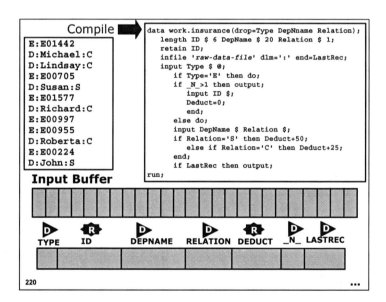

220

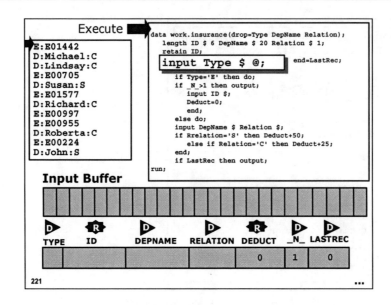

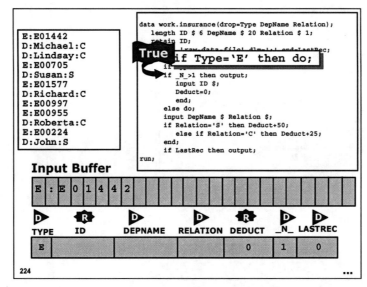

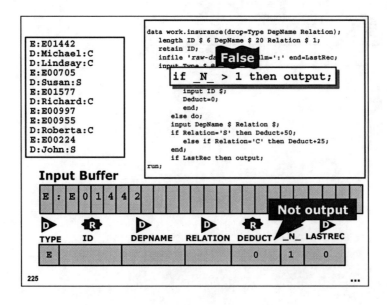

You do not want to output the first header record before reading all the detail information.

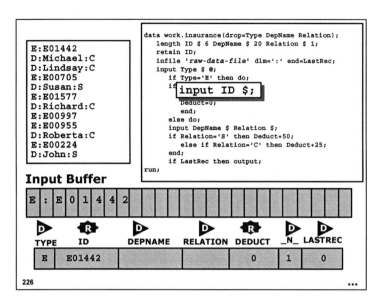

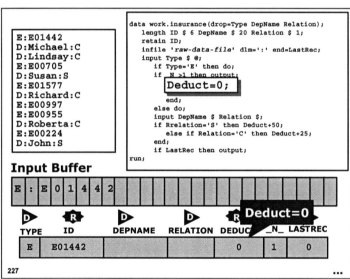

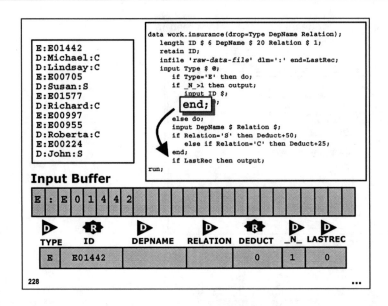

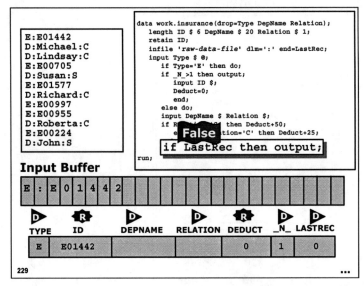

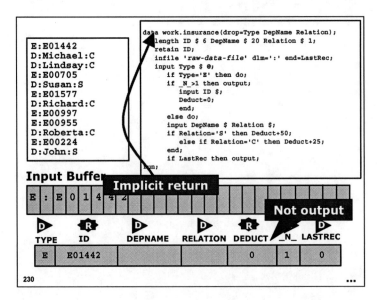

SAS does not output the information, but the RETAIN flags hold it in the PDV.

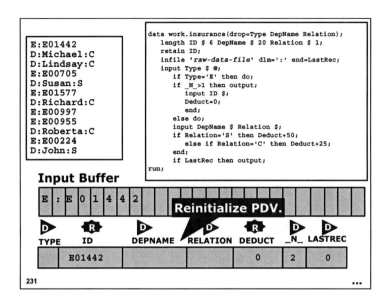

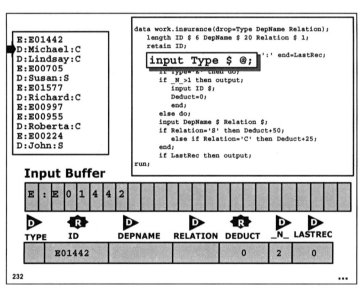

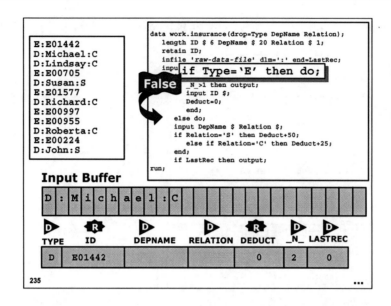

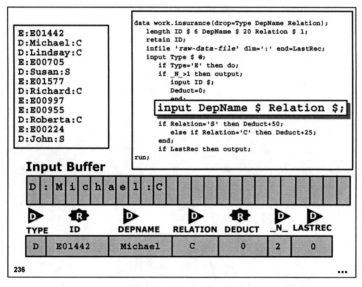

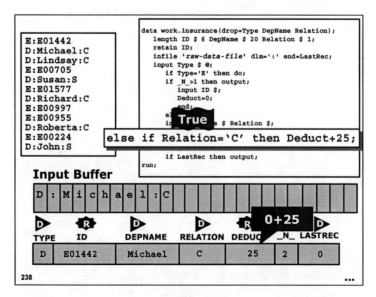

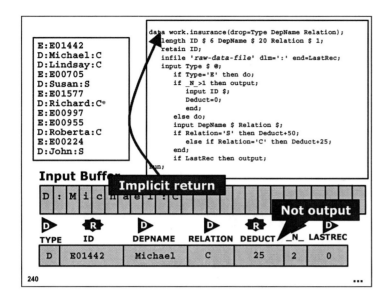

SAS continues reading the detail records associated with the first header.

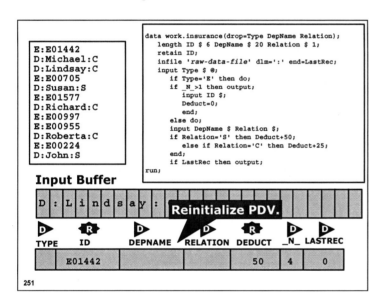

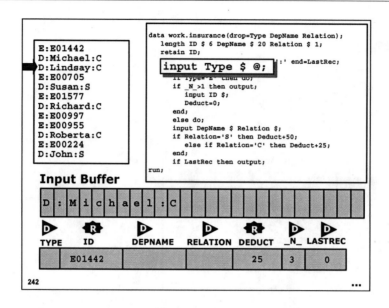

```
data work.insurance(drop=Type DepName Relation);
   length ID $ 6 DepName $ 20 Relation $ 1;
   retain ID;
```
```
input Type $ @;
```
```
   if Type='E' then do;
   if _N_ >1 then output;
      input ID $;
      Deduct=0;
   end;
   else do;
   input DepName $ Relation $;
   if Relation='S' then Deduct+50;
      else if Relation='C' then Deduct+25;
   end;
   if LastRec then output;
run;
```

E:E01442
D:Michael:C
D:Lindsay:C
E:E00705
D:Susan:S
E:E01577
D:Richard:C
E:E00997
E:E00955
D:Roberta:C
E:E00224
D:John:S

Input Buffer

242

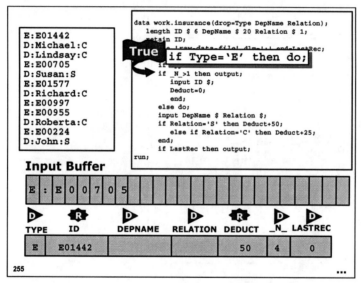

```
data work.insurance(drop=Type DepName Relation);
   length ID $ 6 DepName $ 20 Relation $ 1;
   retain ID;
```
True
```
if Type='E' then do;
```
```
   if _N_ >1 then output;
      input ID $;
      Deduct=0;
   end;
   else do;
   input DepName $ Relation $;
   if Relation='S' then Deduct+50;
      else if Relation='C' then Deduct+25;
   end;
   if LastRec then output;
run;
```

E:E01442
D:Michael:C
D:Lindsay:C
E:E00705
D:Susan:S
E:E01577
D:Richard:C
E:E00997
E:E00955
D:Roberta:C
E:E00224
D:John:S

Input Buffer

255

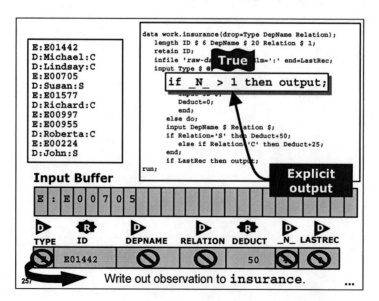

```
data work.insurance(drop=Type DepName Relation);
   length ID $ 6 DepName $ 20 Relation $ 1;
   retain ID;
   infile 'raw-da        dlm=':' end=LastRec;
   input Type $ @
```
True
```
if _N_ > 1 then output;
```
```
      Deduct=0;
   end;
   else do;
   input DepName $ Relation $;
   if Relation='S' then Deduct+50;
      else if Relation='C' then Deduct+25;
   end;
   if LastRec then output;
run;
```

Explicit output

E:E01442
D:Michael:C
D:Lindsay:C
E:E00705
D:Susan:S
E:E01577
D:Richard:C
E:E00997
E:E00955
D:Roberta:C
E:E00224
D:John:S

Input Buffer

Write out observation to `insurance`.

257

When SAS encounters the second header, it outputs the accumulated detail information and the appropriate header information.

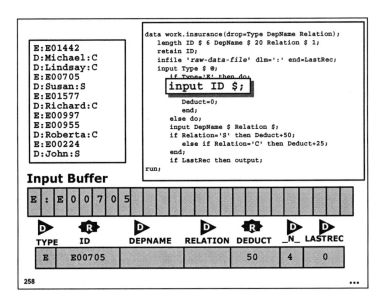

After the information for the last employee has been output, SAS begins to read header information for the next employee.

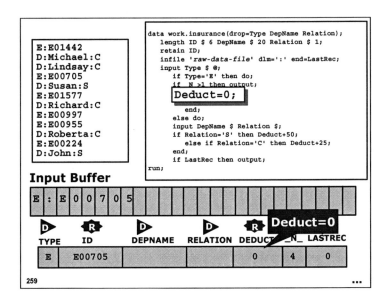

`Deduct` must be reset with each new employee header that is read.

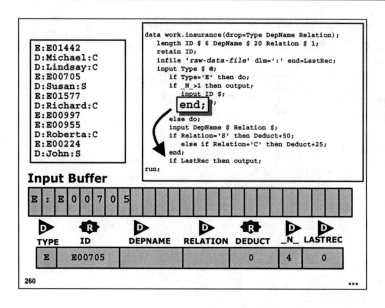

```
                              data work.insurance(drop=Type DepName Relation);
  E:E01442                      length ID $ 6 DepName $ 20 Relation $ 1;
  D:Michael:C                    retain ID;
  D:Lindsay:C                    infile 'raw-data-file' dlm=':' end=LastRec;
  E:E00705                       input Type $ @;
  D:Susan:S                        if Type='E' then do;
  E:E01577                           if _N_>1 then output;
  D:Richard:C                          input ID $;
  E:E00997                        end; ';
  E:E00955                         else do;
  D:Roberta:C                      input DepName $ Relation $;
  E:E00224                         if Relation='S' then Deduct+50;
  D:John:S                           else if Relation='C' then Deduct+25;
                                  end;
                                  if LastRec then output;
                                run;
```

Input Buffer

| E | : | E | 0 | 0 | 7 | 0 | 5 | | | | | | | | | | | | | |

TYPE   ID   DEPNAME   RELATION   DEDUCT   _N_   LASTREC

TYPE	ID	DEPNAME	RELATION	DEDUCT	_N_	LASTREC
E	E00705			0	4	0

260   ...

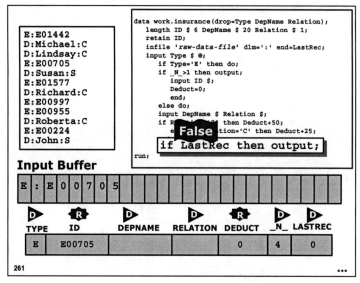

```
                              data work.insurance(drop=Type DepName Relation);
  E:E01442                      length ID $ 6 DepName $ 20 Relation $ 1;
  D:Michael:C                    retain ID;
  D:Lindsay:C                    infile 'raw-data-file' dlm=':' end=LastRec;
  E:E00705                       input Type $ @;
  D:Susan:S                        if Type='E' then do;
  E:E01577                           if _N_>1 then output;
  D:Richard:C                          input ID $;
  E:E00997                            Deduct=0;
  E:E00955                            end;
  D:Roberta:C                       else do;
  E:E00224                         input DepName $ Relation $;
  D:John:S                           if R        then Deduct+50;
                                  e    tion='C' then Deduct+25;
                      False    if LastRec then output;
                                run;
```

Input Buffer

| E | : | E | 0 | 0 | 7 | 0 | 5 | | | | | | | | | | | | | |

TYPE   ID   DEPNAME   RELATION   DEDUCT   _N_   LASTREC

TYPE	ID	DEPNAME	RELATION	DEDUCT	_N_	LASTREC
E	E00705			0	4	0

261   ...

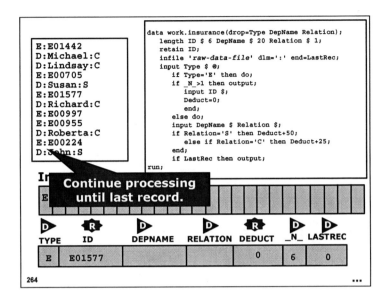

SAS continues processing all the employee records this way until it reaches the last record in the data file.

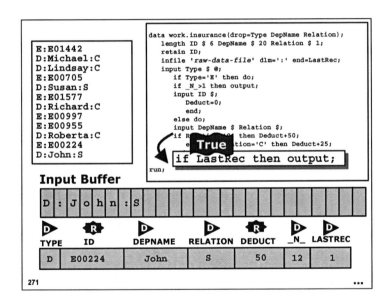

When the last record in the raw data file is read, the value of **LastRec**, which is created with the END= option, changes to 1.

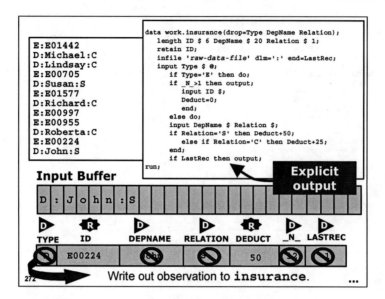

```
                        data work.insurance(drop=Type DepName Relation);
E:E01442                   length ID $ 6 DepName $ 20 Relation $ 1;
D:Michael:C                retain ID;
D:Lindsay:C                infile 'raw-data-file' dlm=':' end=LastRec;
E:E00705                   input Type $ @;
D:Susan:S                     if Type='E' then do;
E:E01577                      if _N_>1 then output;
D:Richard:C                      input ID $;
E:E00997                         Deduct=0;
E:E00955                         end;
D:Roberta:C                   else do;
E:E00224                      input DepName $ Relation $;
D:John:S                      if Relation='S' then Deduct+50;
                                 else if Relation='C' then Deduct+25;
                              end;
                           if LastRec then output;
                        run;
```

Input Buffer

| D | : | J | o | h | n | : | S | | | | | | | | | | | | | |

TYPE   ID   DEPNAME   RELATION   DEDUCT   _N_   LASTREC

| | E00224 | | | 50 | | |

Write out observation to **insurance**.

The condition **if LastRec** (if **LastRec** not equal to 0 and not equal to missing) is true. The explicit output is executed, writing the last employee's information to the SAS data set.

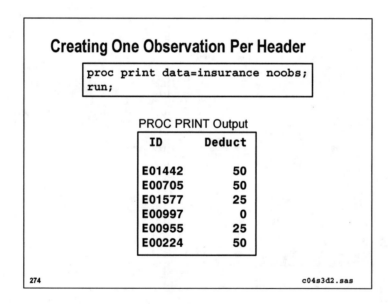

Creating One Observation Per Header

```
proc print data=insurance noobs;
run;
```

PROC PRINT Output

ID	Deduct
E01442	50
E00705	50
E01577	25
E00997	0
E00955	25
E00224	50

274   c04s3d2.sas

 **Exercises**

8. Reading a Hierarchical Raw Data File and Creating One Observation per Detail Record

The raw data file SALARIES is hierarchical. The header record has the employee's identification number, first name, last name, and the date he or she was hired. The detail records have the employee's salary for each year he or she has been employed with the company.

Header Records

Order	Field	Notes
1	Record Type	E = Header record, S = Detail record
2	Employee ID Number	6-character code
3	First Name	Longest value is 8 characters
4	Last Name	Longest value is 8 characters
5	Hire Date	Written in DATE9.

Detail Records

Order	Field	Notes
1	Record Type	E = Header record, S = Detail record
2	Salary Year	4-digit year
3	Salary	Written in COMMA9.

Sample Records

```
E E1232 JOHN SMITH 15OCT1999
S 1999 51,684
S 2000 56,180
S 2001 61,065
E E2341 ALICE JONES 01JUN1997
S 1997 65,684
S 1998 71,396
S 1999 77,604
S 2000 84,353
S 2001 91,688
```

Create the SAS data set **work.salaries** that contains the variables ID, FName, LName, SalYear and Salary. There should be one observation for each year the employee has worked.

Partial Listing of **work.salaries**

Obs	ID	LName	FName	Sal Year	Salary
1	E1232	SMITH	JOHN	1999	51684
2	E1232	SMITH	JOHN	2000	56180
3	E1232	SMITH	JOHN	2001	61065
4	E2341	JONES	ALICE	1997	65684
5	E2341	JONES	ALICE	1998	71396
6	E2341	JONES	ALICE	1999	77604
7	E2341	JONES	ALICE	2000	84353
8	E2341	JONES	ALICE	2001	91688

9. Reading a Hierarchical Raw Data File and Creating One Observation Per Header Record (Optional)

Using the same raw data file as in exercise 7, create a SAS data set named **work.current** with the variables **ID**, **LName**, **FName**, **HireDate**, and **Salary**. There should be one observation for each employee, and the value of **Salary** should be equal to the most recent year's salary.

Listing of **work.current**

Obs	ID	LName	FName	Hire Date	Salary
1	E1232	SMITH	JOHN	14532	61065
2	E2341	JONES	ALICE	13666	91688
3	E3452	MOORE	LES	12352	32639
4	E6781	LEE	JENNIFER	11947	28305
5	E8321	LONG	GAYLE	13479	40440
6	E1052	GREEN	THOMAS	13572	39461
7	E1062	FOREMAN	NEIL	9991	41463
8	E8172	THOMPSON	RANDY	14615	40650
9	E1091	MCKINSEY	STARR	11554	40950

4.4 Solutions to Exercises

1. Reading Nonstandard Data

```
    /*View raw data file before writing code*/
proc fslist fileref='raw-data-file';
run;

data states;
    infile 'raw-data-file' dlm='!';
                    /*Set delimiter with DLM=*/
    length State $16;
    input State $ Population:comma9. Size
EnterDate:date9.;
                /*Use colon modifier and informat to
                    read non-standard fields*/
run;

proc print data=states;
    title 'State Names and Facts';
run;
```

2. Using INFILE Statement Options to Change Defaults

```
/*View raw data file before writing code*/
proc fslist fileref='raw-data-file';
run;

data aromas;
    length Condition $ 11 Cure1 Cure2 Cure3 $ 11;
    infile 'raw-data-file' dsd dlm=' ' missover;
                /*DSD option deals with embedded
                    delimiters
                    DLM= changes delimiter back to a space
                    MISSOVER prevents SAS from going to a
                    new record where Cure2 and Cure3 are
                    missing*/
    input Condition $ Cure1 $ Cure2 $ Cure3 $;
run;

proc print data=aromas;
    title 'Aromatherapy Data Set';
run;
```

3. Reading Multiple Records per Observation

```
/*View raw data file before writing code*/
proc fslist fileref='raw-data-file';
run;

data medical(drop=plan);
   infile 'raw-data-file';
   length ID $ 5 FName LName $ 11 Plan $ 1 Blood $ 3 ;
   input ID $ FName $ Lname $;
   input Plan $ Blood $; /*Second INPUT statement loads
                          next record. A forward slash
                          (/) can also be used.*/
 run;

proc print data=medical;
   title 'Patient Names and Blood Types';
run;
```

4. Reading Mixed Record Types

```
/*View raw data file before writing code*/
proc fslist fileref='raw-data-file';
run;

data allergies;
   length ID $ 5 FName LName $ 11
          Plan $ 1 Blood $ 3 Allergy $ 1 AlgyType $10;
   infile 'raw-data-file';
   input ID $ LName $ FName $ Plan $ Blood $ Allergy $ @;
                        /*Trailing @ prevents new record
                          from being loaded*/
   if allergy='N' then
      input dependents;
   else if allergy='Y' then
        input Algytype $ Dependents;
run;

proc print data=allergies;
   title 'Patients and Allergy Code';
run;
```

5. Subsetting from a Raw Data File (Optional)

```
data allergies2;
   length ID $ 5 FName LName $ 11
          Plan $ 1 Blood $ 3 Allergy $ 1 AlgyType $10;
   infile 'raw-data-file';
   input ID $ LName $ FName $ Plan $ Blood $ Allergy $ @;
   if allergy='Y'; /*subsetting IF*/
      input Algytype $ Dependents;
run;

proc print data=allergies2;
   title 'Patients with Allergies Only';
run;
```

6. Reading Raw Data with Multiple Observations per Record

```
/*View raw data file before writing code*/
proc fslist fileref='raw-data-file';
run;

/*Create two data sets*/

data credits debits;
   infile 'raw-data-file';
   input Date: date9. Type $ Amount : comma9. @@;
                     /*Hold until end of record*/

run;

proc print data=credits;
   title 'Account Transactions';
run;
```

7. Creating Multiple SAS Data Sets from a Single Raw Data File (Optional)

```
   /*View raw data file before writing code*/
proc fslist fileref='raw-data-file';
run;


/*Create two data sets*/

data credits debits;
   infile 'raw-data-file';
   input Date: date9. Type $ Amount : comma9. @@;
                                     /*Hold until end of
                                         record*/
/*Use Type to determine whether credit or debit*/
   if Type='C' then output credits;
   if Type='D' then output debits;
run;

proc print data=credits;
   title 'Credits to Account';
run;

proc print data=debits;
   title 'Debits to Account';
run;
```

8. Reading a Hierarchical Data File and Creating One Observation per Detail Record

```
/*View raw data file before writing code*/
proc fslist fileref='raw-data-file';
run;

data salaries (drop=Type);
   retain ID LName FName;
   length ID $ 6;
   infile 'raw-data-file';
   input Type $ @;
   if Type='E' then  /*This is a header record*/
      input ID $ FName $ LName $;
   else if Type='S' then do;
      input SalYear Salary:comma8.;
      output;
        /*Outputs one observation for each detail record*/
    end;
run;

proc print data=salaries;
   title 'Yearly Salaries Through 2001';
run;
```

9. **Reading a Hierarchical Raw Data File and Creating One Observation per Header Record (Optional)**

```
   /*View raw data file before writing code*/
proc fslist fileref='raw-data-file';
run;

data current(drop=SalYear Type);
   retain ID FName LName HireDate Salary;
    /*Must retain all variables in new data set*/
   length ID $ 6;
   infile 'raw-data-file';
   input Type $ @;
   if Type='E' then do;
      if _n_ ne 1 then output; /*Ouput when next employee
                                      is read*/
      input ID $ FName $ LName $
            HireDate : date9.;
      end;
   else if Type='S' then do;
      input SalYear Salary:comma8.;
      end;
run;

proc print data=current;
   title 'Salaries as of 2001';
run;
```

Chapter 5   Data Transformations

5.1   Introduction

Objectives

- Review the syntax of SAS functions.

3

SAS Functions

The SAS System provides a large library of functions for manipulating data during DATA step execution.

A SAS function is often categorized by the type of data manipulation performed:

- truncation
- character
- date and time
- mathematical
- trigonometric
- special

- sample statistics
- arithmetic
- financial
- random number
- state and ZIP code.

4

See SAS OnlineDoc for Version 8 or *SAS® Language Reference: Dictionary, Version 8,* for a complete list of functions and their syntax.

Syntax for SAS Functions

A *SAS function* is a routine that performs a computation or system manipulation and returns a value. Functions use *arguments* supplied by the user or by the operating environment.

General form of a SAS function:

> *function-name(argument-1,argument-2,...,argument-n)*

5

Each argument is separated from the others by a comma.

Some functions accept

- multiple arguments in any order
- a specific number of arguments in a fixed order
- no arguments.

Functions that require arguments accept

- constants
- variables
- functions
- expressions.

Using SAS Functions

You can use functions in executable DATA step statements anywhere an expression can appear.

```
data contrib;
   set prog2.donate;
   Total=sum(Qtr1,Qtr2,Qtr3,Qtr4);
   if Total ge 50;
run;

proc print data=contrib noobs;
run;
```

6

Using SAS Functions

Partial Output

ID	Qtr1	Qtr2	Qtr3	Qtr4	Total
E00224	12	33	22	.	67
E00367	35	48	40	30	153
E00441	.	63	89	90	242
E00587	16	19	30	29	94
E00621	10	12	15	25	62

What if you want to sum Qtr1 through Qtr400, instead of Qtr1 through Qtr4?

7

Many functions ignore arguments that contain a missing value.

SAS Variable Lists

A *SAS variable list* is an abbreviated method of referring to a list of variable names. SAS enables you to use the following variable lists:

- numbered range lists
- name range lists
- name prefix lists
- special SAS name lists.

8

Numbered range lists	`x1-xn`	specifies all variables from X1 to Xn inclusive. You can begin with any number and end with any number as long as you do not violate the rules for user-supplied variable names and the numbers are consecutive.
Name range lists	`x--a`	specifies all variables ordered as they are in the program data vector, from X to A inclusive.
	`x-numeric-a`	specifies all numeric variables from X to A inclusive.
	`x-character-a`	specifies all character variables from X to A inclusive.
Name prefix lists	`sum(of REV:)`	tells SAS to calculate the sum of all the variables that begin with "REV," such as REVJAN, REVFEB, and REVMAR.
Special SAS name lists	`_ALL_`	specifies all variables that are already defined in the current DATA step.
	`_NUMERIC_`	specifies all numeric variables that are currently defined in the current DATA step.
	`_CHARACTER_`	specifies all character variables that are currently defined in the current DATA step.

SAS Variable Lists

When you use a numbered range list in a SAS function, use the keyword OF in front of the first variable name in the list.

```
data contrib;
   set prog2.donate;
   Total=sum(of Qtr1-Qtr4);
   if Total ge 50;
run;
```

Omitting the keyword OF causes subtraction to occur.

9

5.2 Manipulating Character Values

Objectives

- Use SAS functions and operators to extract, edit, and search character values.

11

A Mailing Label Application

The `prog2.freqfliers` data set contains information about frequent fliers. Use this data set to create another data set suitable for mailing labels.

12

A Mailing Label Application

ID is a character variable. Its last digit represents the
gender (1 denotes female, 2 denotes male) of the
frequent flier.

prog2.freqfliers

ID	Name	Address1	Address2
F31351	Farr,Sue	15 Harvey Rd.	Macon,Bibb,GA,31298
F161	Cox,Kay B.	163 McNeil Pl.	Kern,Pond,CA,93280
F212	Mason,Ron	442 Glen Ave.	Miami,Dade,FL,33054
F25122	Ruth,G. H.	2491 Brady St.	Munger,Bay,MI,48747

13

A Mailing Label Application

labels

FullName	Address1	Address2
Ms. Sue Farr	15 Harvey Rd.	Macon, GA 31298
Ms. Kay B. Cox	163 McNeil Pl.	Kern, CA 93280
Mr. Ron Mason	442 Glen Ave.	Miami, FL 33054
Mr. G. H. Ruth	2491 Brady St.	Munger, MI 48747

The first task is to create a title of "Mr." or "Ms." based on
the last digit of ID.

14

The SUBSTR Function (Right Side)

The SUBSTR function is used to extract or insert characters.

> *NewVar*=SUBSTR(*string*,*start*<,*length*>);

This form of the SUBSTR function (right side of assignment statement) extracts characters.

15

string   can be a character constant, variable, or expression.

start   specifies the starting position.

length   specifies the number of characters to extract. If omitted, the substring consists of the remainder of *string*.

✎   If the length of the created variable is not previously defined with a LENGTH statement, it is the same as the length of the first argument to SUBSTR.

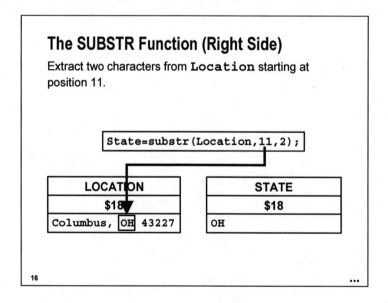

The SUBSTR Function (Right Side)

Extract two characters from `Location` starting at position 11.

`State=substr(Location,11,2);`

LOCATION
$18
Columbus, OH 43227

STATE
$18
OH

16

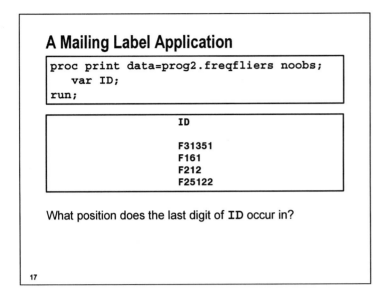

A Mailing Label Application

```
proc print data=prog2.freqfliers noobs;
    var ID;
run;
```

ID
F31351
F161
F212
F25122

What position does the last digit of ID occur in?

17

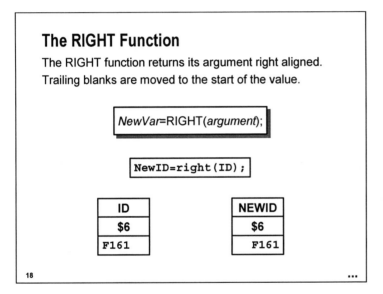

The RIGHT Function

The RIGHT function returns its argument right aligned.
Trailing blanks are moved to the start of the value.

NewVar=RIGHT(*argument*);

```
NewID=right(ID);
```

ID		NEWID
$6		$6
F161		F161

18   •••

argument   can be a character constant, variable, or expression.

    If the length of the created variable is not previously defined with a
LENGTH statement, it is the same as the length of *argument*.

The LEFT function returns its argument left aligned. Trailing blanks are
moved to the end of the value. The argument's length does not change.

NewVar=LEFT(*argument*);

A Mailing Label Application

```
data labels;
   set prog2.freqfliers;
   if substr(right(ID),6)='1' then
      Title='Ms.';
   else if substr(right(ID),6)='2'
      then Title='Mr.';
run;

proc print data=labels noobs;
   var ID Title;
run;
```

19

A Mailing Label Application

ID	Title
F31351	Ms.
F161	Ms.
F212	Mr.
F25122	Mr.

20

A Mailing Label Application

The next task is to separate the names of the frequent fliers into two parts.

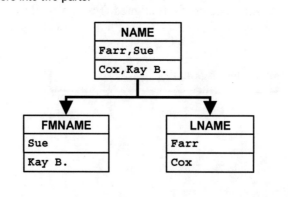

21

The SCAN Function

The SCAN function returns the *n*th word of a character value.

It is used to extract words from a character value when the relative order of words is known, but their starting positions are not.

> *NewVar*=SCAN(*string,n<,delimiters>*);

22

string   can be a character constant, variable, or expression.

n   specifies the *n*th word to extract from *string*. If *n* is negative, SCAN selects the word in the character string starting from the end of the string.

delimiters   defines characters that delimit (separate) words.

   If the third argument is omitted, the default delimiters are

ASCII (PC, UNIX)	blank . < (+ | & ! $ *) ; - / , % ^
EBCDIC (OS/390)	blank . < (+ | & ! $ *) ; - / , % | ¢ ¬

The SCAN Function

When using the SCAN function,

- the length of the created variable is 200 bytes if it is not previously defined with a LENGTH statement
- delimiters before the first word have no effect
- any character or set of characters can serve as delimiters
- two or more contiguous delimiters are treated as a single delimiter
- a missing value is returned if there are fewer than *n* words in *string*.

23

The SCAN Function

Extract the second word of **Phrase**.

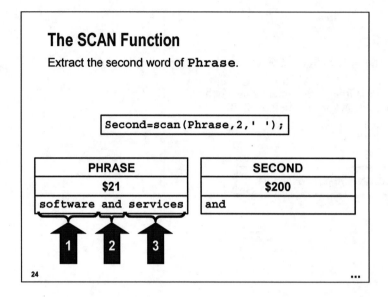

```
Second=scan(Phrase,2,' ');
```

PHRASE
$21
software and services

SECOND
$200
and

24

The SCAN Function

Extract the second word of **Phrase**.

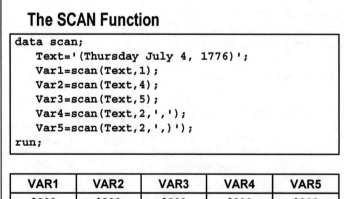

```
Second=scan(Phrase,2,':');
```

PHRASE
$21
software and:services

SECOND
$200
services

25

The SCAN Function

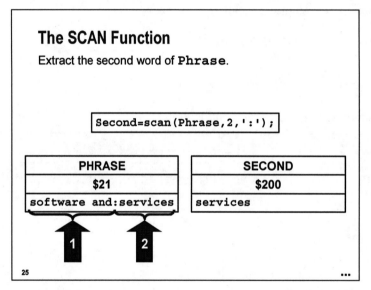

```
data scan;
   Text='(Thursday July 4, 1776)';
   Var1=scan(Text,1);
   Var2=scan(Text,4);
   Var3=scan(Text,5);
   Var4=scan(Text,2,',');
   Var5=scan(Text,2,',)');
run;
```

VAR1	VAR2	VAR3	VAR4	VAR5
$200	$200	$200	$200	$200
Thursday	1776		1776)	1776

29

A Mailing Label Application

```
data labels;
   length FMName LName $ 10;
   set prog2.freqfliers;
   if substr(right(ID),6)='1' then
      Title='Ms.';
   else if substr(right(ID),6)='2'
        then Title='Mr.';
   FMName=scan(Name,2,',');
   LName=scan(Name,1,',');
run;
```

30

A Mailing Label Application

```
proc print data=labels noobs;
   var ID Title Name FMName LName;
run;
```

ID	Title	Name	FMName	LName
F31351	Ms.	Farr,Sue	Sue	Farr
F161	Ms.	Cox,Kay B.	Kay B.	Cox
F212	Mr.	Mason,Ron	Ron	Mason
F25122	Mr.	Ruth,G. H.	G. H.	Ruth

The next task is to join the values of `Title`, `FMName`, and `LName` into another variable.

31

Concatenation Operator

The *concatenation operator* joins character strings.

Depending on the characters available on your keyboard, the symbol to concatenate character values can be two exclamation points (!!), two vertical bars (||), or two broken vertical bars (¦¦).

> *NewVar=string1 !! string2;*

32

✒ If the length of the created variable is not previously defined with a LENGTH statement, it is the sum of the lengths of the concatenated constants, variables, and expressions.

Concatenation cannot be accomplished with a SAS function. You must use the concatenation operator.

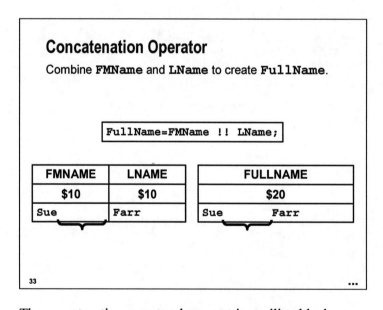

Concatenation Operator

Combine **FMName** and **LName** to create **FullName**.

`FullName=FMName !! LName;`

FMNAME	LNAME	FULLNAME
$10	$10	$20
Sue	Farr	Sue Farr

33

The concatenation operator does not trim trailing blanks.

The TRIM Function

The TRIM function removes trailing blanks from its argument.

> *NewVar*=TRIM(*argument1*) !! *argument2*;

If the argument is blank, TRIM returns one blank.

34

argument can be a character constant, variable, or expression.

 If the length of the created variable is not previously defined with a LENGTH statement, the length of the new variable is the length of *argument*.

The TRIMN and TRIM functions are similar. TRIMN returns a null string (zero blanks) if the argument is blank.

The COMPBL function is also used to remove multiple blanks in a character string. COMPBL translates each occurrence of two or more consecutive blanks into a single blank. The value that the COMPBL function returns has a default length of 200.

The TRIM Function

```
data trim;
   length FMName LName $ 10;
   FMName='Sue';
   LName='Farr';
   FullName1=trim(FMName);
   FullName2=trim(FMName) !! LName;
   FullName3=trim(FMName) !! ' ' !! LName;
run;
```

FULLNAME1	FULLNAME2	FULLNAME3
$10	$20	$21
Sue	SueFarr	Sue Farr

36   c05s2d1.sas

The TRIM function does not remove leading blanks from a character argument. Use a combination of the TRIM and LEFT functions to remove leading and trailing blanks from a character argument.

For example, if **FMName** contained leading blanks, the following assignment statement would correctly concatenate **FMName** and **LName** into **FullName**:

```
FullName=trim(left(FMName)) !! ' ' !! LName;
```

 **Exercises**

1. Manipulating Character Values

Read the variable **Name** from **prog2.people** to create a temporary SAS data set named **flname** that contains the variables **NewName** and **CityState**. The values of **NewName** should be the concatenation of each person's first name and last name with a single blank between them.

Listing of **prog2.people**

```
              Name                        CityState

              LAFF, STANLEY X.            SPRINGFIELD,IL.
              FLORENTINO, HELEN-ASHE H.   WASHINGTON:DC.
              VAN ALLSBURG, JAN F.        SHORT HILLS-NJ.
              DEAN, LINDSAY A.            PASADENA(MD.)
              RIZEN, GEORGE Q.            CHICAGO(IL.)
              MITCHELL, MARC J.           CHICAGO-IL.
              MILLS, DOROTHY E.           JOE,MT.
              WEBB, JONATHAN W.           MORRISVILLE:(NC.)
              BAGGETT, ROSEMARY C.        CLEMMONS,NC.
              LACK, PHYLLIS M.            WOODLAND HILLS[CA.]
              HICKS, CLARENCE C.          IRVINE,CA.
              COX, DOROTHY E.             TIMONIUM(MD.)
              SEPTOFF, DONALD E.          BOSTON;MA.
              PHOENIX, JANICE A.          SOMERVILLE/NJ.
              HUNEYCUTT, MURRAY Y.        DIME BOX-TX.
              ERICKSON, SHERRY A.         EL PASO--TX.
              SCHNEIDER, CLIVE J.         WEST PALM BEACH/FL.
              PUTNAM, KIMBERLY M.         DUNWOODY(GA.)
              PITTMAN, JENNIFER R.        BENNINGTON-VT.
              ROLEN, STACY D.             CODY/WY.
```

All values of **Name** in **prog2.people** consist of a first name, middle initial, and last name.

✏ Some names contain hyphenated first names or multiple-word last names.

Print the **flname** data set to verify your results.

Partial Listing of **flname**

```
        Obs    NewName                   CityState

         1     STANLEY LAFF              SPRINGFIELD,IL.
         2     HELEN-ASHE FLORENTINO     WASHINGTON:DC.
         3     JAN VAN ALLSBURG          SHORT HILLS-NJ.
         4     LINDSAY DEAN              PASADENA(MD.)
         5     GEORGE RIZEN              CHICAGO(IL.)
```

2. Performing Additional Character Manipulations

Read the variable **Name** from **prog2.people** to create a temporary SAS data set named **init** that contains the variables **Name**, **Initials**, and **CityState**. The values of **Initials** should be the concatenation of the first character from each person's first name, middle name, and last name with no delimiters separating the characters.

Print the **init** data set to verify your results.

Partial Listing of **init**

Obs	Name	CityState	Initials
1	LAFF, STANLEY X.	SPRINGFIELD,IL.	SXL
2	FLORENTINO, HELEN-ASHE H.	WASHINGTON:DC.	HHF
3	VAN ALLSBURG, JAN F.	SHORT HILLS-NJ.	JFV
4	DEAN, LINDSAY A.	PASADENA(MD.)	LAD
5	RIZEN, GEORGE Q.	CHICAGO(IL.)	GQR

A Search Application

The `prog2.ffhistory` data set contains information about the history of each frequent flier.

This history information consists of

- each membership level the flier has attained (bronze, silver, or gold)
- the year the flier attained each level.

Create a report showing all frequent fliers who have attained silver membership status and the year each of them became silver members.

38

A Search Application

`prog2.ffhistory`

ID	Status	Seat Pref
F31351	Silver 1998,Gold 2000	AISLE
F161	Bronze 1999	WINDOW
F212	Bronze 1992,silver 1995	WINDOW
F25122	Bronze 1994,Silver 1996,Gold 1998	AISLE

To determine who has attained silver membership status, you must search the `Status` variable for the value "`Silver`".

39

The INDEX Function

The INDEX function searches a character argument for the location of a specified character value and returns its location.

Position=INDEX(*target*,*value*);

The INDEX function returns
- the starting position of the first occurrence of *value* within *target*, if *value* is found.
- 0, if *value* is not found.

40

target　specifies the character expression to search.

value　specifies the string of characters to search for in the character expression.

The search for *value* is literal. Capitalization and blanks (leading, embedded, and trailing) are considered.

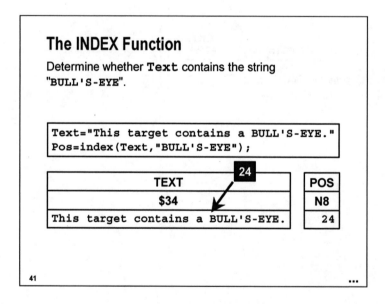

The INDEX Function

Determine whether `Text` contains the string
`"BULL'S-EYE"`.

```
Text="This target contains a BULL'S-EYE."
Pos=index(Text,"BULL'S-EYE");
```

TEXT	POS
$34	N8
This target contains a BULL'S-EYE.	24

41

The INDEX Function

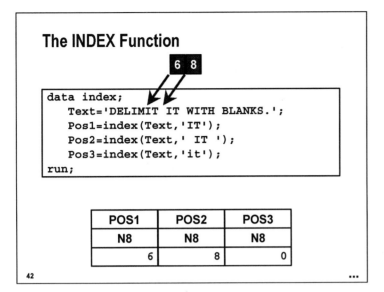

```
data index;
   Text='DELIMIT IT WITH BLANKS.';
   Pos1=index(Text,'IT');
   Pos2=index(Text,' IT ');
   Pos3=index(Text,'it');
run;
```

POS1	POS2	POS3
N8	N8	N8
6	8	0

42 ...

The INDEX Function

```
data index2;
   length String $ 5;
   String='IT';
   Text='DELIMIT IT WITH BLANKS.';
   Pos4=index(Text,String);
   Pos5=index(Text,trim(String));
   Pos6=index(Text,' ' !! trim(String) !! ' ');
run;
```

STRING	POS4	POS5	POS6
$5	N8	N8	N8
IT	0	6	8

43 ...

A Search Application

`prog2.ffhistory`

```
                                          Seat
   ID       Status                        Pref

   F31351   Silver 1998,Gold 2000         AISLE
   F161     Bronze 1999                   WINDOW
   F212     Bronze 1992,silver 1995       WINDOW
   F25122   Bronze 1994,Silver 1996,Gold 1998  AISLE
```

```
data silver;
   set prog2.ffhistory;
   if index(Status,'Silver') > 0;
run;
```

44

A Search Application

```
proc print data=silver noobs;
run;
```

ID	Status	Seat Pref
F31351	Silver 1998,Gold 2000	AISLE
F25122	Bronze 1994,Silver 1996,Gold 1998	AISLE

Why was F212 not selected?

45

The UPCASE Function

The UPCASE function

- converts all letters in its argument to uppercase
- has no effect on digits and special characters.

NewVal=UPCASE(*argument*);

46

argument   specifies any character argument.

A Search Application

```
data silver(drop=Location);
   length Year $ 4;
   set prog2.ffhistory;
   Location=index(upcase(Status),'SILVER');
   if Location > 0;
   Year=substr(Status,Location+7,4);
run;

proc print data=silver noobs;
   var ID Status Year SeatPref;
run;
```

47

A Search Application

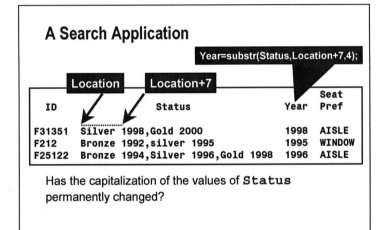

Has the capitalization of the values of `Status` permanently changed?

48   ...

The TRANWRD Function

The TRANWRD function replaces or removes all occurrences of a given word (or a pattern of characters) within a character string.

> *NewVal*=TRANWRD(*source,target,replacement*);

The TRANWRD function does not remove trailing blanks in *target* or *replacement*.

49

source   specifies the source string that you want to translate.

target   specifies the string searched for in *source*.

replacement   specifies the string that replaces *target*.

 If the length of the created variable is not previously defined with a LENGTH statement, it is 200 bytes.

The TRANWRD Function

Replace the first word of **Dessert**.

> ```
> Dessert=tranwrd(Dessert,'Pumpkin','Apple');
> ```

DESSERT
$20
Pumpkin pie

DESSERT
$20
Apple pie

50   ...

Using the TRANWRD function to replace an existing string with a longer string may cause truncation of the resulting value if a LENGTH statement is not used.

A Search Application

```
data silver(drop=Location);
   length Year $ 4;
   set prog2.ffhistory;
   Status=tranwrd(Status,'silver','Silver');
   Location=index(Status,'Silver');
   if Location > 0;
   Year=substr(Status,Location+7,4);
run;

proc print data=silver noobs;
   var ID Status Year SeatPref;
run;
```

51

A Search Application

ID	Status	Year	Seat Pref
F31351	Silver 1998,Gold 2000	1998	AISLE
F212	Bronze 1992,Silver 1995	1995	WINDOW
F25122	Bronze 1994,Silver 1996,Gold 1998	1996	AISLE

52

The LOWCASE Function

The LOWCASE function

- converts all letters in its argument to lowercase
- has no effect on digits and special characters.

NewVal=LOWCASE(*argument*);

53

---

argument   specifies any character argument.

The SUBSTR Function (Left Side)

The SUBSTR function is used to extract or insert characters.

SUBSTR(*string,start<,length>*)=*value;*

This form of the SUBSTR function (left side of assignment statement) replaces characters in a character variable.

54

---

string   specifies a character variable.

start   specifies a numeric expression that is the beginning character position.

length   specifies a numeric expression that is the length of the substring that will be replaced.

✎   *length* cannot be larger than the remaining length of *string* (including trailing blanks) after *start*.

If you omit *length*, SAS uses all of the characters on the right side of the assignment statement to replace the values of *string*, up to the limit indicated by the previous note.

The SUBSTR Function (Left Side)

Replace two characters from `Location` starting at position 11.

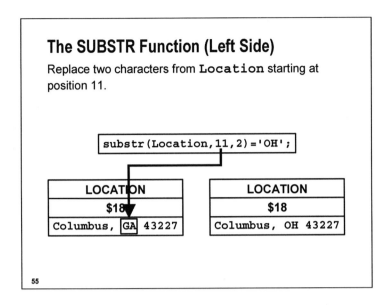

55

The LOWCASE Function

```
data silver;
   set silver;
   substr(SeatPref,2)=
      lowcase(substr(SeatPref,2));
run;
```

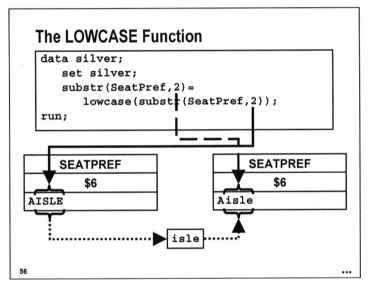

56   ...

A Search Application

```
proc print data=silver noobs;
   var ID Year SeatPref;
run;
```

ID	Year	Seat Pref
F31351	1998	Aisle
F212	1995	Window
F25122	1996	Aisle

c05s2d2.sas

57

 **Exercises**

3. Searching for a Character Value

Read the variable **CityState** from **prog2.people** to create a temporary SAS data set named **prairie** that contains only those people who live in the state of Illinois (IL). Use the INDEX function to search through the values of CityState.

Partial Listing of **prog2.people**

Name	CityState
LAFF, STANLEY X.	SPRINGFIELD,IL.
FLORENTINO, HELEN-ASHE H.	WASHINGTON:DC.
VAN ALLSBURG, JAN F.	SHORT HILLS-NJ.
DEAN, LINDSAY A.	PASADENA(MD.)
RIZEN, GEORGE Q.	CHICAGO(IL.)

Print the **prairie** data set to verify your results. There should be three observations.

Listing of **prairie**

Obs	Name	CityState
1	LAFF, STANLEY X.	SPRINGFIELD,IL.
2	RIZEN, GEORGE Q.	CHICAGO(IL.)
3	MITCHELL, MARC J.	CHICAGO-IL.

✒ Illinois is unofficially known as the "Prairie State." This nickname originates from the practice of declaring the third full week in September each year as Illinois Prairie Week to demonstrate the value of preserving and re-establishing native Illinois prairies.

4. Performing Additional Character Manipulations

Read the variable **Name** from **prairie** to create a temporary SAS data set named **mixedprairie** that contains the values of **Name** converted from all uppercase to mixed case as shown below.

Print the **mixedprairie** data set to verify your results.

Listing of **mixedprairie**

Obs	Name	CityState
1	Laff, Stanley X.	SPRINGFIELD,IL.
2	Rizen, George Q.	CHICAGO(IL.)
3	Mitchell, Marc J.	CHICAGO-IL.

5. Using Additional Character Functions (Optional)

Read the variable **CityState** from **prog2.people** to create a temporary SAS data set named **postal**. Use the STNAMEL function to convert the state postal code in **CityState** to the corresponding **uppercase** state name.

The STNAMEL function converts a two-character state postal code (or world-wide GSA geographic code for U.S. territories), such as IL, for Illinois, to the corresponding state name in **mixed** case. Returned values can contain up to 20 characters.

> NewState=STNAMEL(*postal-code*);

postal-code specifies a character expression that contains the two-character standard state postal code. Characters can be mixed case.

> ✎ STNAMEL ignores trailing blanks but generates an error if the expression contains leading blanks.

Partial Listing of **postal**

```
Obs    Name                        CityState

 1     LAFF, STANLEY X.            SPRINGFIELD, ILLINOIS
 2     FLORENTINO, HELEN-ASHE H.   WASHINGTON, DISTRICT OF COLUMBIA
 3     VAN ALLSBURG, JAN F.        SHORT HILLS, NEW JERSEY
 4     DEAN, LINDSAY A.            PASADENA, MARYLAND
 5     RIZEN, GEORGE Q.            CHICAGO, ILLINOIS
```

6. Performing Additional Character Manipulations (Optional)

Read the variable **Name** from **prog2.people** to create a temporary SAS data set named **mixedall** that contains the values of **Name** converted from all uppercase to mixed case as shown below.

Print the **mixedall** data set to verify your results.

Partial Listing of **mixedall**

```
Obs    Name                        CityState

 1     Laff, Stanley X.            SPRINGFIELD,IL.
 2     Florentino, Helen-Ashe H.   WASHINGTON:DC.
 3     Van Allsburg, Jan F.        SHORT HILLS-NJ.
 4     Dean, Lindsay A.            PASADENA(MD.)
 5     Rizen, George Q.            CHICAGO(IL.)
```

> ✎ Some names contain hyphenated first names or multiple-word last names.

5.3 Manipulating Numeric Values

Objectives

- Use SAS functions to truncate numeric values.
- Use SAS functions to compute sample statistics of numeric values.

60

Truncation Functions

Selected functions that truncate numeric values include

- ROUND function
- CEIL function
- FLOOR function
- INT function.

61

The ROUND Function

The ROUND function returns a value rounded to the nearest round-off unit.

> *NewVar*=ROUND(*argument*<,*round-off-unit*>);

If *round-off-unit* is not provided, *argument* is rounded to the nearest integer.

62

argument   is numeric.

round-off-unit   is numeric and nonnegative.

The ROUND Function

```
data truncate;
   NewVar1=round(12.12);
   NewVar2=round(42.65,.1);
   NewVar3=round(6.478,.01);
   NewVar4=round(96.47,10);
run;
```

NEWVAR1	NEWVAR2	NEWVAR3	NEWVAR4
12	42.7	6.48	100

63   ...

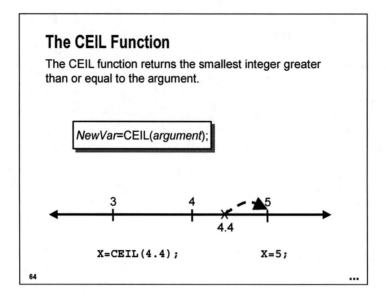

argument is numeric.

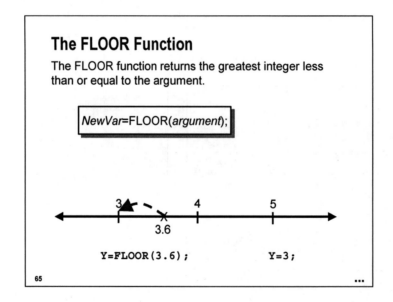

argument is numeric.

The INT Function

The INT function returns the integer portion of the
argument.

NewVar=INT(*argument*);

66

argument is numeric.

Truncation Functions

```
data truncate;
   Var1=6.478;
   NewVar1=ceil(Var1);
   NewVar2=floor(Var1);
   NewVar3=int(Var1);
run;
```

VAR1	NEWVAR1	NEWVAR2	NEWVAR3
6.478	7	6	6

67   ...

Truncation Functions

```
data Truncate2;
   Var1=-6.478;
   NewVar1=ceil(Var1);
   NewVar2=floor(Var1);
   NewVar3=int(Var1);
run;
```

VAR1	NEWVAR1	NEWVAR2	NEWVAR3
-6.478	-6	-7	-6

68   ...

For values greater than 0, FLOOR and INT return the same value. For values less than 0, CEIL and INT return the same value.

Functions That Compute Statistics

Selected functions that compute sample statistics based on a group of values include

- SUM function (total of values)
- MEAN function (average of values)
- MIN function (lowest value)
- MAX function (highest value).

69

These functions

- accept multiple arguments in any order
- use the same algorithm as SAS statistical procedures
- ignore missing values.

The SUM Function

The SUM function
- adds values together
- ignores missing values.

NewVar=SUM(*argument-1,argument-2,…,argument-n*);

VAR1	VAR2	VAR3	NewVar=	NEWVAR
12	.	6	sum(Var1,Var2,Var3);	18

What would be the value of `NewVar=Var1+Var2+Var3;`?

70   ...

argument-1 through *argument-n* are numeric.

The assignment statement can be rewritten to take advantage of SAS variable lists:

```
NewVar=sum(of Var1-Var3);
```

The MEAN Function

The MEAN function
- calculates the arithmetic mean (average) of values
- ignores missing values.

NewVar=MEAN(*argument-1,argument-2,…,argument-n*);

Example:

VAR1	VAR2	VAR3	NewVar=	NEWVAR
12	.	6	mean(Var1,Var2,Var3);	9

71   ...

argument-1 through *argument-n* are numeric.

The assignment statement can be rewritten to take advantage of SAS variable lists:

```
NewVar=mean(of Var1-Var3);
```

Exercises

7. Manipulating Numeric Values

Create a data set named **final** from **prog2.grade**. The **final** data set should contain a new variable **Overall** that is the semester average grade. Calculate **Overall** by averaging all the tests plus the final. The final is weighted twice as much as any of the other tests, so count the final twice when calculating **Overall**. Store **Overall** rounded to the nearest integer. Print the **final** data set.

Partial Listing of **prog2.grade**

SSN	Course	Test1	Test2	Test3	Final
012-40-4928	BUS450	80	70	80	80
012-83-3816	BUS450	90	90	60	80
341-44-0781	MATH400	78	87	90	91
423-01-7721	BUS450	80	70	75	95
448-23-8111	MATH400	88	91	100	95

Partial Listing of **final**

Obs	SSN	Course	Test1	Test2	Test3	Final	Overall
1	012-40-4928	BUS450	80	70	80	80	78
2	012-83-3816	BUS450	90	90	60	80	80
3	341-44-0781	MATH400	78	87	90	91	87
4	423-01-7721	BUS450	80	70	75	95	83
5	448-23-8111	MATH400	88	91	100	95	94

8. Performing Additional Numeric Manipulations (Optional)

Modify the DATA step created in the previous exercise so the value of **Overall** is the average of the two highest test scores and the final. (The lowest test score should not be used to calculate **Overall**.) As before, the final should be counted twice. Store **Overall** rounded to the nearest integer. Print the **final** data set.

Partial Listing of **final**

Obs	SSN	Course	Test1	Test2	Test3	Final	Overall
1	012-40-4928	BUS450	80	70	80	80	80
2	012-83-3816	BUS450	90	90	60	80	85
3	341-44-0781	MATH400	78	87	90	91	90
4	423-01-7721	BUS450	80	70	75	95	86
5	448-23-8111	MATH400	88	91	100	95	95

5.4 Manipulating Numeric Values Based on Dates

Objectives
- Review SAS functions used to create SAS date values.
- Review SAS functions to extract information from SAS date values.
- Use SAS functions to determine intervals between two SAS date values.

74

Creating SAS Date Values

You can use the MDY or TODAY functions to create SAS date values.

The MDY function creates a SAS date value from month, day, and year values.

    NewDate=MDY(month,day,year);

The TODAY function returns the current date as a SAS date value.

    NewDate=TODAY();

75

month   specifies a numeric expression representing an integer from 1 to 12.

day   specifies a numeric expression representing an integer from 1 to 31.

year   specifies a numeric expression representing an integer that identifies a specific year.

✐   The DATE function is synonymous with the TODAY function.

Extracting Information

You can use the MONTH, DAY, and YEAR functions to extract information from SAS date values.

The MONTH function creates a numeric value (1-12) that represents the month of a SAS date value.

> *NewMonth*=MONTH(*SAS-date-value*);

continued...

76

Extracting Information

The DAY function creates a numeric value (1-31) that represents the day of a SAS date value.

> *NewDay*=DAY(*SAS-date-value*);

The YEAR function creates a four-digit numeric value that represents the year.

> *NewYear*=YEAR(*SAS-date-value*);

77

Other similar functions include

QTR	Returns the quarter of the SAS date value (1-4; 1 represents January through March, 2 represents April thru June, and so on).
WEEKDAY	Returns the day of the week of a SAS date value (1-7; 1 represents Sunday, 7 represents Saturday).

Calculating an Interval of Years

The YRDIF function returns the number of years between two SAS date values.

NewVal=YRDIF(*sdate,edate,basis*);

78

sdate   specifies a SAS date value that identifies the starting date.

edate   specifies a SAS date value that identifies the ending date.

basis   identifies a character constant or variable that describes how SAS calculates the date difference. The following character strings are valid:

'ACT/ACT'	uses the actual number of days between dates in calculating the number of years. SAS calculates this value as the number of days that fall in 365-day years divided by 365 plus the number of days that fall in 366-day years divided by 366. You can use 'ACTUAL' as an alias.
'30/360'	specifies a 30-day month and a 360-day year in calculating the number of years. Each month is considered to have 30 days and each year 360 days, regardless of the actual number of days in each month or year. SAS treats the last day of any month as the last day of a 30-day month. You can use '360' as an alias.
'ACT/360'	uses the actual number of days between dates in calculating the number of years. SAS calculates this value as the number of days divided by 360, regardless of the actual number of days in each year.
'ACT/365'	uses the actual number of days between dates in calculating the number of years. SAS calculates this value as the number of days divided by 365, regardless of the actual number of days in each year.

To calculate the actual number of months between two dates, use the YRDIF function and multiply by 12.

```
NumMonths=yrdif(Date1,Date2,'ACT/ACT')*12;
```

The YRDIF Function

The variable DOB represents a person's date of birth. Assume today's date is May 3, 2008, and DOB is 8 November 1972. What is this person's age?

```
MyVal=yrdif(DOB,'3may2008'd,'act/act');
```

MYVAL
35.483606557

How can you alter this program to

- compute each employee's age based on today's date?
- truncate all of the decimal places without rounding?

79   ...

The DATDIF function can be used to return the number of days between two SAS date values. Only two basis values are valid for the DATDIF function, 'ACT/ACT' and '30/360'.

 **Exercises**

9. Manipulating Numeric Values Based on Dates

The **prog2.noday** data set contains information about employees. Use **prog2.noday** to create **emphire**.

Use the existing **Hiredmonth** and **Hiredyear** variables to create a new variable, **Hired**, that stores the SAS date value for each employee's date of hire. Assume each employee was hired on the 15th of each month.

Create a second new variable, **Years**, that stores the number of years between each employee's date of hire and today's date.

The values of **Hired** should be displayed using a DATE9. format. The values of **Years** should be truncated to remove all decimals without rounding.

emphire should contain three variables: **ID**, **Hired**, and **Years**. Print the data set to verify your results.

Listing of **prog2.noday**

ID	Hired Month	Hired Year
E03464	3	1994
E06523	8	1996
E07346	1	1997
E09965	10	1999
E13467	2	2000

Listing of **emphire**

Obs	ID	Hired	Years
1	E03464	15MAR1994	7
2	E06523	15AUG1996	4
3	E07346	15JAN1997	4
4	E09965	15OCT1999	1
5	E13467	15FEB2000	1

The results above were generated in 2001. Your values of **Years** may differ.

5.5   Converting Variable Type

Objectives

- Understand automatic conversion of character data into numeric data.
- Explicitly convert character data into numeric data.
- Understand automatic conversion of numeric data into character data.
- Explicitly convert numeric data into character data.

82

Data Conversion

In many applications, you may need to convert one data type to another.

- You may need to read digits in character form into a numeric value.
- You may need to write a numeric value to a character string.

83

Data Conversion

You can convert data types
- implicitly by allowing the SAS System to do it for you
- explicitly with these functions:
  - INPUT   character-to-numeric conversion
  - PUT   numeric-to-character conversion.

84

The INPUT statement uses an informat to read a data value and then optionally stores that value in a variable. The INPUT function returns the value produced when a SAS expression is read using a specified informat.

The PUT statement writes a value to an external destination (either the SAS log or a destination you specify). The PUT function returns a value using a specified format.

Automatic Character-to-Numeric Conversion

The `prog2.salary1` data set contains a character variable `Grosspay`. Compute a 10 percent bonus for each employee.

What will happen when the character values of `Grosspay` are used in an arithmetic expression?

85

Automatic Character-to-Numeric Conversion

`prog2.salary1`

ID	GrossPay
$11	$5
201-92-2498	52000
482-87-7945	32000
330-40-7172	49000

```
data bonuses;
   set prog2.salary1;
   Bonus=.10*GrossPay;
run;
```

86

Automatic Character-to-Numeric Conversion

Partial Log

```
2    data bonuses;
3       set prog2.salary1;
4       Bonus=.10*GrossPay;
5    run;

NOTE: Character values have been converted to numeric
values at the places given by: (Line):(Column).
     4:14
NOTE: The data set WORK.BONUSES has 3 observations and
3 variables.
```

87

Automatic Character-to-Numeric Conversion

SAS automatically converts a character value to a numeric value when the character value is used in a numeric context, such as

- assignment to a numeric variable
- an arithmetic operation
- logical comparison with a numeric value
- a function that takes numeric arguments.

89

The WHERE statement and WHERE= data set option do not perform any automatic conversion in comparisons.

Automatic Character-to-Numeric Conversion

The automatic conversion

- uses the *w.* informat
- produces a numeric missing value from a character value that does not conform to standard numeric notation (digits with optional decimal point and/or leading sign and/or E-notation).

90

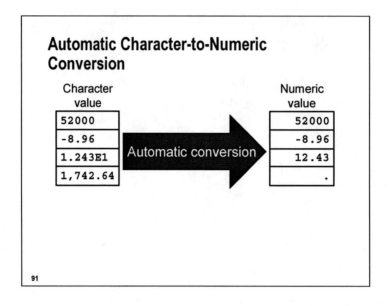

The INPUT Function

The INPUT function is used primarily for converting character values to numeric values.

> *NumVar*=INPUT(*source,informat*);

The INPUT function returns *source* read with *informat*.

source   is a constant, variable, or expression (numeric or character).

informat   is any SAS format or user-defined informat. It must agree with *source* in type.

If you use the INPUT function to create a variable not previously defined, the type and length of the variable is defined by the informat.

     No conversion messages are written to the SAS log by the INPUT function.

The INPUT Function

```
data conversion;
   CVar1='32000';
   CVar2='32,000';
   CVar3='03may2008';
   CVar4='050308';
   NVar1=input(CVar1,5.);
   NVar2=input(CVar2,comma6.);
   NVar3=input(CVar3,date9.);
   NVar4=input(CVar4,mmddyy6.);
run;

proc contents data=conversion;
run;
```

93

The INPUT Function

Partial PROC CONTENTS Output

```
-----Alphabetic List of Variables and Attributes-----

        #    Variable    Type    Len    Pos

        1    CVar1       Char     5      32
        2    CVar2       Char     6      37
        3    CVar3       Char     9      43
        4    CVar4       Char     6      52
        5    NVar1       Num      8       0
        6    NVar2       Num      8       8
        7    NVar3       Num      8      16
        8    NVar4       Num      8      24
```

94

The INPUT Function

```
proc print data=conversion noobs;
run;
```

PROC PRINT Output

CVar1	CVar2	CVar3	CVar4	NVar1
32000	32,000	03may2008	050308	32000

NVar2	NVar3	NVar4
32000	17655	17655

95

Explicit Character-to-Numeric Conversion

The values of the variable **Grosspay** in the SAS data set **prog2.salary2** contain commas. Attempt to use automatic conversion to compute a 10 percent bonus.

prog2.salary2

Id $11	GrossPay $5
201-92-2498	52,000
482-87-7945	32,000
330-40-7172	49,000

96

Explicit Character-to-Numeric Conversion

```
data bonuses;
   set prog2.salary2;
   Bonus=.10*GrossPay;
run;

proc print data=bonuses;
run;
```

PROC PRINT Output

ID	GrossPay	Bonus
201-92-2498	52,000	.
482-87-7945	32,000	.
330-40-7172	49,000	.

97

Explicit Character-to-Numeric Conversion

```
data bonuses;
   set prog2.salary2;
   Bonus=.10*input(GrossPay,comma6.);
run;

proc print data=bonuses;
run;
```

PROC PRINT Output

ID	GrossPay	Bonus
201-92-2498	52,000	5200
482-87-7945	32,000	3200
330-40-7172	49,000	4900

98

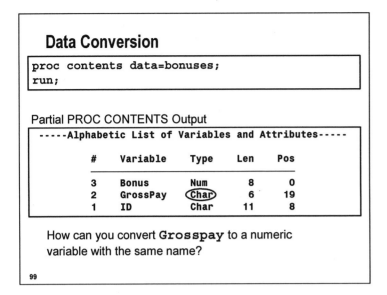

The values of the **Grosspay** variable were explicitly converted to numeric values to create the **Bonus** variable. However, **Grosspay** remains a character variable.

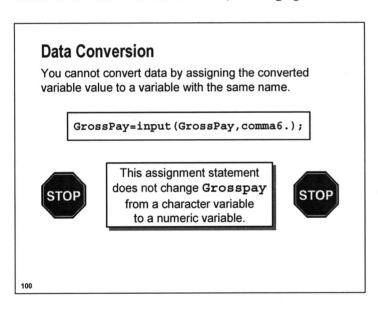

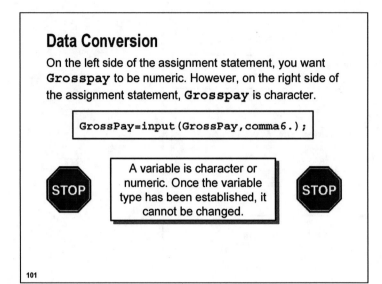

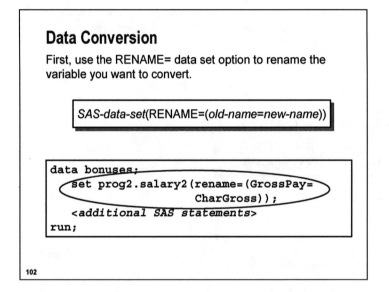

old-name specifies the variable you want to rename.

new-name specifies the new name of the variable. It must be a valid SAS name.

✎ The new name of the variable you want to convert is arbitrary. In this example, the existing variable is renamed **Chargross** to emphasize that a character variable is being converted.

To rename more than one variable from the same data set, separate the variables you want to rename with a space. For example, to rename not only **GrossPay**, but also **ID**, use the following statement.

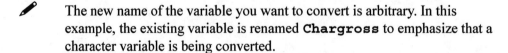

Data Conversion

Second, use the INPUT function in an assignment statement to create a new variable whose name is the original name of the variable you renamed previously.

```
data bonuses;
   set prog2.salary2(rename=(GrossPay=
                       CharGross));
   GrossPay=input(CharGross,comma6.);
   <additional SAS statements>
run;
```

103

Data Conversion

Third, use a DROP= data set option in the DATA statement to exclude the original variable from the output SAS data set.

```
data bonuses(drop=CharGross);
   set prog2.salary2(rename=(GrossPay=
                       CharGross));
   GrossPay=input(CharGross,comma6.);
   Bonus=.10*GrossPay;
run;
```

104

Data Conversion

```
data bonuses(drop=CharGross);
   set prog2.salary2(rename=(GrossPay=
                       CharGross));
   GrossPay=input(CharGross,comma6.);
   Bonus=.10*GrossPay;
run;
```

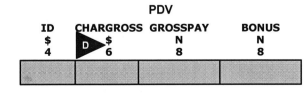

PDV

ID	CHARGROSS	GROSSPAY	BONUS
$	D $	N	N
4	6	8	8

109   c05s5d1.sas ...

Converting Character Dates to SAS Dates

`prog2.born`

Name	Date
$12	$7
Ruth, G. H.	13apr72
Delgado, Ed	25aug68
Overby, Phil	08jun71

```
data birth(drop=Date);
   set prog2.born;
   Birthday=input(Date,date7.);
   Age=int(yrdif(Birthday,'3may2008'd,
         'ACT/ACT'));
run;
```

How can you alter this program to compute each person's age based on today's date?

110

Converting Character Dates to SAS Dates

```
proc print data=birth noobs;
run;
```

PROC PRINT Output

Name	Birthday	Age
Ruth, G. H.	4486	36
Delgado, Ed	3159	39
Overby, Phil	4176	36

111

Automatic Numeric-to-Character Conversion

The `prog2.phones` data set contains a numeric variable `Code` (area code) and a character variable `Telephone` (telephone number). Create a character variable that contains the area code in parentheses followed by the telephone number.

112

Automatic Numeric-to-Character Conversion

```
prog2.phones
```

Code	Telephone
8	$8
303	393-0956
919	770-8292
301	449-5239

```
data phonenumbers;
   set prog2.phones;
   Phone='(' !! Code !! ') ' !! Telephone;
run;
```

113

What will happen when the numeric variable **Code** is used in a character expression?

Automatic Numeric-to-Character Conversion

Partial Log

```
13    data phonenumbers;
14       set prog2.phones;
15       Phone='(' !! Code !! ') ' !! Telephone;
16    run;

NOTE: Numeric values have been converted to character
values at the places given by: (Line):(Column).
      15:17
NOTE: The data set WORK.PHONENUMBERS has 3 observations
and 3 variables.
```

114

Automatic Numeric-to-Character Conversion

```
proc print data=phonenumbers noobs;
run;
```

Code	Telephone		Phone
303	393-0956	(	303) 393-0956
919	770-8292	(	919) 770-8292
301	449-5239	(	301) 449-5239

115

Automatic Numeric-to-Character Conversion

SAS automatically converts a numeric value to a character value when the numeric value is used in a character context, such as

- assignment to a character variable
- a concatenation operation
- a function that takes character arguments.

116

The WHERE statement and WHERE= data set option do not perform any automatic conversion in comparisons.

Automatic Numeric-to-Character Conversion

The automatic conversion

- uses the BEST12. format
- right-aligns the resulting character value.

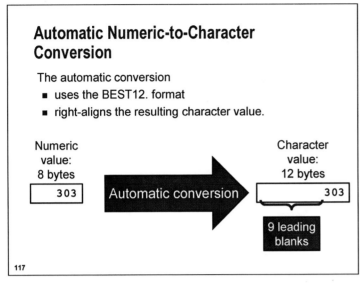

117

Automatic Numeric-to-Character Conversion

```
data phonenumbers;
   set prog2.phones;
   Phone='(' !! Code !! ') ' !! Telephone;
run;
```

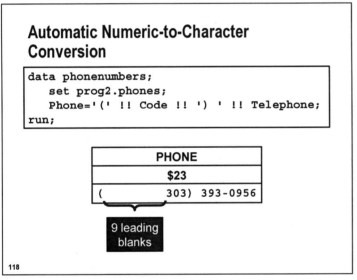

118

The PUT Function

The PUT function writes values with a specific format.

> *CharVar*=PUT(*source,format*);

The PUT function returns *source* written with *format*.

119

---

source   is a constant, variable, or expression (numeric or character).

format   is any SAS format or user-defined format. It must agree with *source* in type.

The PUT function always returns a character string.

Numeric formats right-align the results. Character formats left-align the results.

If you use the PUT function to create a variable not previously defined, it creates a character variable with a length equal to the format width.

 No conversion messages are written to the SAS log by the PUT function.

The PUT Function

```
data conversion;
   NVar1=614;
   NVar2=55000;
   NVar3=366;
   CVar1=put(NVar1,3.);
   CVar2=put(NVar2,dollar7.);
   CVar3=put(NVar3,date9.);
run;

proc contents data=conversion;
run;
```

120

The PUT Function

Partial PROC CONTENTS Output

```
-----Alphabetic List of Variables and Attributes-----

       #    Variable    Type    Len    Pos

       4    CVar1       Char      3     24
       5    CVar2       Char      7     27
       6    CVar3       Char      9     34
       1    NVar1       Num       8      0
       2    NVar2       Num       8      8
       3    NVar3       Num       8     16
```

121

The PUT Function

```
proc print data=conversion noobs;
run;
```

PROC PRINT Output

```
NVar1     NVar2     NVar3     CVar1     CVar2     CVar3
 614      55000      366       614     $55,000   01JAN1961
```

122

Explicit Numeric-to-Character Conversion

```
data phonenumbers;
   set prog2.phones;
   Phone='(' !! put(Code,3.) !! ') ' !!
           Telephone;
run;
```

Partial Log

```
20    data phonenumbers;
21       set prog2.phone;
22       Phone='(' !! put(Code,3.) !! ') ' !! Telephone;
23    run;

NOTE: The data set WORK.PHONENUMBERS has 3 observations
and 3 variables.
```

123

Explicit Numeric-to-Character Conversion

```
proc print data=phonenumbers noobs;
run;
```

PROC PRINT Output

Code	Telephone	Phone
303	393-0956	(303) 393-0956
919	770-8292	(919) 770-8292
301	449-5239	(301) 449-5239

How can you change **Code** to a character variable with length 3?

124

c05s5d2.sas

Exercises

10. Converting Variable Type

The data set **prog2.students** contains information about students.

Partial PROC CONTENTS Output of **prog2.students**

```
-----Alphabetic List of Variables and Attributes-----

     #    Variable    Type    Len    Pos

     3    DOB         Char      8     19
     2    Number      Num       8      0
     1    SSN         Char     11      8
```

Partial Listing of **prog2.students**

```
          SSN          Number      DOB

       012-40-4928    5467887    12-05-68
       012-83-3816    6888321    05-03-65
       341-44-0781    9418123    11-23-72
       423-01-7721    7839191    06-28-67
       448-23-8111    9428122    11-30-60
```

Create a new data set named **students** from **prog2.students**. Create a new character variable **Telephone** that has this pattern: XXX-XXXX, where XXXXXXX is the value of **Number**. Print the **students** data set listing all the variables to verify the data conversion.

Recall the previous program and alter it to create a new numeric variable **Birthday** from the DOB variable. **Birthday** should contain SAS date values and have a format of DATE9. Print the **students** data set and list all the variables to verify the data conversion.

When you are confident that both variables have been converted correctly, use a DROP= or KEEP= data set option to ensure that the only variables in the **students** data set are SSN, **Telephone**, and **Birthday**.

Print your data set to verify your results.

Partial Listing of **students**

```
    Obs      SSN          Telephone     Birthday

     1     012-40-4928    546-7887     05DEC1968
     2     012-83-3816    688-8321     03MAY1965
     3     341-44-0781    941-8123     23NOV1972
     4     423-01-7721    783-9191     28JUN1967
     5     448-23-8111    942-8122     30NOV1960
```

5.6 Solutions to Exercises

1. Manipulating Character Values

```
data flname(keep=NewName CityState);
   length FMNames FName LName $ 30;
   set prog2.people;

   /* Last name is everything before the comma.
      Everything after the comma is first and
      middle name. First name is followed by a blank
      Middle name is preceded by a blank */

   FMNames=left(scan(Name,2,','));
   FName=scan(FMNames,1,' ');
   LName=scan(Name,1,',');
   NewName=trim(FName) !! ' ' !! Lname;
run;

proc print data=flname;
   var NewName CityState;
run;
```

2. Performing Additional Character Manipulations

```
data init(drop=FName MName LName FMNames);
   length Initials $ 3 LName FMNames FName MName $ 30;
   set prog2.people;

   /* Last name is everything before the comma.
      Everything after the comma is first and
      middle name. First name is followed by a blank
      Middle name is preceded by a blank. */

   LName=scan(Name,1,',');
   FMNames=scan(Name,2,',');
   FName=scan(FMNames,1,' ');
   MName=scan(FMNames,2,' ');

   /* Put together just the first letters */

   Initials=substr(FName,1,1) ||
            substr(MName,1,1) ||
            substr(LName,1,1);
run;
```

```
proc print data=init;
   var Name CityState initials;
run;
```

🖉   Each value of **Name** contains a middle initial. The assignment statement that
creates INITIALS can be altered if some values of **Name** contain a middle
initial, and other values of **Name** do not contain a middle initial. The
remainder of the DATA step does not need to be changed.

```
Initials=FI || trimn(MI) || LI;
```

The TRIMN function returns a null string (zero blanks) for a blank string.
The TRIM function returns a single blank.

3. Searching for a Character Value

```
data prairie;
   set prog2.people;

   /* Second argument to INDEX function must include
      a period to avoid extraneous results. */

   if index(CityState,', IL.') > 0;
run;

proc print data=prairie;
run;
```

4. Performing Additional Character Manipulations

```
data mixedprairie(drop=FName MName LName FMNames);
   length LName FMNames FName MName $ 30;
   set prairie;
   LName=scan(Name,1,',');
   FMnames=scan(Name,2,',');
   FName=scan(FMnames,1,' ');
   MName=scan(FMnames,2,' ');
   substr(FName,2)=lowcase(substr(FName,2));
   substr(LName,2)=lowcase(substr(LName,2));
   Name=trim(LName) || ', ' ||
        trim(FName) || ' ' || MName;
run;

proc print data=mixedprairie;
run;
```

5. Using Additional Character Functions (Optional)

```
data postal(keep=Name CityState);
   length State $40;
   set prog2.people;

   /* Comma, left parenthesis, colon, semicolon, left
      bracket, and slash are used as third argument to
      SCAN function, instead of comma and space, or
      space to account for multiple word city names,
      such as "SHORT HILLS," and the various delimiters
      used.

      Resulting second word of CITYSTATE is left aligned
      to eliminate leading blank.

      The SUBSTR function is used to extract the first
      two characters only, avoiding the trailing
      period. */

   State=substr(left(scan(CityState,2,',(-:;/[')),1,2);
   StateName=upcase(stnamel(State));
   CityState=scan(CityState,1,',(-:;/') !! ', '
                  !! StateName;
run;

proc print data=postal;
   var Name CityState;
run;
```

6.   Performing Additional Character Manipulations (Optional)

```
data mixedall(keep=Name CityState);
   set prog2.people;

   /* The entire value of Name is transformed into
      lowercase letters because, in your final results,
      most of the letters in the value of Name are
      lowercase. */

   Name=lowcase(Name);

   /* Extract the last name, and place its first
      character back into uppercase. */

   LName=scan(Name,1,',');
   substr(LName,1,1)=upcase(substr(LName,1,1));

   /* Use the INDEX function to search for a blank
      within the value of LName.  If a blank is found,
      uppercase the character one position to its right.
      This is the first character of the second word
      of a multiple-word last name. */

   BlankPos=index(LName,' ');
   if BlankPos gt 0 then
      substr(LName,BlankPos+1,1)=
           upcase(substr(LName,BlankPos+1,1));

   /* Extract the first and middle names, and place
      their first characters back into uppercase. */

   FMNames=left(scan(Name,2,','));
   FName=scan(FMNames,1,' ');
   MName=scan(FMNames,2,' ');
   substr(FName,1,1)=upcase(substr(FName,1,1));
   substr(MName,1,1)=upcase(substr(MName,1,1));

   /* Use the INDEX function to search for a hypen
      within the value of LName.  If a hyphen is found,
      uppercase the character one position to its right.
      This is the first character of the second word
      of a multiple-word last name. */

   DashPos=index(FName,'-');
   if DashPos gt 0 then
      substr(FName,DashPos+1,1)=
           upcase(substr(FName,DashPos+1,1));
   Name=trim(LName) !! ', ' !! trim(FName) !!
           ' ' !! MName;
run;
```

```
proc print data=mixedall;
run;
```

7. Manipulating Numeric Values

```
data final;
   set prog2.grade;
   Overall=round(mean(Test1,Test2,Test3,Final,Final));
run;

   /* The assignment statement above
      could be replaced with

      Overall=mean(of Test1-Test3,Final,Final); */

proc print data=final;
run;
```

8. Performing Additional Numeric Manipulations (Optional)

```
data final;
   set prog2.grade;
   OverallTotal=sum(Test1,Test2,Test3,Final,Final)-
               min(Test1,Test2,Test3);
   Overall=round(OverallTotal/4);
run;

   /* The first assignment statement above
      could be replaced with

      Overall=sum(of Test1-Test3,Final,Final)-
               min(of Test1-Test3); */

proc print data=final;
run;
```

9. Manipulating Numeric Values Based on Dates

```
data emphire(keep=ID Hired Years);
   set prog2.noday;
   Hired=mdy(HiredMonth,15,HiredYear);

   /* The FLOOR function could be used in the following
      assignment statement: */

   Years=int(yrdif(Hired,today(),'act/act'));
   format Hired date9.;
run;

proc print data=emphire;
run;
```

10. Converting Variable Type

```
data students(drop=Number DOB);
   set prog2.students;

   /* The PUT function is used to convert NUMBER from
      numeric to character, and then the resulting
      character value is manipulated with the SUBSTR
      function to extract the first three characters
      and the last four characters. */

   Telephone=substr(put(Number,7.),1,3) || '-' ||
             substr(put(Number,7.),4);

   /* The INPUT function is used to convert DOB from
      character to numeric. Because the character values
      are in the form MM-DD-YY, the MMDDYY8. format is
      used in the conversion. */

   Birthday=input(DOB,mmddyy8.);
   format Birthday date9.;
run;

proc print data=students;
run;
```

Chapter 6   Debugging Techniques (Self-Study)

6.1 Using the PUT Statement

Objectives

- Use the PUT statement in the DATA step to help identify logic problems.

3

Scenario

You have taken a new position in the company. Your predecessor wrote some code that was not working at the time he left. You need to identify what the program code is currently doing and determine where the problem is.

4

Input Data

```
CityCountry                    State

Auckland, New Zealand
Amsterdam, Netherlands
Anchorage, USA                 Alaska
Canberra, Australia            Australian Capital
Athens (Athinai), Greece
Birmingham, USA                Alabama
Bangkok, Thailand
Nashville, USA                 Tennessee
Boston, USA                    Massachusetts
Kansas City, USA               Missouri
```

5

Current Program

```
data work.agents2;
   set prog2.agents;
   length Country $ 20;
   Country=scan(CityCountry,2,',');
   if Country='USA'
      then TrueLocation
              = scan(CityCountry,1,',')
              !! ', ' !! State;
   else /* not USA */
      TrueLocation = CityCountry;
run;
```

7

Expected Results

```
          TrueLocation

Auckland, New Zealand
Amsterdam, Netherlands
Anchorage, Alaska
Canberra, Australia
Athens (Athinai), Greece
Birmingham, Alabama
Bangkok, Thailand
Nashville, Tennessee
Boston, Massachusetts
Kansas City, Missouri
```

6

Current Results

```
         TrueLocation

Auckland, New Zealand
Amsterdam, Netherlands
Anchorage, USA
Canberra, Australia
Athens (Athinai), Greece
Birmingham, USA
Bangkok, Thailand
Nashville, USA
Boston, USA
Kansas City, USA
```

8

Syntax Errors Versus Logic Errors

- A *syntax error* occurs when program statements do not conform to the rules of the SAS language. An error message is produced by the SAS System and written to the log.

- A *logic error* occurs when the program statements follow the rules, but the results are not correct.

This section focuses on logic errors.

9

Because logic errors do not produce notes in the log, they are often difficult to detect and correct. The PUT statement and the SAS debugger (discussed in the next section) are two methods for detecting logic errors.

The PUT Statement

If you do not specify a FILE statement, the PUT statement writes information to the log. This is useful to determine

- which piece of code is executing
- which piece of code is not executing
- the current value of a particular variable
- the current values of all variables.

10

General Forms of the PUT Statement

PUT *'text'*;

writes the text string literal.

Example:

```
put 'I am here.';
```

writes `I am here.` to the log.

11

General Forms of the PUT Statement

PUT *variable-name=*;

writes the name of the variable followed by an equal sign and the value.

Example:

If the value of the variable **Var** is 5, the statement

```
put Var=;
```

writes **Var**=5 to the log.

12

General Forms of the PUT Statement

> **PUT** *variable-name format-name.*;

writes the variable value with the indicated format.

Example:

If the value of the variable `ChVar` is `THIS` with a leading space, the statement

```
put ChVar $quote20.;
```

writes " `THIS`" to the log.

13

 The format $QUOTE*w*. writes a character value, preserving any leading spaces, with quotes around it.

General Forms of the PUT Statement

> **PUT** _ALL_;

writes the name of each variable in the PDV followed by an equal sign and the value of the variable.

14

 The PUT statement can be used in SAS in both the batch and interactive modes.

Determining Logic Errors

Programs: c06s1d1.sas, c06s1d2.sas

This demonstration shows how to detect and correct logic errors using the PUT statement.

```
data work.agents2;
   set prog2.agents;
   length Country $ 20 TrueLocation $ 40;
   Country = scan(CityCountry,2,',');
   if country = 'USA'
      then TrueLocation = scan(CityCountry,1,',')
           !! ', ' !! State;
   else /* not USA */
      TrueLocation = CityCountry;
run;

proc print data=work.agents2 noobs;
   var TrueLocation CityCountry State;
   title 'Current Output from Program';
run;
```

PROC PRINT Output

```
                    Current Output from Program

CityCountry                 TrueLocation                State


Auckland, New Zealand       Auckland, New Zealand
Amsterdam, Netherlands      Amsterdam, Netherlands
Anchorage, USA              Anchorage, USA              Alaska
Canberra, Australia         Canberra, Australia         Australian Capital
Athens (Athinai), Greece    Athens (Athinai), Greece
Birmingham, USA             Birmingham, USA             Alabama
Bangkok, Thailand           Bangkok, Thailand
Nashville, USA              Nashville, USA              Tennessee
Boston, USA                 Boston, USA                 Massachusetts
Kansas City, USA            Kansas City, USA            Missouri
```

Bring the code into the Editor window.

1. Determine what code is executing.

   Convert the IF-THEN statement that creates **TrueLocation** for USA branches into a DO group, and insert a PUT statement to determine whether the code is executing:

```
data work.agents2;
   set prog2.agents;
   length Country $ 20 TrueLocation $ 40;
   Country=scan(CityCountry,2,',');
   if Country='USA' then do;
      TrueLocation = scan(CityCountry,1,',')
                        !! ', ' !! State;
      put 'Country is USA';
   end;
   else /* not USA */
      TrueLocation = CityCountry;
run;
```

   Submit the code. The text string in the PUT statement does not appear in the log.

2. Determine the value of **Country** just before the IF-THEN statement.

   Insert a PUT statement between the assignment statement for **Country** and the IF-THEN statement that creates **TrueLocation** for USA branches.

```
data work.agents2;
   set prog2.agents;
   length Country $ 20 TrueLocation $ 40;
   Country=scan(CityCountry,2,',');
   put Country=;
   if Country='USA' then do;
      TrueLocation = scan(CityCountry,1,',')
                        !! ', ' !! State;
      put 'Country is USA';
   end;
else /* not USA */
   TrueLocation = CityCountry;
run;
```

   Submit the code. The values of **Country** seem to be created appropriately.

Partial Log

```
Country=New Zealand
Country=Netherlands
Country=USA
Country=Australia
Country=Greece
Country=USA
```

3.   Use the $QUOTE*w*. format to check for leading blanks.

By default, character values are written with the standard character format ($*w*., where *w* is the length of the character variable). The standard character format left-justifies the value (removes leading blanks).

To check for leading blanks in the value for `Country`, change the PUT statement as shown below:

```
data work.agents2;
    set prog2.agents;
    length Country $ 20 TrueLocation $ 40;
    Country=scan(CityCountry,2,',');
    put Country $quote20.;
    if Country='USA' then do;
        TrueLocation = scan(CityCountry,1,',')
                            !! ', ' !! State;
        put 'Country is USA';
    end;
    else /* not USA */
        TrueLocation = CityCountry;
run;
```

Submit the code and check the log. Notice that each value shows one leading blank.

Partial Log

```
" New Zealand"
" Netherlands"
" USA"
" Australia"
" Greece"
" USA"
```

4.   Use the LEFT function to remove leading blanks from the values of `Country`.

```
data work.agents2;
    set prog2.agents;
    length Country $ 20 TrueLocation $ 40;
    Country=left(scan(CityCountry,2,','));
    put Country $quote20.;
    if Country='USA' then do;
        TrueLocation = scan(CityCountry,1,',')
                            !! ', ' !! State;
        put 'Country is USA';
    end;
    else /* not USA */
        TrueLocation = CityCountry;
run;
```

Submit the code and check the log. The PUT statement in the DO group is now writing to the log at the appropriate time.

Partial Log

```
"New Zealand"
"Netherlands"
"USA"
Country is USA
"Australia"
"Greece"
"USA"
Country is USA
```

```
proc print data=work.agents2 noobs;
    var TrueLocation CityCountry State;
    title 'Output with Leading Spaces Removed';
run;
```

PROC PRINT Output

```
                Output with Leading Spaces Removed

      TrueLocation           CityCountry              State

Auckland, New Zealand     Auckland, New Zealand
Amsterdam, Netherlands    Amsterdam, Netherlands
Anchorage, Alaska         Anchorage, USA            Alaska
Canberra, Australia       Canberra, Australia       Australian Capital
Athens (Athinai), Greece  Athens (Athinai), Greece
Birmingham, Alabama       Birmingham, USA           Alabama
Bangkok, Thailand         Bangkok, Thailand
Nashville, Tennessee      Nashville, USA            Tennessee
Boston, Massachusetts     Boston, USA               Massachusetts
Kansas City, Missouri     Kansas City, USA          Missouri
```

5. Remove the PUT statements from the DATA step.

```
data work.agents2 (drop=Country);
    set prog2.agents;
    length Country $ 20 TrueLocation $ 40;
    Country=left(scan(CityCountry,2,','));
    if Country='USA' then
        TrueLocation = scan(CityCountry,1,',')
                        !! ', ' !! State;
    else /* not USA */
        TrueLocation = CityCountry;
run;

proc print data=work.agents2 noobs;
    var TrueLocation CityCountry State;
    title 'Corrected Output';
run;
```

Submit the code and check the log and output.

PROC PRINT Output

```
                          Corrected Output

         TrueLocation            CityCountry              State

      Auckland, New Zealand     Auckland, New Zealand
      Amsterdam, Netherlands    Amsterdam, Netherlands
      Anchorage, Alaska         Anchorage, USA           Alaska
      Canberra, Australia       Canberra, Australia      Australian Capital
      Athens (Athinai), Greece  Athens (Athinai), Greece
      Birmingham, Alabama       Birmingham, USA          Alabama
      Bangkok, Thailand         Bangkok, Thailand
      Nashville, Tennessee      Nashville, USA           Tennessee
      Boston, Massachusetts     Boston, USA              Massachusetts
      Kansas City, Missouri     Kansas City, USA         Missouri
```

6.2 Using the DEBUG Option

Objectives

- Use the DEBUG option in the DATA statement to help identify logic problems.

17

Scenario

You have taken a new position in the company. Your predecessor wrote some code that was not working at the time he left. You need to identify what the program code is currently doing and determine where the problem is.

18

Input Data

```
CityCountry                State

Auckland, New Zealand
Amsterdam, Netherlands
Anchorage, USA             Alaska
Canberra, Australia        Australian Capital
Athens (Athinai), Greece
Birmingham, USA            Alabama
Bangkok, Thailand
Nashville, USA             Tennessee
Boston, USA                Massachusetts
Kansas City, USA           Missouri
```

19

Expected Results

```
           TrueLocation

Auckland, New Zealand
Amsterdam, Netherlands
Anchorage, Alaska
Canberra, Australia
Athens (Athinai), Greece
Birmingham, Alabama
Bangkok, Thailand
Nashville, Tennessee
Boston, Massachusetts
Kansas City, Missouri
```

20

Current Program

```
data work.agents2;
   set prog2.agents;
   length Country $ 20;
   Country=scan(CityCountry,2,',');
   if Country='USA'
      then TrueLocation
            = scan(CityCountry,1,',')
              !! ', ' !! State;
   else /* not USA */
      TrueLocation = CityCountry;
run;
```

21

Current Results

```
        TrueLocation

Auckland, New Zealand
Amsterdam, Netherlands
Anchorage, USA
Canberra, Australia
Athens (Athinai), Greece
Birmingham, USA
Bangkok, Thailand
Nashville, USA
Boston, USA
Kansas City, USA
```

22

The DEBUG Option

The DEBUG option is an interactive interface to the DATA step during DATA step execution. This option is useful to determine

- which piece of code is executing
- which piece of code is not executing
- the current value of a particular variable
- when the value of a variable changes.

23

The DEBUG option can be used only in the SAS System's interactive mode.

The DEBUG Option

General form of the DEBUG option:

> **DATA** *data-set-name* **/ DEBUG;**

24

DEBUG Commands

Common commands used with the DEBUG option.

Command	Abbreviation	Action
STEP	ENTER key	Steps through a program one statement at a time.
EXAMINE	E *variable(s)*	Displays the value of the variable.
WATCH	W *variable(s)*	Suspends execution when the value of the variable changes.
LIST WATCH	L W	List variables that are watched.
QUIT	Q	Halts execution of the DATA step.

25

The W and E commands precede the name of the variable, for example:

```
w Country
```

To view the values of all variables, use the command

```
e _all_
```

 You can also select these commands from the pull-down menu if it is turned on.

 **Determining Logic Errors**

Program: c06s2d1.sas

Use the DEBUG option to detect the logic error in the following program:

```
data work.agents2;
   set prog2.agents;
   length Country $ 20 TrueLocation $ 40;
   Country=scan(CityCountry,2,',');
   if Country='USA'
      then TrueLocation = scan(CityCountry,1,',')
                            !! ', ' !! State;
   else /* not USA */
      TrueLocation = CityCountry;
run;

proc print data=work.agents2 noobs;
   var TrueLocation State;
   title 'Locations of Ticket Agents';
run;
```

PROC PRINT Output

```
                  Locations of Ticket Agents


TrueLocation                CityCountry                 State


Auckland, New Zealand       Auckland, New Zealand
Amsterdam, Netherlands      Amsterdam, Netherlands
Anchorage, USA              Anchorage, USA              Alaska
Canberra, Australia         Canberra, Australia         Australian Capital
Athens (Athinai), Greece    Athens (Athinai), Greece
Birmingham, USA             Birmingham, USA             Alabama
Bangkok, Thailand           Bangkok, Thailand
Nashville, USA              Nashville, USA              Tennessee
Boston, USA                 Boston, USA                 Massachusetts
Kansas City, USA            Kansas City, USA            Missouri
```

The correct output is shown below:

```
                              Locations of Ticket Agents

            TrueLocation              CityCountry               State

     Auckland, New Zealand      Auckland, New Zealand
     Amsterdam, Netherlands     Amsterdam, Netherlands
     Anchorage, Alaska          Anchorage, USA            Alaska
     Canberra, Australia        Canberra, Australia       Australian Capital
     Athens (Athinai), Greece   Athens (Athinai), Greece
     Birmingham, Alabama        Birmingham, USA           Alabama
     Bangkok, Thailand          Bangkok, Thailand
     Nashville, Tennessee       Nashville, USA            Tennessee
     Boston, Massachusetts      Boston, USA               Massachusetts
     Kansas City, Missouri      Kansas City, USA          Missouri
```

1. Add the DEBUG option to the end of the DATA statement.

```
data work.agents2 / debug;
   set prog2.agents;
   length Country $ 20 TrueLocation $ 40;
   Country=scan(CityCountry,2,',');
   if Country='USA'
      then TrueLocation = scan(CityCountry,1,',')
                              !! ', ' !! State;
   else /* not USA */
      TrueLocation = CityCountry;
run;
```

2. Submit the DATA step.

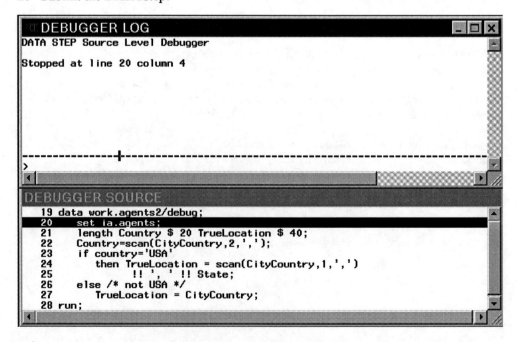

✏ The debugger source highlights the next statement to be executed.

3. Press the Enter key to execute the SET statement.

4. Use the Examine command to examine the value of `CityCountry`:

    `e citycountry`

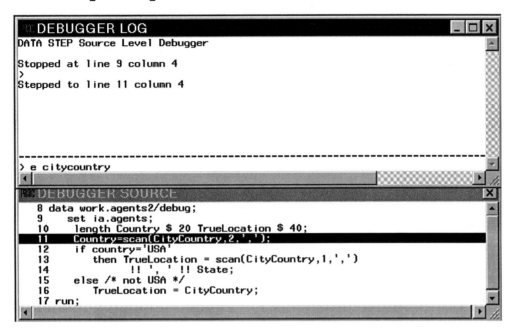

5. Press Enter to execute the assignment statement for `Country`.

6. Use the Examine command to examine the value of `Country`:

    `e country`

```
DEBUGGER LOG                                              _ □ ✕
DATA STEP Source Level Debugger

Stopped at line 9 column 4
>
Stepped to line 11 column 4
> e citycountry
CityCountry = Auckland, New Zealand
>
Stepped to line 12 column 4
> e country
Country =  New Zealand
-------------------------------------------------------------
>
```

```
DEBUGGER SOURCE                                            ✕
    8 data work.agents2/debug;
    9    set ia.agents;
   10    length Country $ 20 TrueLocation $ 40;
   11    Country=scan(CityCountry,2,',');
   12    if country='USA'
   13       then TrueLocation = scan(CityCountry,1,',')
   14              !! ', ' !! State;
   15    else /* not USA */
   16       TrueLocation = CityCountry;
   17 run;
```

7. Press Enter to check the conditional statement.

8. Press Enter to execute the ELSE statement.

9. Use the Examine command to examine the value of **TrueLocation**:

    e truelocation

10. Use the Watch command to monitor the values of **TrueLocation**, **Country**, and **CityCountry**:

    w truelocation country citycountry

11. Press Enter until you execute the SET statement again.

12. Press Enter until **Country** changes to USA.

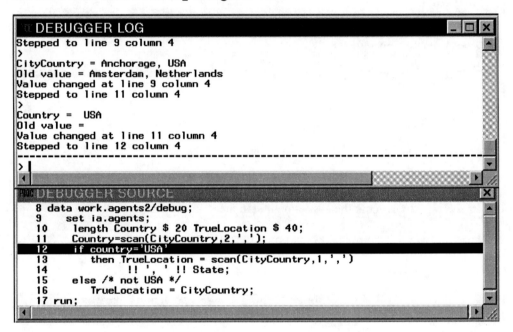

13. Press Enter to check the IF-THEN statements.

14. Note the changes in the values of the watched variables from step 10.

15. Use the Examine command to check the value of `Country` for leading spaces:

    e country $quote20.

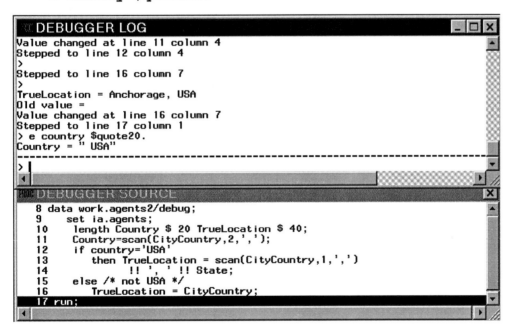

16. Press Enter until SAS reaches the bottom of the DATA step.

17. Use the Quit command to halt the DATA step.

18. Remove the DEBUG option from the DATA step and use the LEFT function to remove the leading space.

```
data work.agents2(drop=CityCountry Country);
    set prog2.agents;
    length Country $ 20 TrueLocation $ 40;
    Country=left(scan(CityCountry,2,','));
    if Country='USA'
        then TrueLocation = scan(CityCountry,1,',')
                                !! ', ' !! State;
    else /* not USA */
        TrueLocation = CityCountry;
run;

proc print data=work.agents2 noobs;
    var TrueLocation CityCountry State;
    title 'Locations of Ticket Agents';
run;
```

PROC PRINT Output

```
                       Locations of Ticket Agents

        TrueLocation              CityCountry              State

   Auckland, New Zealand     Auckland, New Zealand
   Amsterdam, Netherlands    Amsterdam, Netherlands
   Anchorage, Alaska         Anchorage, USA            Alaska
   Canberra, Australia       Canberra, Australia       Australian Capital
   Athens (Athinai), Greece  Athens (Athinai), Greece
   Birmingham, Alabama       Birmingham, USA           Alabama
   Bangkok, Thailand         Bangkok, Thailand
   Nashville, Tennessee      Nashville, USA            Tennessee
   Boston, Massachusetts     Boston, USA               Massachusetts
   Kansas City, Missouri     Kansas City, USA          Missouri
```

Chapter 7 Processing Data Iteratively

7.1   DO Loop Processing

Objectives

- Understand iterative DO loops.
- Use DO loops to generate data.
- Use DO loops to eliminate redundant code.
- Use DO loop processing to conditionally execute code.

3

DO Loop Processing

Statements within a DO loop execute for a specific number of iterations or until a specific condition stops the loop.

```
DATA statement;
   SAS statements
   DO statement;
       iterated SAS statements
   END statement;
   SAS statements
RUN statement;
```

4

DO Loop Processing

You can use DO loops to

- perform repetitive calculations
- generate data
- eliminate redundant code
- execute SAS code conditionally.

5

Repetitive Coding

Compare the interest for yearly versus quarterly compounding on a $50,000 investment made for one year at 7.5 percent interest. How much money will a person accrue in each situation?

6

Repetitive Coding

```
data compound;
   Amount=50000;
   Rate=.075;
   Yearly=Amount*Rate;
   Quarterly+((Quarterly+Amount)*Rate/4);
   Quarterly+((Quarterly+Amount)*Rate/4);
   Quarterly+((Quarterly+Amount)*Rate/4);
   Quarterly+((Quarterly+Amount)*Rate/4);
run;
```

7

DATA steps that do not read data execute only once.

Repetitive Coding

```
proc print data=compound noobs;
run;
```

PROC PRINT Output

Amount	Rate	Yearly	Quarterly
50000	0.075	3750	3856.79

What if you wanted to determine the quarterly compounded interest after a period of 20 years (80 quarters)?

8

DO Loop Processing

```
data compound(drop=Qtr);
   Amount=50000;
   Rate=.075;
   Yearly=Amount*Rate;
   do Qtr=1 to 4;
      Quarterly+(Quarterly+Amount)*Rate/4;
   end;
run;
```

9

✐ The name of the index variable, QTR, was chosen for clarity. Any valid SAS variable name could have been used.

The Iterative DO Statement

The iterative DO statement executes statements between DO and END statements repetitively based on the value of an index variable.

> **DO** *index-variable=specification-1 <,...specification-n>*;
>   *<additional SAS statements>*
> **END;**

specification-1...specification-n can represent a range of values or a list of specific values.

10

---

index-variable   names a variable whose value governs execution of the DO loop. The *index-variable* argument is required.

specification   denotes an expression or a series of expressions. The iterative DO statement requires at least one *specification* argument.

✐ The index variable, unless dropped, is included in the data set that is being created.

Avoid changing the value of the index variable within the DO loop. If you modify the value of the index variable within the DO loop, you may cause infinite looping.

The Iterative DO Statement

DO *index-variable=start* TO *stop* <BY *increment*>;

The values of *start*, *stop*, and *increment* are established before executing the loop.

start, *stop*, and *increment* must be numbers or expressions that yield numbers.

Any changes to the values of *stop* or *increment* made within the DO loop do not affect the number of iterations.

11

start specifies the initial value of the index variable.

stop specifies the ending value of the index variable.

increment optionally specifies a positive or negative number to control the incrementing of *index-variable*. If no increment is specified, the index variable is increased by 1.

When *increment* is positive, *start* must be the lower bound and *stop*, if present, must be the upper bound for the loop. If *increment* is negative, *start* must be the upper bound and *stop*, if present, must be the lower bound for the loop.

The Iterative DO Statement

```
do i=1 to 12;                              Out of range
      1 2 3 4 5 6 7 8 9 10 11 12 13
do j=2 to 10 by 2;  Out of range
      2 4 6 8 10 12
do k=14 to 2 by -2;      Out of range
      14 12 10 8 6 4 2 0
do m=3.6 to 3.8 by .05;            Out of range
      3.60 3.65 3.70 3.75 3.80 3.85
```

What are the values of each of the four index variables?

12   ...

The Iterative DO Statement

> **DO** *index-variable=item-1 <,...item-n>;*

item-1 through *item-n* can be either all numeric or all character constants, or they can be variables.
The DO loop is executed once for each value in the list.

13

Enclose character constants in quotation marks.

The Iterative DO Statement

How many times will each DO loop execute?

```
do Month='JAN','FEB','MAR';
      3 times.
do Fib=1,2,3,5,8,13,21;
      7 times.
do i=Var1,Var2,Var3;
      3 times.
do j=BeginDate to Today() by 7;
      Unknown. The number of iterations depends on
      the values of BeginDate and Today().
do k=Test1-Test50;
      1 time. A single value of K is determined by
      subtracting Test50 from Test1.
```

14   ...

DO Loop Logic

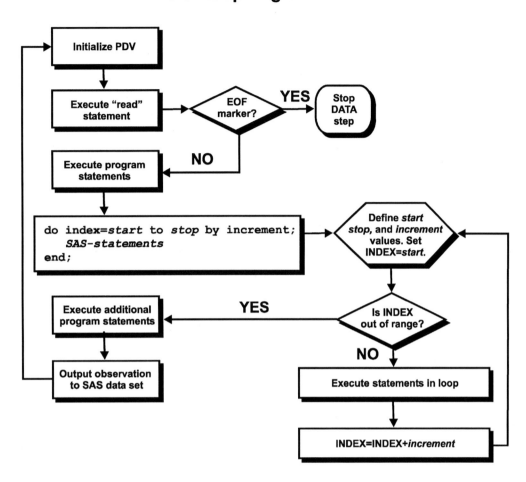

Performing Repetitive Calculations

On January 1 of each year, $5,000 is invested in an account. Determine the value of the account after three years based on a constant annual interest rate of 7.5 percent.

```
data invest;
   do Year=2001 to 2003;
      Capital+5000;
      Capital+(Capital*.075);
   end;
run;
```

20

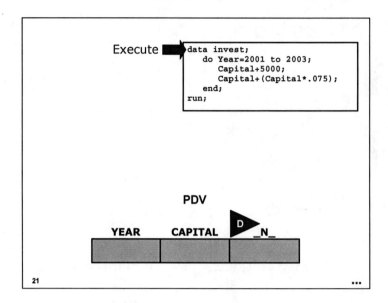

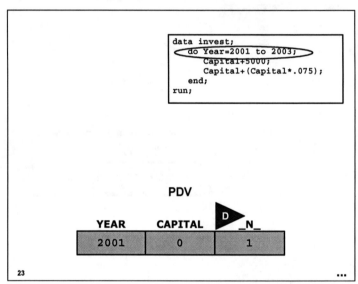

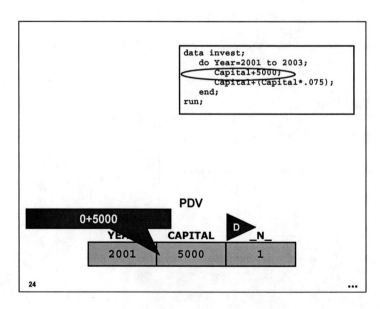

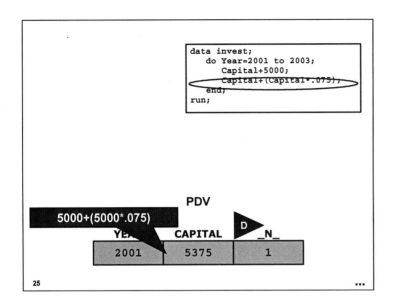

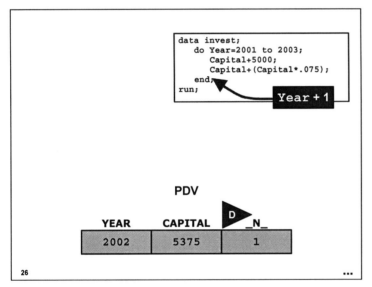

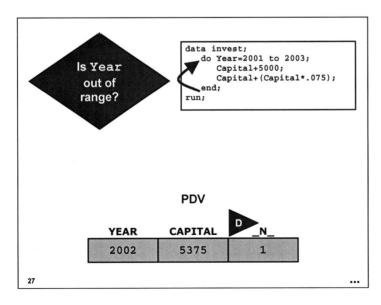

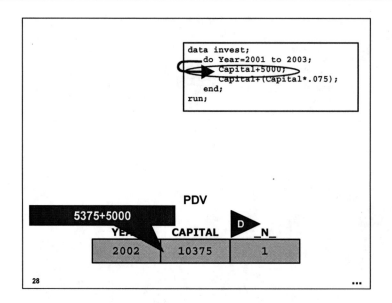

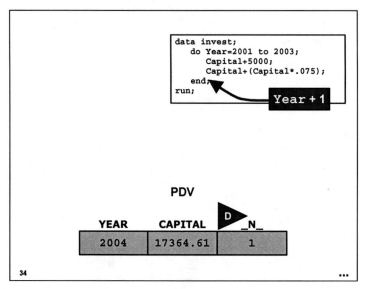

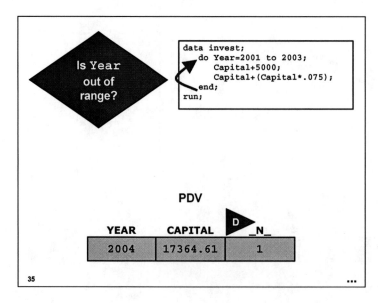

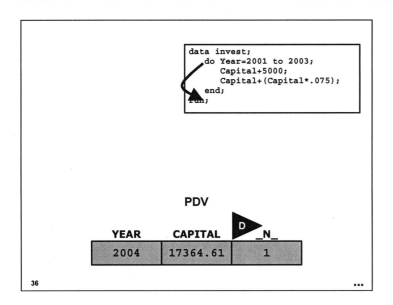

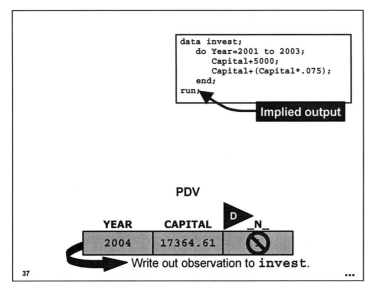

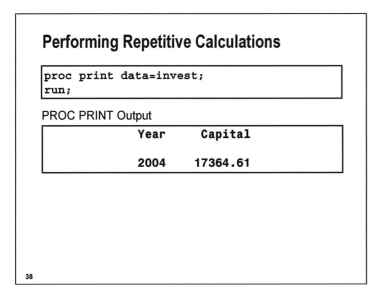

Performing Repetitive Calculations

```
proc print data=invest;
run;
```

PROC PRINT Output

Year	Capital
2004	17364.61

38

Performing Repetitive Calculations

Generate a separate observation for each year.

```
data invest;
   do Year=2001 to 2003;
      Capital+5000;
      Capital+(Capital*.075);
      output;
   end;
run;

proc print data=invest noobs;
run;
```

39

Performing Repetitive Calculations

PROC PRINT Output

Year	Capital
2001	5375.00
2002	11153.13
2003	17364.61

Why is the value of `Year` not equal to 2004 in the last observation?

40

The explicit OUTPUT statement within the DO loop writes one observation for each of the ten iterations of the DO loop. In the previous example, implicit output wrote only one observation.

The final values of **Capital** are identical regardless of how many observations are output.

Reducing Redundant Code

Recall the example that forecast the growth of each division of International Airlines.

Partial Listing of `prog2.growth`

Division	Num Emps	Increase
APTOPS	205	0.075
FINACE	198	0.040
FLTOPS	187	0.080

41

A Forecasting Application (Review)

```
data forecast;
   set prog2.growth(rename=(NumEmps=NewTotal));
   Year=1;
   NewTotal=NewTotal*(1+Increase);
   output;
   Year=2;
   NewTotal=NewTotal*(1+Increase);
   output;
   Year=3;
   NewTotal=NewTotal*(1+Increase);
   output;
run;
```

What if you wanted to forecast growth over the next 30 years?

42

 This program differs slightly from the program introduced in Chapter 2. A RENAME= data set option has been added in the SET statement. As a result, the three assignment statements that assign values to **NewTotal** are identical. Therefore, a DROP statement is no longer necessary.

Reducing Redundant Code

Use a DO loop to eliminate the redundant code in the previous example.

```
data forecast;
   set prog2.growth(rename=(NumEmps=NewTotal));
   do Year=1 to 3;
      NewTotal=NewTotal*(1+Increase);
      output;
   end;
run;
```

43

Growth over the next 30 years could be forecast by changing the iterative DO statement:

```
do Year=1 to 30;
```

Reducing Redundant Code

```
proc print data=forecast noobs;
run;
```

Partial PROC PRINT Output

Division	New Total	Increase	Year
APTOPS	220.38	0.075	1
APTOPS	236.90	0.075	2
APTOPS	254.67	0.075	3
FINACE	205.92	0.040	1

What if you wanted to forecast the number of years it would take for the size of the Airport Operations division to exceed 300 people?

44

Conditional Iterative Processing

You can use DO WHILE and DO UNTIL statements to stop the loop when a condition is met rather than when the index variable exceeds a specific value.

To avoid infinite loops, be sure that the condition specified will be met.

45

The DO WHILE Statement

The DO WHILE statement executes statements in a DO loop while a condition is true.

> **DO WHILE** (*expression*);
>   <*additional SAS statements*>
> **END**;

expression is evaluated at the top of the loop.

The statements in the loop never execute if the expression is initially false.

46

The DO UNTIL Statement

The DO UNTIL statement executes statements in a DO loop until a condition is true.

> **DO UNTIL** (*expression*);
>   <*additional SAS statements*>
> **END**;

expression is evaluated at the bottom of the loop.

The statements in the loop are executed at least once.

47

Conditional Iterative Processing

Determine the number of years it would take for an account to exceed $1,000,000 if $5,000 is invested annually at 7.5 percent.

48

Conditional Iterative Processing

```
data invest;
   do until(Capital>1000000);
      Year+1;
      Capital+5000;
      Capital+(Capital*.075);
   end;
run;

proc print data=invest noobs;
run;
```

49

Conditional Iterative Processing

PROC PRINT Output

Capital	Year
1047355.91	38

How could you generate the same result with a DO WHILE statement?

50

The Iterative DO Statement with a Conditional Clause

You can combine DO WHILE and DO UNTIL statements with the iterative DO statement.

> **DO** *index-variable=start* TO *stop* <BY *increment*>
>   **WHILE | UNTIL** (*expression*);
>   <*additional SAS statements*>
> **END**;

This is one method of avoiding an infinite loop in DO WHILE or DO UNTIL statements.

51

In a DO WHILE statement, the conditional clause is checked **after** the index variable has been incremented.

In a DO UNTIL statement, the conditional clause is checked **before** the index variable has been incremented.

The Iterative DO Statement with a Conditional Clause

Determine the return of the account again.

Stop the loop if 25 years is reached or more than $250,000 is accumulated.

52

The Iterative DO Statement with a Conditional Clause

```
data invest;
   do Year=1 to 25 until(Capital>250000);
      Capital+5000;
      Capital+(Capital*.075);
   end;
run;

proc print data=invest noobs;
run;
```

53

The Iterative DO Statement with a Conditional Clause

PROC PRINT Output

Year	Capital
21	255594.86

54

Nested DO Loops

Nested DO loops are loops within loops.

When you nest DO loops,

- use different index variables for each loop
- make sure each DO statement has a corresponding END statement.

55

Nested DO Loops

Create one observation per year for five years showing the earnings if you invest $5,000 per year with 7.5 percent annual interest compounded quarterly.

56

Nested DO Loops

```
data invest(drop=Quarter);
   do Year=1 to 5;
      Capital+5000;
      do Quarter=1 to 4;
         Capital+((.075/4)*Capital);
      end;
      output;
   end;
run;

proc print data=invest noobs;
run;
```

5x 4x

57 ...

Nested DO Loops

PROC PRINT Output

Year	Capital
1	5385.68
2	11186.79
3	17435.37
4	24165.94
5	31415.68

How could you generate one observation for each quarterly amount?

58

Nested DO Loops

Compare the final results of investing $5,000 a year for
five years in three different banks that compound
quarterly. Assume each bank has a fixed interest rate.

prog2.Banks

Name	Rate
Calhoun Bank and Trust	0.0718
State Savings Bank	0.0721
National Savings and Trust	0.0728

59

Nested DO Loops

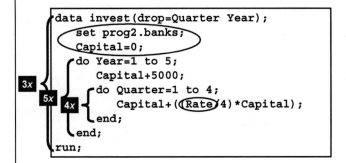

```
data invest(drop=Quarter Year);
   set prog2.banks;
   Capital=0;
   do Year=1 to 5;
      Capital+5000;
      do Quarter=1 to 4;
         Capital+((Rate/4)*Capital);
      end;
   end;
run;
```

This program is similar to the previous program. The
changes are circled.

60   ...

Nested DO Loops

```
data invest(drop=Quarter Year);
   set prog2.banks;
   Capital=0;
   do Year=1 to 5;
      Capital+5000;
      do Quarter=1 to 4;
         Capital+((0.718/4)*Capital);
      end;
   end;
run;
```

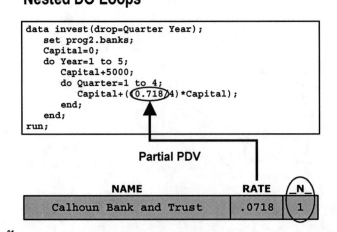

Partial PDV

NAME	RATE	_N_
Calhoun Bank and Trust	.0718	1

61   ...

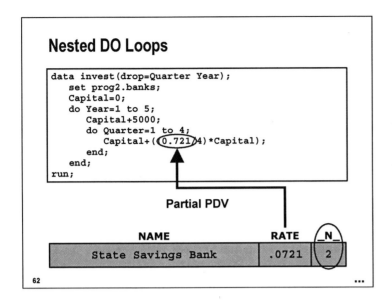

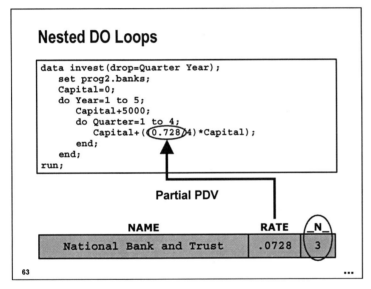

Nested DO Loops

```
proc print data=invest noobs;
run;
```

PROC PRINT Output

Name	Rate	Capital
Calhoun Bank and Trust	0.0718	31106.73
State Savings Bank	0.0721	31135.55
National Savings and Trust	0.0728	31202.91

c07s1d1.sas

Exercises

1. Performing Computations with DO Loops

The payroll department needs to project total employee costs (wages, retirement benefits, and medical benefits) through future years based on assumed increases.

a. Create a SAS data set named **future** with four variables: **Year** and the three variables shown below.

Initialize each of the variables below to their current values, and use a DO loop to calculate their estimated values for the next ten years. For example, next year's wage expense will be this year's wage expense plus 6 percent of this year's amount; in two years, the wage expense will be next year's amount plus 6 percent; and so on. Create one observation for each year.

Variable	Current level	Estimated Annual Increase
Wages	**$12,874,000**	**6.0%**
Retire	**1,765,000**	**1.4%**
Medical	**649,000**	**9.5%**

Use SAS date functions to guarantee that the value of **Year** in the first observation is the upcoming year, regardless of the current year. (If the current year is 2001, the value of **Year** in the first observation will be 2002. If the program is run in 2006 without any modifications, the value of YEAR in the first observation will be 2007.)

Print the data set to verify your results.

Obs	Year	Wages	Retire	Medical
1	2002	13646440.00	1789710.00	710655.00
2	2003	14465226.40	1814765.94	778167.23
3	2004	15333139.98	1840172.66	852093.11
4	2005	16253128.38	1865935.08	933041.96
5	2006	17228316.09	1892058.17	1021680.94
6	2007	18262015.05	1918546.99	1118740.63
7	2008	19357735.95	1945406.64	1225020.99
8	2009	20519200.11	1972642.34	1341397.99
9	2010	21750352.12	2000259.33	1468830.80
10	2011	23055373.25	2028262.96	1608369.72

The results above were generated in 2001. Your values of **Year** may differ.

b. Modify the previous program to create a new variable named **Totcost** that is the sum of the wage, retirement, and medical costs for each year.

Print the data set.

Obs	Year	Wages	Retire	Medical	TotCost
1	2001	13646440.00	1789710.00	710655.00	16146805.00
2	2002	14465226.40	1814765.94	778167.23	17058159.57
3	2003	15333139.98	1840172.66	852093.11	18025405.76
4	2004	16253128.38	1865935.08	933041.96	19052105.42
5	2005	17228316.09	1892058.17	1021680.94	20142055.20
6	2006	18262015.05	1918546.99	1118740.63	21299302.67
7	2007	19357735.95	1945406.64	1225020.99	22528163.59
8	2008	20519200.11	1972642.34	1341397.99	23833240.44
9	2009	21750352.12	2000259.33	1468830.80	25219442.24
10	2010	23055373.25	2028262.96	1608369.72	26692005.93
11	2011	24438695.64	2056658.64	1761164.84	28256519.13

The results above were generated in 2001. Your values of **Year** may differ.

c. Corporate income for last year was $50,000,000. Income is projected to increase at 1 percent per year. Modify the previous program so that the DO loop stops when the year's total costs exceed the year's income.

Print the data set to verify that total costs exceed income after 26 observations.

Obs	Year	Income	TotCost
1	2002	50500000.00	16146805.00
2	2003	51005000.00	17058159.57
3	2004	51515050.00	18025405.76
4	2005	52030200.50	19052105.42
5	2006	52550502.51	20142055.20
6	2007	53076007.53	21299302.67
7	2008	53606767.61	22528163.59
8	2009	54142835.28	23833240.44
9	2010	54684263.63	25219442.24
10	2011	55231106.27	26692005.93
11	2012	55783417.33	28256519.13
12	2013	56341251.51	29918944.75
13	2014	56904664.02	31685647.29
14	2015	57473710.66	33563421.13
15	2016	58048447.77	35559520.91
16	2017	58628932.25	37681694.14
17	2018	59215221.57	39938216.30
18	2019	59807373.78	42337928.49
19	2020	60405447.52	44890278.01
20	2021	61009502.00	47605361.89
21	2022	61619597.02	50493973.81
22	2023	62235792.99	53567654.57
23	2024	62858150.92	56838746.30
24	2025	63486732.43	60320451.03
25	2026	64121599.75	64026893.56
26	2027	64762815.75	67973189.29

The results above were generated in 2001. Your values of **Year** may differ.

7.2   SAS Array Processing

Objectives

- Understand what a SAS array is.
- Use SAS arrays to perform repetitive calculations.

67

Performing Repetitive Calculations

Employees contribute an amount to charity every quarter. The SAS data set `prog2.donate` contains contribution data for each employee. The employer supplements each contribution by 25 percent. Calculate each employee's quarterly contribution including the company supplement.

Partial Listing of `prog2.donate`

ID	Qtr1	Qtr2	Qtr3	Qtr4
E00224	12	33	22	.
E00367	35	48	40	30

68

Performing Repetitive Calculations

```
data charity;
   set prog2.donate;
   Qtr1=Qtr1*1.25;
   Qtr2=Qtr2*1.25;
   Qtr3=Qtr3*1.25;
   Qtr4=Qtr4*1.25;
run;

proc print data=charity noobs;
run;
```

69

Performing Repetitive Calculations

Partial PROC PRINT Output

ID	Qtr1	Qtr2	Qtr3	Qtr4
E00224	15.00	41.25	27.50	.
E00367	43.75	60.00	50.00	37.50
E00441	.	78.75	111.25	112.50
E00587	20.00	23.75	37.50	36.25
E00598	5.00	10.00	7.50	1.25

What if you wanted to similarly modify 52 weeks of data stored in **Week1** through **Week52**?

70

Array Processing

You can use arrays to simplify programs that

- perform repetitive calculations
- create many variables with the same attributes
- read data
- rotate SAS data sets by making variables into observations or observations into variables
- compare variables
- perform a table lookup.

71

What Is a SAS Array?

A *SAS array*

- is a temporary grouping of SAS variables that are arranged in a particular order
- is identified by an *array name*
- exists only for the duration of the current DATA step
- is not a variable.

72

SAS arrays are different from those in many other programming languages. In the SAS System, an array is **not** a data structure. It is simply a convenient way of temporarily identifying a group of variables.

What Is a SAS Array?

Each variable in an array is

- called an *element*
- identified by a *subscript* that represents the position of the element in the array.

When you use an *array reference*, the corresponding variable is substituted for the reference.

73

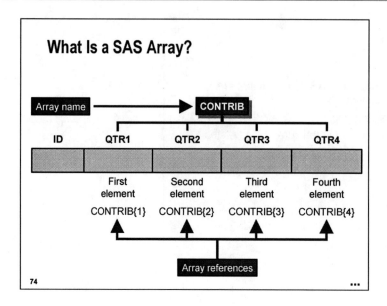

The ARRAY Statement

The ARRAY statement defines the elements in an array. These elements will be processed as a group. You refer to elements of the array by the array name and subscript.

> **ARRAY** *array-name {subscript} <$><length> <array-elements> <(initial-value-list)>;*

75

array-name	specifies the name of the array.
{subscript}	describes the number and arrangement of elements in the array by using an asterisk, a number, or a range of numbers. *subscript* is enclosed in braces ({}). Brackets ([ ]) and parentheses (( )) are also allowed. *subscript* often has the form *{dimension-size(s)}*. *{dimension-size(s)}* is used to indicate a numeric representation of either the number of elements in a one-dimensional array or the number of elements in each dimension of a multidimensional array.
$	indicates that the elements in the array are character elements. The dollar sign is not necessary if the elements in the array have been previously defined as character elements.
length	specifies the length of elements in the array that have not been previously assigned a length.
array-elements	names the elements that make up the array. Array elements can be listed in any order.
(initial-value-list)	gives initial values for the corresponding elements in the array. The values for elements can be numbers or character strings. You must enclose all character strings in quotation marks.

✎ Array names cannot be used in LABEL, FORMAT, DROP, KEEP, or LENGTH statements.

If you use a function name as the name of the array, SAS treats parenthetical references that involve the name as array references, not function references, for the duration of the DATA step.

The ARRAY Statement

The ARRAY statement

- must contain all numeric or all character elements
- must be used to define an array before the array name can be referenced
- creates variables if they do not already exist in the PDV
- is a compile-time statement.

76

✎ You can use special SAS name lists to reference variables that have been previously defined in the same DATA step. The _CHARACTER_ variable lists character values only. The _NUMERIC_ variable lists numeric values only.

Avoid using the _ALL_ special SAS name list to reference variables, because the elements in an array must be either all character or all numeric values.

Defining an Array

Write an ARRAY statement that defines the four quarterly contribution variables as elements of an array.

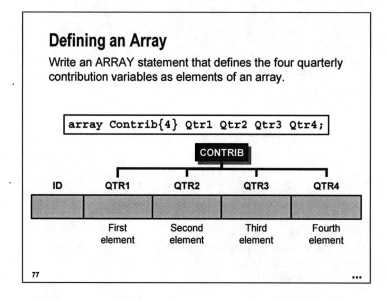

```
array Contrib{4} Qtr1 Qtr2 Qtr3 Qtr4;
```

77 ...

✎ The four variables, **Qtr1**, **Qtr2**, **Qtr3**, and **Qtr4**, can now be referenced via the array name **Contrib**.

Defining an Array

Variables that are elements of an array need not have similar, related, or numbered names.

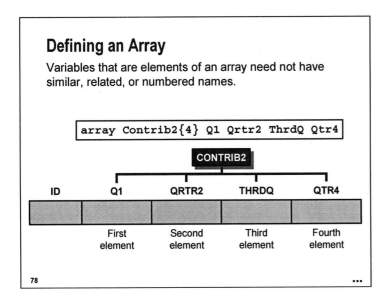

78 ...

Processing an Array

Array processing often occurs within DO loops. An iterative DO loop that processes an array has the following form:

> **DO** *index-variable*=1 **TO** *number-of-elements-in-array*;
>   *additional SAS statements*
>   *using array-name{index-variable}...*
> **END**;

To execute the loop as many times as there are elements in the array, specify that the values of *index-variable* range from 1 to *number-of-elements-in-array*.

79

You must tell SAS which variable in the array to use in each iteration of the loop. You can write programming statements so that the index variable of the DO loop is the subscript of the array reference (for example, *array-name{index-variable}*). When the value of the index variable changes, the subscript of the array reference (and therefore the variable that is referenced) also changes.

To process particular elements of an array, specify those elements as the range of the iterative DO statement.

By default, SAS includes *index-variable* in the output data set. Use a DROP statement or the DROP= data set option to prevent the index variable from being written to your output data set.

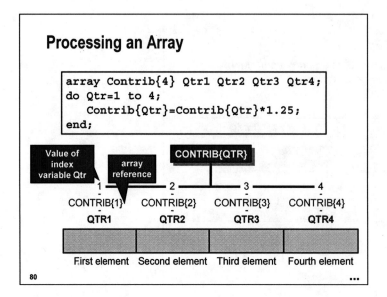

✎ The name of the index variable, **Qtr**, was chosen for clarity. Any valid SAS variable name could have been used.

Performing Repetitive Calculations

```
data charity(drop=Qtr);
   set prog2.donate;
   array Contrib{4} Qtr1 Qtr2 Qtr3 Qtr4;
   do Qtr=1 to 4;
      Contrib{Qtr}=Contrib{Qtr}*1.25;
   end;
run;
```

81   ...

Performing Repetitive Calculations

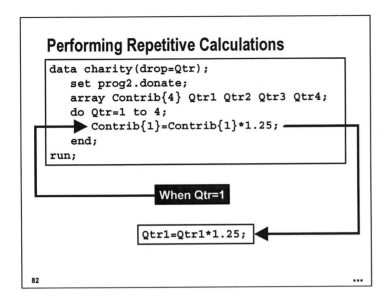

```
data charity(drop=Qtr);
   set prog2.donate;
   array Contrib{4} Qtr1 Qtr2 Qtr3 Qtr4;
   do Qtr=1 to 4;
      Contrib{1}=Contrib{1}*1.25;
   end;
run;
```

When Qtr=1

```
Qtr1=Qtr1*1.25;
```

82   ...

Performing Repetitive Calculations

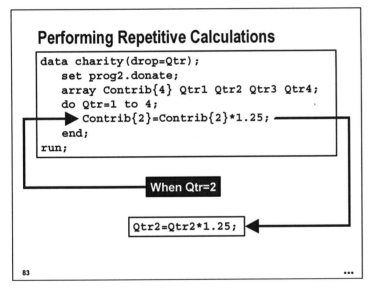

```
data charity(drop=Qtr);
   set prog2.donate;
   array Contrib{4} Qtr1 Qtr2 Qtr3 Qtr4;
   do Qtr=1 to 4;
      Contrib{2}=Contrib{2}*1.25;
   end;
run;
```

When Qtr=2

```
Qtr2=Qtr2*1.25;
```

83   ...

Performing Repetitive Calculations

```
proc print data=charity noobs;
run;
```

Partial PROC PRINT Output

ID	Qtr1	Qtr2	Qtr3	Qtr4
E00224	15.00	41.25	27.50	.
E00367	43.75	60.00	50.00	37.50
E00441	.	78.75	111.25	112.50
E00587	20.00	23.75	37.50	36.25
E00598	5.00	10.00	7.50	1.25

86   c07s2d1.sas

 **Exercises**

2. Using Arrays for Repetitive Computations

A ski resort has a weather-recording device that writes an observation to a SAS data set every day. Each observation in the data set **prog2.ski** contains the date and 24 hourly readings of the temperature in degrees Fahrenheit starting at 1:00 AM.

Partial Listing of **prog2.ski**

Date	T1	T2	T3	T4	T5	T6	T7	T8	T9	T10	T11	T12
18FEB2000	23	22	20	20	21	24	26	28	28	29	31	31
19FEB2000	25	25	26	30	31	33	33	35	36	37	39	40
20FEB2000	31	31	30	29	29	28	29	30	30	31	30	30
21FEB2000	13	15	16	17	19	20	20	21	23	24	26	27
22FEB2000	20	22	23	25	26	27	29	31	33	35	36	36

T13	T14	T15	T16	T17	T18	T19	T20	T21	T22	T23	T24
32	32	31	32	31	33	32	31	29	27	26	25
40	41	42	42	43	42	41	40	38	36	34	32
30	29	28	26	25	23	22	21	19	17	15	13
29	30	31	30	30	31	30	27	23	22	21	20
37	38	37	34	32	31	30	26	24	25	21	20

Create a data set named **celsius** by reading the **prog2.ski** data set. Convert all of the temperatures stored in T1 through T24 to Celsius by using this formula:

$$\text{Celsius temperature} = 5*(\text{Fahrenheit temperature} - 32)/9$$

These Celsius temperatures will be stored back in T1 through T24. (You do not need to create 24 new variables for the Celsius temperatures.)

Create a variable that contains the daily cost of running a snowmaking machine if the machine automatically runs for one hour when the detected temperature is lower than 2 degrees Celsius. It costs $125.00 per hour to run the machine.

Print the data set. Round the temperature values to the first decimal place.

Partial PROC PRINT Output

Obs	Date	T1	T2	T3	T4	T5	T6	T7
1	18FEB2000	-5.0	-5.6	-6.7	-6.7	-6.1	-4.4	-3.3
2	19FEB2000	-3.9	-3.9	-3.3	-1.1	-0.6	0.6	0.6
3	20FEB2000	-0.6	-0.6	-1.1	-1.7	-1.7	-2.2	-1.7
4	21FEB2000	-10.6	-9.4	-8.9	-8.3	-7.2	-6.7	-6.7
5	22FEB2000	-6.7	-5.6	-5.0	-3.9	-3.3	-2.8	-1.7

Obs	T8	T9	T10	T11	T12	T13	T14	T15	T16	T17
1	-2.2	-2.2	-1.7	-0.6	-0.6	0.0	0.0	-0.6	0.0	-0.6
2	1.7	2.2	2.8	3.9	4.4	4.4	5.0	5.6	5.6	6.1
3	-1.1	-1.1	-0.6	-1.1	-1.1	-1.1	-1.7	-2.2	-3.3	-3.9
4	-6.1	-5.0	-4.4	-3.3	-2.8	-1.7	-1.1	-0.6	-1.1	-1.1
5	-0.6	0.6	1.7	2.2	2.2	2.8	3.3	2.8	1.1	0.0

Obs	T18	T19	T20	T21	T22	T23	T24	Cost
1	0.6	0.0	-0.6	-1.7	-2.8	-3.3	-3.9	3000
2	5.6	5.0	4.4	3.3	2.2	1.1	0.0	1250
3	-5.0	-5.6	-6.1	-7.2	-8.3	-9.4	-10.6	3000
4	-0.6	-1.1	-2.8	-5.0	-5.6	-6.1	-6.7	3000
5	-0.6	-1.1	-3.3	-4.4	-3.9	-6.1	-6.7	2375

7.3 Using SAS Arrays

Objectives

- Use SAS arrays to create new variables.
- Use SAS arrays to perform a table lookup.
- Use SAS arrays to rotate a SAS data set.

89

Creating Variables with Arrays

Calculate the percentage that each quarter's contribution represents of the employee's total annual contribution. Base the percentage only on the employee's actual contribution and ignore the company contributions.

Partial Listing of `prog2.donate`

ID	Qtr1	Qtr2	Qtr3	Qtr4
E00224	12	33	22	.
E00367	35	48	40	30

90

Creating Variables with Arrays

```
data percent(drop=Qtr);
   set prog2.donate;
   Total=sum(of Qtr1-Qtr4);
   array Contrib{4} Qtr1-Qtr4;
   array Percent{4};
   do Qtr=1 to 4;
      Percent{Qtr}=Contrib{Qtr}/Total;
   end;
run;
```

The second ARRAY statement creates four numeric
variables: **Percent1**, **Percent2**, **Percent3**, and
Percent4.

91

The first ARRAY statement uses the existing variables **Qtr1**, **Qtr2**, **Qtr3**, and
Qtr4. In that ARRAY statement, a numbered range SAS variable list is used.

Creating Variables with Arrays

```
proc print data=percent noobs;
   var ID Percent1-Percent4;
   format Percent1-Percent4 percent5.;
run;
```

Partial PROC PRINT Output

ID	Percent1	Percent2	Percent3	Percent4
E00224	18%	49%	33%	.
E00367	23%	31%	26%	20%
E00441	.	26%	37%	37%
E00587	17%	20%	32%	31%
E00598	21%	42%	32%	5%

92

The PERCENT*w.d* format multiplies values by 100, formats them the same as the
BEST*w.d* format, and adds a percent sign (%) to the end of the formatted value.
Negative values are enclosed in parentheses. The PERCENT*w.d* format allows room
for a percent sign and parentheses, even if the value is not negative.

Creating Variables with Arrays

Calculate the difference in each employee's actual contribution from one quarter to the next.

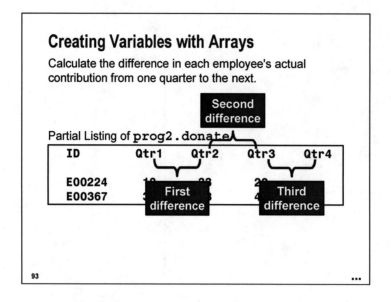

Partial Listing of `prog2.donate`

```
   ID          Qtr1      Qtr2      Qtr3     Qtr4

   E00224
   E00367
```

Creating Variables with Arrays

```
data change(drop=i);
   set prog2.donate;
   array Contrib{4} Qtr1-Qtr4;
   array Diff{3};
   do i=1 to 3;
      Diff{i}=Contrib{i+1}-Contrib{i};
   end;
run;
```

Creating Variables with Arrays

```
data change(drop=i);
   set prog2.donate;
   array Contrib{4} Qtr1-Qtr4;
   array Diff{3};
   do i=1 to 3;
      Diff{1}=Contrib{2}-Contrib{1};
   end;
run;
```

When i=1

```
Diff1=Qtr2-Qtr1;
```

Creating Variables with Arrays

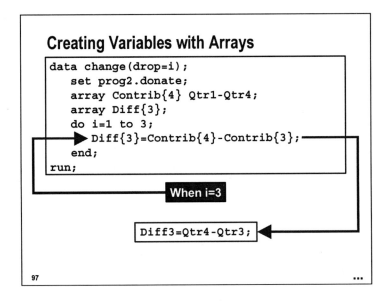

```
data change(drop=i);
   set prog2.donate;
   array Contrib{4} Qtr1-Qtr4;
   array Diff{3};
   do i=1 to 3;
      Diff{3}=Contrib{4}-Contrib{3};
   end;
run;
```

When i=3

```
Diff3=Qtr4-Qtr3;
```

97   •••

Creating Variables with Arrays

```
proc print data=change noobs;
   var ID Diff1-Diff3;
run;
```

Partial PROC PRINT Output

ID	Diff1	Diff2	Diff3
E00224	21	-11	.
E00367	13	-8	-10
E00441	.	26	1
E00587	3	11	-1
E00598	4	-2	-5

98

Assigning Initial Values

Determine the difference between employee contributions and last year's average quarterly goals of $10, $15, $5, and $10 per employee.

```
data compare(drop=Qtr Goal1-Goal4);
   set prog2.donate;
   array Contrib{4} Qtr1-Qtr4;
   array Diff{4};
   array Goal{4} Goal1-Goal4 (10,15,5,10);
   do Qtr=1 to 4;
      Diff{Qtr}=Contrib{Qtr}-Goal{Qtr};
   end;
run;
```

99

Elements and values are matched by position. If there are more array elements than initial values, the remaining array elements are assigned missing values and SAS issues a warning.

You can separate the values in the initial value list with either a comma or a blank space.

 Initial values are retained until a new value is assigned to the array element.

This is an example of a simple *table lookup* program.

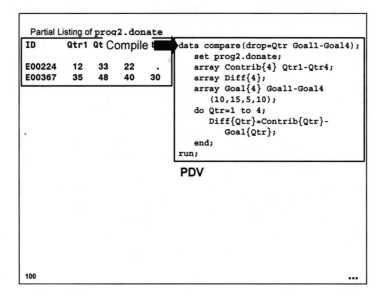

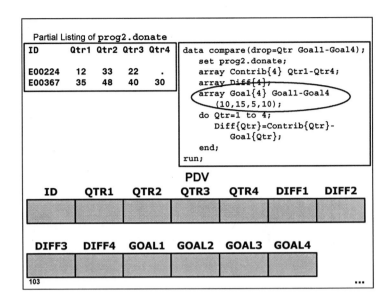

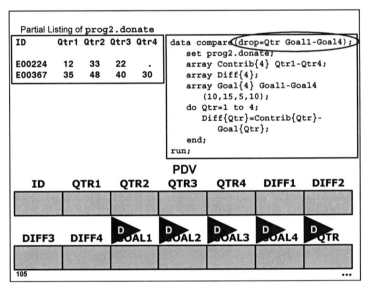

The elements in the **Goal** array, **Goal1**, **Goal2**, **Goal3**, and **Goal4**, are created in the PDV. These variables are used to calculate the values of **Diff1**, **Diff2**, **Diff3**, and **Diff4**, and subsequently excluded from the output data set **compare** using the DROP= data set option in the DATA statement.

Assigning Initial Values

```
proc print data=compare noobs;
   var ID Diff1 Diff2 Diff3 Diff4;
run;
```

PROC PRINT Output

ID	Diff1	Diff2	Diff3	Diff4
E00224	2	18	17	.
E00367	25	33	35	20
E00441	.	48	84	80
E00587	6	4	25	19
E00598	-6	-7	1	-9

106

Performing a Table Lookup

You can use the keyword _TEMPORARY_ instead of
specifying variable names when you create an array to
define temporary array elements.

```
data compare(drop=Qtr);
   set prog2.donate;
   array Contrib{4} Qtr1-Qtr4;
   array Diff{4};
   array Goal{4} _temporary_ (10,15,5,10);
   do Qtr=1 to 4;
      Diff{Qtr}=Contrib{Qtr}-Goal{Qtr};
   end;
run;
```

107

Arrays of temporary elements are useful when the only purpose for creating an array
is to perform a calculation. To preserve the result of the calculation, assign it to a
variable.

   Temporary data elements do not appear in the output data set.

Temporary data element values are always automatically retained.

Performing a Table Lookup

```
proc print data=compare noobs;
   var ID Diff1 Diff2 Diff3 Diff4;
run;
```

PROC PRINT Output

ID	Diff1	Diff2	Diff3	Diff4
E00224	2	18	17	.
E00367	25	33	35	20
E00441	.	48	84	80
E00587	6	4	25	19
E00598	-6	-7	1	-9

108

Rotating a SAS Data Set

Rotating, or transposing, a SAS data set can be accomplished by using array processing. When a data set is rotated, the values of an observation in the input data set become values of a variable in the output data set.

Partial Listing of `prog2.donate`

ID	Qtr1	Qtr2	Qtr3	Qtr4
E00224	12	33	22	.
E00367	35	48	40	30

109

The TRANSPOSE procedure is also used to create an output data set by restructuring the values in a SAS data set, transposing selected variables into observations.

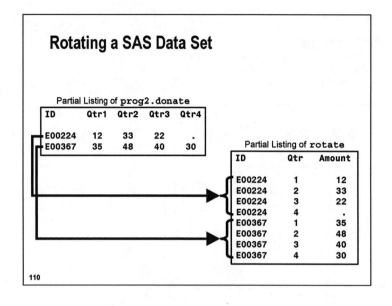

Rotating a SAS Data Set

```
data rotate(drop=Qtr1-Qtr4);
   set prog2.donate;
   array Contrib{4} Qtr1-Qtr4;
   do Qtr=1 to 4;
      Amount=Contrib{Qtr};
      output;
   end;
run;
```

111

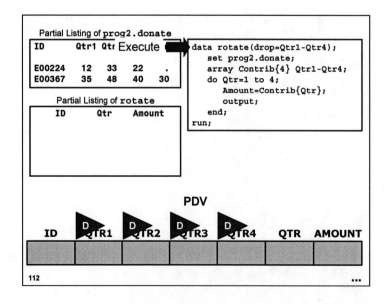

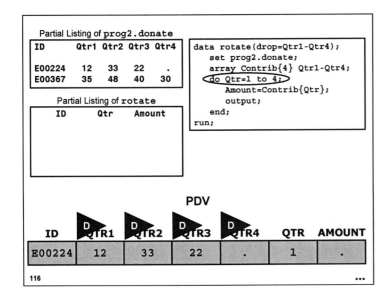

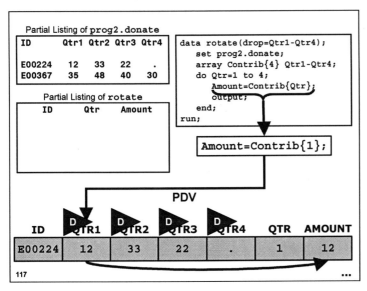

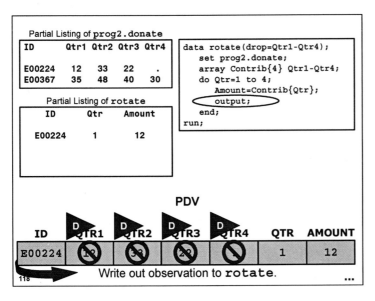

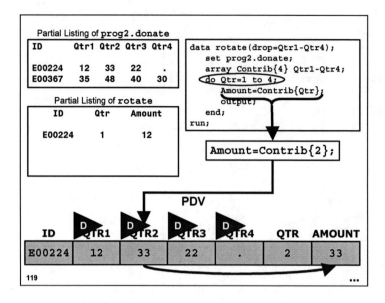

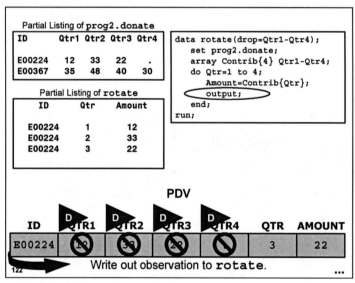

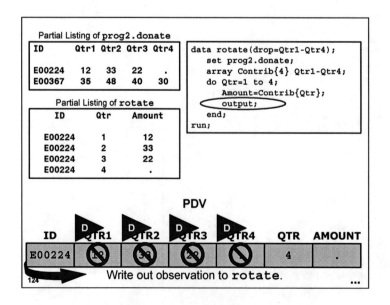

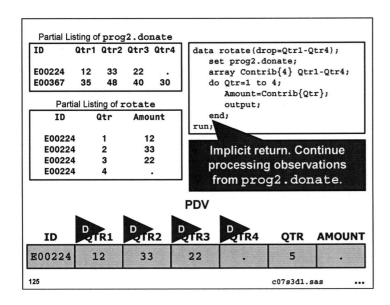

c07s3d1.sas   ...

Exercises

3. Using Arrays to Create Variables

Write a DATA step that reads the SAS data set **prog2.donate** and creates a
SAS data set named **quarter**. Calculate the average contribution for an
employee across all four quarters, and then calculate the difference between each
quarterly contribution and the average. Use arrays to help perform the
calculation.

Partial Listing of **prog2.donate**

ID	Qtr1	Qtr2	Qtr3	Qtr4
E00224	12	33	22	.
E00367	35	48	40	30
E00441	.	63	89	90
E00587	16	19	30	29
E00598	4	8	6	1

Print the data set. The desired report is shown below.

Partial PROC PRINT Output

Obs	ID	Average	Diff1	Diff2	Diff3	Diff4
1	E00224	22.3333	-10.3333	10.6667	-0.3333	.
2	E00367	38.2500	-3.2500	9.7500	1.7500	-8.2500
3	E00441	80.6667	.	-17.6667	8.3333	9.3333
4	E00587	23.5000	-7.5000	-4.5000	6.5000	5.5000
5	E00598	4.7500	-0.7500	3.2500	1.2500	-3.7500

4. Using Arrays for Table Lookup (Optional)

A driver's license renewal test consists of ten multiple-choice questions. Each question has five choices (A-E). Each day, all test results are entered into the SAS data set **prog2.testans** shown below. Each observation in **prog2.testans** contains a single person's answers.

Listing of **prog2.testans**

ID	Q1	Q2	Q3	Q4	Q5	Q6	Q7	Q8	Q9	Q10
291192	A	C	C	B	D	E	D	B	B	A
593137	B	C	C		E	E	D	B	A	A
721311	A	C	C	B	D	D	E	B	B	C
345221	B	C	C	A	D	B	B	C	A	D
193920	A	C	C	B	E	E	D	B	B	A
257672	B	C	C	B	D	D	D	B	B	A
357899	C	C	C	B	E	E	E	B	B	A
564332	A	C	C	B	E	E	D	B	B	A
111033		A	C	B	D	D	D	B	B	A
445732	C	C	C	C	E	E	D	B	B	B
824610	B	B	E	B	E	E	D	B	B	A
774235	A	C	C	B	E	E	D	B	B	A
943244	C	C	C	B	E	E	D	B	B	A
647893	A	C	C	B	E	E	E	B	B	A
432118	A	C	C	B	E	E	D	B	B	A

The correct answers for the questions are shown below:

Question:	1	2	3	4	5	6	7	8	9	10
Answer:	A	C	C	B	E	E	D	B	B	A

Read **prog2.testans** and determine whether each person passed or failed the test. Compute a variable **score** that contains the total correct answers for each person.

 Create a temporary array for the answer key.

If a person scores 7 or higher, write their observation to a data set named **passed**. Print the data set to verify that there are 12 observations in **passed**.

PROC PRINT Output

Obs	ID	Q1	Q2	Q3	Q4	Q5	Q6	Q7	Q8	Q9	Q10	Score
1	291192	A	C	C	B	D	E	D	B	B	A	9
2	593137	B	C	C		E	E	D	B	A	A	7
3	193920	A	C	C	B	E	E	D	B	B	A	10
4	257672	B	C	C	B	D	D	D	B	B	A	7
5	357899	C	C	C	B	E	E	E	B	B	A	8
6	564332	A	C	C	B	E	E	D	B	B	A	10
7	445732	C	C	C	C	E	E	D	B	B	B	7
8	824610	B	B	E	B	E	E	D	B	B	A	7
9	774235	A	C	C	B	E	E	D	B	B	A	10
10	943244	C	C	C	B	E	E	D	B	B	A	9
11	647893	A	C	C	B	E	E	E	B	B	A	9
12	432118	A	C	C	B	E	E	D	B	B	A	10

If a person scores less than 7, write their observation to a data set named **failed**. Print the data set to verify that there are 3 observations in **failed**.

PROC PRINT Output

Obs	ID	Q1	Q2	Q3	Q4	Q5	Q6	Q7	Q8	Q9	Q10	Score
1	721311	A	C	C	B	D	D	E	B	B	C	6
2	345221	B	C	C	A	D	B	B	C	A	D	2
3	111033		A	C	B	D	D	D	B	B	A	6

7.4   Solutions to Exercises

1.   Performing Computations with DO Loops

a.

```
data future;
   Wages=12874000;
   Retire=1765000;
   Medical=649000;
   Year=year(today());
   do until(Year=year(today())+10);
      Year+1;

   /* If a DO UNTIL statement is used, you
      must remember to increment the value of
      Year. */

      Wages+(Wages*.06);
      Retire+(Retire*.014);
      Medical+(Medical*.095);
      output;
   end;
run;

proc print data=future;
run;
```

Alternative solution:

```
data future;
   Wages=12874000;
   Retire=1765000;
   Medical=649000;
   do Year=year(today())+1 to year(today())+10;
      Wages+Wages*.06;
      Retire+Retire*.014;
      Medical+Medical*.095;
      output;
   end;
run;

proc print data=future;
run;
```

b.

```
data future;
   Wages=12874000;
   Retire=1765000;
   Medical=649000;
   do Year=year(today()) to year(today())+10;
      Wages+(Wages*.06);
      Retire+(Retire*.014);
      Medical+(Medical*.095);
      TotCost=sum(Wages,Retire,Medical);
      output;
   end;
run;

proc print data=future;
   var Year Wages Retire Medical TotCost;
run;
```

c.

```
data future;
   Year=year(today());
   Wages=12874000;
   Retire=1765000;
   Medical=649000;
   Income=50000000;
   do until(TotCost gt Income);
      Wages+(Wages*.06);
      Retire+(Retire*.014);
      Medical+(Medical*.095);
      TotCost=sum(Wages,Retire,Medical);
      Income+(Income*.01);
      Year+1;
      output;
   end;
run;

proc print data=future;
   var Year Income TotCost;
run;
```

2.   Using Arrays for Repetitive Computations

```
data celsius(drop=i);
   set prog2.ski;

   /* You must reset cost to zero every time
      an observation from prog2.ski is read. */

   Cost=0;
   array Temps{24} T1-T24;
   do i=1 to 24;
      Temps{i}=round(5*(Temps{i}-32)/9,.1);
      if Temps{i} lt 2 then
      Cost+125;
   end;
run;

proc print data=celsius;
run;
```

3.   Using Arrays to Create Variables

```
data quarter(drop=Qtr);
   set prog2.donate;

   /* Two ARRAY statements are necessary. The
      first ARRAY statement creates a SAS array
      that contains the four quarterly
      contributions. The second ARRAY statement
      creates a SAS array that contains the
      four differences that will be calculated
      during the DATA step. */

   array Contrib{4} Qtr1-Qtr4;
   array Diff{4};

   Average=mean(of Qtr1-Qtr4);
   do Qtr=1 to 4;
      Diff{Qtr}=Contrib{Qtr}-Average;
   end;
run;

proc print data=quarter;
   var ID Average Diff1-Diff4;
run;
```

4. Using Arrays for Table Lookup (Optional)

```
data passed(drop=i) failed(drop=i);
   set prog2.testans;

   /* Two ARRAY statements are necessary. The
      first ARRAY statement creates a SAS array
      that contains the ten responses each
      test-taker selected. The second ARRAY
      statement creates a SAS array that contains
      the ten correct answers for each of the
      ten questions. */

   array Response{10} Q1-Q10;
   array Answer{10} $ 1 _temporary_ ('A','C','C','B','E',
                                     'E','D','B','B','A');

   Score=0;
   do i=1 to 10;
      if Answer{i}=Response{i} then
      Score+1;
   end;
   if Score ge 7 then
      output passed;
   else output failed;
run;

proc print data=passed;
run;

proc print data=failed;
run;
```

Chapter 8   Combining SAS® Data Sets

8.1 Match-Merging Two or More SAS Data Sets

Objectives

- Perform a match-merge.
- Perform explicit output for matching and non-matching observations.

3

Merging Data Sets

A merge combines two or more existing data sets by joining observations side-by-side.

4

Match-Merge

The most common type of merge is a match-merge, which uses a common variable to join observations.

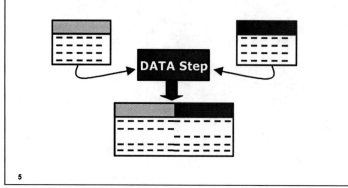

5

Match-Merging

When you are match-merging two or more data sets, it is common to have

- repeated BY values
- non-matches

6

Match-Merging

The data set `prog2.transact` contains an account number and information on transactions for a week. The data set `prog2.branches` contains an account number and the branch location for that account.

Act Num	Trans	Amnt	Act Num	Branch
56891	D	126.32	56891	N. Lincoln
56891	C	560	56900	S. Cicero
57900	C	235	58876	W. Argyle
58876	D	14.56	59900	N. Damen
59987	C	371.69	59987	E. Wacker

7

Desired Output

The bank manager wants to see reports based on three data sets.

A data set named **newtrans** shows this week's transactions.

```
Act
Num       Trans        Amnt     Branch

56891       D         126.32    N. Lincoln
56891       C            560    N. Lincoln
58876       D          14.56    W. Argyle
59987       C         371.69    E. Wacker
```

8

Desired Output

A data set named **noactiv** shows accounts with no transactions this week.

```
Act
Num        Branch

56900      S. Cicero
59900      N. Damen
```

9

Desired Output

A data set named **noacct** shows transactions with no matching account number.

```
Act
Num       Trans        Amnt

57900       C            235
```

10

The MERGE Statement

You can use the MERGE statement to combine observations from two or more SAS data sets.

General form of the MERGE statement with a BY statement:

```
DATA SAS-data-set ... ;
    MERGE SAS-data-set-1 SAS-data-set-2 ...;
    BY BY-variable-1 ...;
    <additional SAS statements>
RUN;
```

11

There is no limit on the number of data sets that can be merged in one DATA step.

The SORT Procedure (Review)

When you use the BY statement with a MERGE statement, the data set must be sorted or indexed according to the BY variable(s).

You can sort the data using the SORT procedure.

General form of a PROC SORT step:

```
PROC SORT DATA=SAS-data-set1
            <OUT=SAS-data-set2>;
    BY <DESCENDING> BY-variable ...;
RUN;
```

12

If you are merging a SAS data set with a DBMS table from another database, the DBMS tables does not have to be sorted.

DATA Step Merge

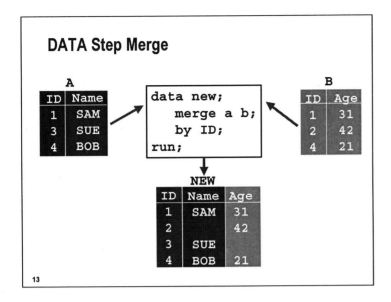

Identifying Data Set Contributors

When you read multiple SAS data sets in one DATA step, you can use the IN= data set option to detect which data set contributed to an observation.

General form of the IN= data set option:

> *SAS-data-set*(IN=*variable*)

where *variable* is any valid SAS variable name.

14

The variable name can be any unique, valid variable name. The variable name must be supplied by the programmer. The value is supplied by the SAS System.

The IN= Data Set Option

variable   is a temporary numeric variable with a
                  value of:

    0   to indicate false; the data set did not
                  contribute to the current observation

    1   to indicate true; the data set did contribute
                  to the current observation

15

Variables created with IN= are automatically dropped from the output data set.

Using the IN= Data Set Option

```
data newtrans
     noactiv (drop=Trans Amnt)
     noacct  (drop=Branch);
  merge prog2.transact(in=InTrans)
        prog2.branches(in=InBanks);
  by ActNum;
  additional SAS statements
run;
```

16

If the Observation Is a Match

`prog2.transact` and `prog2.branches` both contributed to the observation.

InTrans=1 and InBanks=1

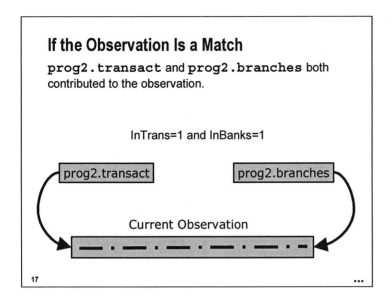

17   •••

If the Observation Is Not a Match

`prog2.branches` contributed to the observation. `prog2.transact` did not. (The account had no transactions this week.)

InTrans=0 and InBanks=1

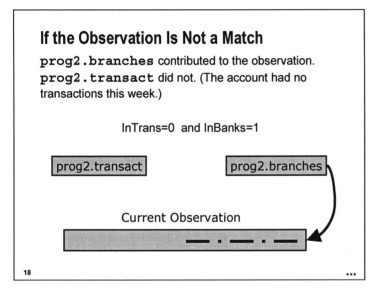

18   •••

If the Observation Is Not a Match

`prog2.transact` contributed to the observation. `prog2.branches` did not. (A transaction occurred, but the account number was invalid.)

InTrans=1 and InBanks=0

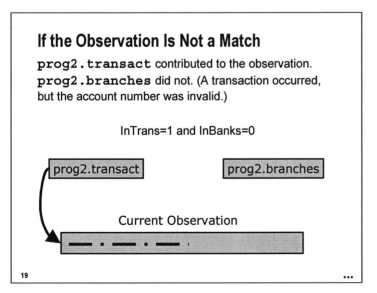

19   •••

Using IN= to Identify Matches and Non-Matches

```
data newtrans
     noactiv (drop=Trans Amnt)
     noacct  (drop=Branch);
   merge prog2.transact(in=InTrans)
         prog2.branches(in=InBanks);
   by ActNum;
   if InTrans and InBanks
      then output newtrans;
         else if InBanks and not InTrans
                 then output noactiv;
         else if intrans and not InBanks
                 then output noacct;
   run;
```
20

Act Num	Trans	Amnt
56891	D	126.32
56891	C	560
57900	C	235
58876	D	14.56
59987	C	371.69

Act Num	Branch
56891	N. Lincoln
56900	S. Cicero
58876	W. Argyle
59900	N. Damen
59987	E. Wacker

```
data newtrans noactiv (drop=Trans Amnt) noacct (        ◄■ Compile
  merge prog2.transact(in=InTrans) prog2.branches(in=InBanks);
  by ActNum;
  if InTrans and InBanks then output newtrans;
     else if InBanks and not InTrans then output noactiv;
     else if InTrans and not InBanks then output noacct;
  run;
```

INTRANS	ACTNUM	TRANS	AMNT	INBANKS	BRANCH

21   ...

Act Num	Trans	Amnt
56891	D	126.32
56891	C	560
57900	C	235
58876	D	14.56
59987	C	371.69

Act Num	Branch
56891	N. Lincoln
56900	S. Cicero
58876	W. Argyle
59900	N. Damen
59987	E. Wacker

```
data newtrans noactiv (drop=Trans Amnt) noacct (        ◄■ Execute
  merge prog2.transact(in=InTrans) prog2.branches(in=InBanks);
  by ActNum;
  if InTrans and InBanks then output newtrans;
     else if InBanks and not InTrans then output noactiv;
     else if InTrans and not InBanks then output noacct;
  run;
```

INTRANS	ACTNUM	TRANS	AMNT	INBANKS	BRANCH
0			.	0	

22   ...

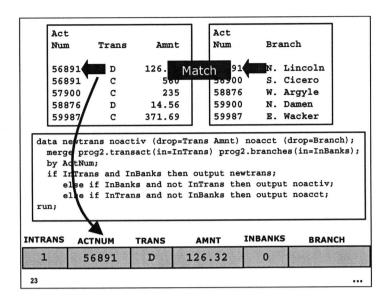

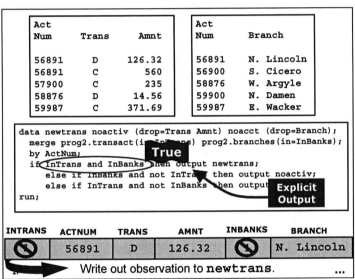

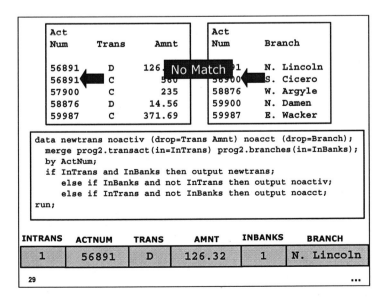

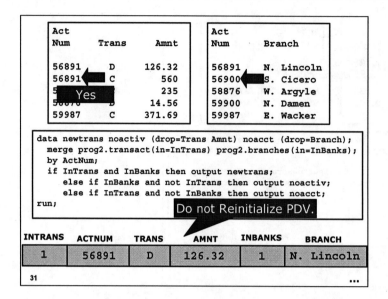

When SAS is performing a match-merge, it only reinitializes values being read from the merged data sets if the BY values in all data sets change.

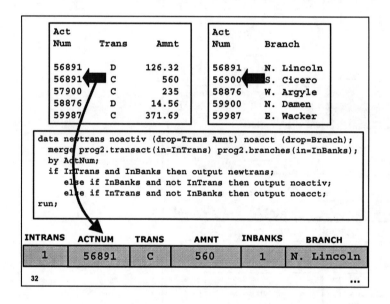

```
Act
Num      Trans      Amnt            Act
                                    Num      Branch
56891     D       126.32
56891     C          560           56891    N. Lincoln
57900     C          235           56900    S. Cicero
58876     D        14.56           58876    W. Argyle
59987     C       371.69           59900    N. Damen
                                    59987    E. Wacker
```

```
data newtrans noactiv (drop=Trans Amnt) noacct (drop=Branch);
  merge prog2.transact(in=InTrans) prog2.branches(in=InBanks);
  by ActNum;
  if InTrans and InBanks then output newtrans;        True
      else if InBanks and not InTrans then output noactiv;
      else if InTrans and not InBanks then output      Explicit
run;                                                    Output
```

INTRANS	ACTNUM	TRANS	AMNT	INBANKS	BRANCH
🚫	56891	C	560	🚫	N. Lincoln

Write out observation to **newtrans**.   ...

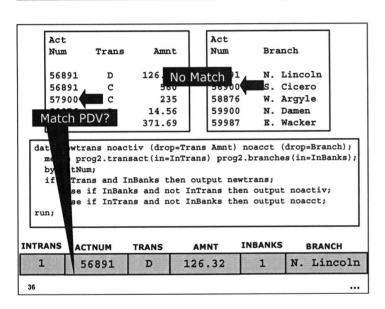

```
Act
Num      Trans      Amnt            Act
                                    Num      Branch
56891     D       126.    No Match  1    N. Lincoln
56891     C          560    56900   S. Cicero
57900     C          235    58876   W. Argyle
          Match PDV?         14.56   59900    N. Damen
                          371.69     59987    E. Wacker
```

```
dat   wtrans noactiv (drop=Trans Amnt) noacct (drop=Branch);
  me   prog2.transact(in=InTrans) prog2.branches(in=InBanks);
  by   tNum;
  if   Trans and InBanks then output newtrans;
       se if InBanks and not InTrans then output noactiv;
       se if InTrans and not InBanks then output noacct;
run;
```

INTRANS	ACTNUM	TRANS	AMNT	INBANKS	BRANCH
1	56891	D	126.32	1	N. Lincoln

36   ...

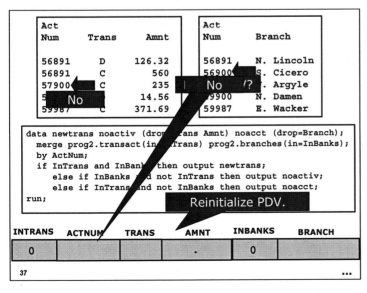

```
Act
Num      Trans      Amnt            Act
                                    Num      Branch
56891     D       126.32
56891     C          560            56891    N. Lincoln
57900     C          235            56900    S. Cicero
5               14.56     No    /?  . Argyle
59987     C       371.69           9900    N. Damen
          No                        59987    E. Wacker
```

```
data newtrans noactiv (drop   ans Amnt) noacct (drop=Branch);
  merge prog2.transact(in   Trans) prog2.branches(in=InBanks);
  by ActNum;
  if InTrans and InBan   then output newtrans;
      else if InBanks    d not InTrans then output noactiv;
      else if InTrans   and not InBanks then output noacct;
run;                        Reinitialize PDV.
```

INTRANS	ACTNUM	TRANS	AMNT	INBANKS	BRANCH
0			.	0	

37   ...

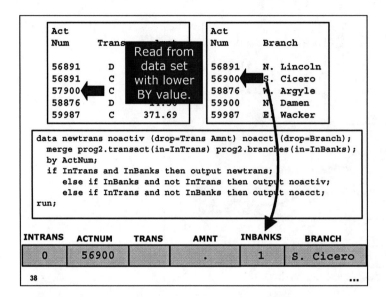

When the BY values do not match each other and do not match the BY value in the PDV, SAS reads the observation with the lowest BY value. Because the data is sorted, this ensures that SAS does not encounter a BY value, later in the data set, that it has already read.

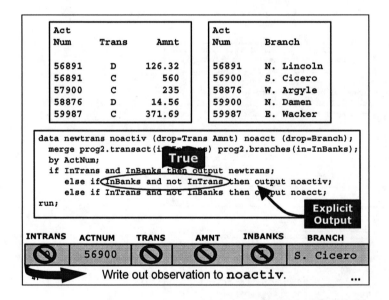

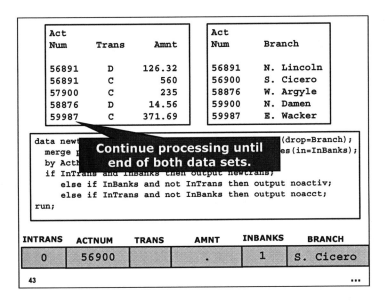

```
data newt                                           (drop=Branch);
  merge                              es(in=InBanks);
  by Act
  if InTrans and InBanks then output newtrans;
    else if InBanks and not InTrans then output noactiv;
    else if InTrans and not InBanks then output noacct;
run;
```

Continue processing until end of both data sets.

INTRANS	ACTNUM	TRANS	AMNT	INBANKS	BRANCH
0	56900		.	1	S. Cicero

43   ...

Viewing Only the Matches

```
proc print data=newtrans noobs;
run;
```

PROC PRINT Output

Act Num	Trans	Amnt	Branch
56891	D	126.32	N. Lincoln
56891	C	560	N. Lincoln
58876	D	14.56	W. Argyle
59987	C	371.69	E. Wacker

44

Non-Matches from prog2.branches

```
proc print data=noactiv noobs;
run;
```

PROC PRINT Output

Act Num	Branch
56900	S. Cicero
59900	N. Damen

45

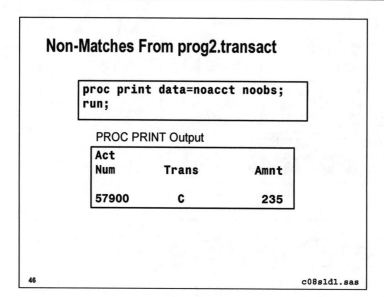

Non-Matches From prog2.transact

```
proc print data=noacct noobs;
run;
```

PROC PRINT Output

Act Num	Trans	Amnt
57900	C	235

46

c08s1d1.sas

 **Exercises**

1. Match-Merging Two Data Sets

The data set **prog2.prices** is a master data set containing a product code
(**ProdCode**) and a unit price (**Price**) for each product sold by a particular
company. The SAS data set **prog2.todaysales** contains a product code and
quantity sold for each sale made on a given day.

Partial Listing of **prog2.prices**

Prod Code	Price
17237	89.64
29978	114.47
10496	128.99
08849	12.23
33060	162.99
05846	107.74
27731	140.75
30967	38.73
16344	181.51
11220	160.49

Partial Listing of **prog2.todaysales**

Prod Code	Qty
17237	5
15078	23
10496	15
33060	1
33060	23
33060	16
33060	30
05846	13
05846	13
05846	10

   The two data sets are not sorted.

Create **three** data sets:

1. A data set named **revenue** that contains the product code (**ProdCode**), the price (**Price**), the quantity sold (**Qty**), and the revenue generated from each sale (**Revenue**). **Revenue** is a new variable that is equal to **Price*Qty**.

2. A data set named **notsold** that contains the product code (**ProdCode**) and price (**Price**) for each product that was not sold.

3. A data set named **invalidcode** that contains the product code (**ProdCode**) and quantity (**Qty**) for each observation in the **todaysales** data set that does not have a corresponding product code in the **prices** data set.

The data sets should contain 39, 7, and 4 observations, respectively.

Partial Listing of **revenue** Data Set (should have 39 observations)

Obs	Prod Code	Price	Qty	Revenue
1	05288	53.26	16	852.16
2	05288	53.26	19	1011.94
3	05846	107.74	13	1400.62
4	05846	107.74	13	1400.62
5	05846	107.74	10	1077.40
6	08766	40.96	13	532.48
7	10496	128.99	15	1934.85
8	11220	160.49	13	2086.37

Listing of **notsold** Data Set (should have 7 observations)

Obs	Prod Code	Price
1	04333	114.36
2	08849	12.23
3	11211	69.16
4	17183	164.82
5	29978	114.47
6	30339	31.74
7	30967	38.73

Listing of **invalidcode** Data Set (should have 4 observations)

Obs	Prod Code	Qty
1	11465	13
2	12556	7
3	15078	23
4	26278	10

8.2   Simple Joins Using the SQL Procedure (Self-Study)

Objectives

- Perform a simple join using the SQL procedure.

49

The SQL Procedure

The SQL procedure enables you to write ANSI standard SQL code within the SAS System and use it to process SAS tables.

50

This section covers basic SQL syntax for an inner join. To learn more about the SQL procedure, see the SAS OnlineDoc for Version 8.

PROC SQL Versus the DATA Step: Benefits

The SQL procedure allows you to

- merge tables and produce a report in one step without creating a SAS data set
- merge tables without sorted data
- use complex matching criteria.

By default, PROC SQL returns a report, not a SAS data set.

51

PROC SQL versus DATA Step: Costs

In general, the SQL procedure requires more CPU time and disk space than a DATA step merge.

52

Joining Two Tables with PROC SQL

Act Num	Trans	Amnt
56891	D	126.32
56891	C	560
57900	C	235
58876	D	14.56
59987	C	371.69

Act Num	Branch
56891	N. Lincoln
56900	S. Cicero
58876	W. Argyle
59900	N. Damen
59987	E. Wacker

The table `prog2.transact` contains an account number and information on transactions for a week. The table `prog2.branches` contains an account number and the branch location for that account.

53

Desired Output

The bank manager wants to see only the accounts that have valid transactions (only rows with matching values of `ActNum`).

ActNum	Trans	Amnt	Branch
56891	D	126.32	N. Lincoln
56891	C	560	N. Lincoln
58876	D	14.56	W. Argyle
59987	C	371.69	E. Wacker

54

The PROC SQL produces a query report, not a SAS table.

The SQL Procedure: Syntax Overview

The PROC SQL statement signals the start of the SQL procedure.

```
PROC SQL;
```

55

The SQL Procedure: Syntax Overview

The QUIT statement ends the SQL step.

QUIT;

56

In PROC SQL syntax, SAS executes a statement as soon as it encounters a semicolon. No RUN statement is required.

The SQL Procedure: Syntax Overview

Statements within the SQL step (also called *queries*) are made of smaller building blocks called *clauses*.

Clauses covered in this section:
- SELECT
- FROM
- WHERE

There is one semicolon at the end of each query **not** at the end of each clause.

57

The SELECT Clause

The SELECT clause identifies columns to include in the query result or table.

SELECT *var-1 , var-2 ...*

Columns listed in the SELECT clause are separated by commas. There is no comma following the last variable in the list.

SELECT *

To select all columns read, use an * in place of the column names.

58

The FROM Clause

The FROM clause identifies the SAS table(s) to read from.

FROM *SAS-data-set ...*

59

Using PROC SQL to Join Tables

To join two or more SAS tables, list them all in the FROM clause separated by commas.

General form of an SQL join:

```
PROC SQL;
   SELECT var-1, var-2...
      FROM SAS-data-set-1, SAS-data-set-2...
   ;
```

60

> You can join up to 32 data sets using PROC SQL.

SQL Joins without a WHERE Clause

By default, an SQL join results in a Cartesian product. All possible combinations are output.

```
proc sql;
   select *
      from prog2.transact,
           prog2.branches
   ;
quit;
```

61

SQL Join without a WHERE Clause

Partial Output

ActNum	Trans	Amnt	Act Num	Branch
56891	D	126.32	56891	N. Lincoln
56891	C	560	56891	N. Lincoln
57900	C	235	56891	N. Lincoln
58876	D	14.56	56891	N. Lincoln
59987	C	371.69	56891	N. Lincoln
56891	D	126.32	56900	S. Cicero
56891	C	560	56900	S. Cicero
57900	C	235	56900	S. Cicero
58876	D	14.56	56900	S. Cicero

62

In the above example, each table contains 5 rows. Therefore, the resulting Cartesian product contains 5*5 or 25 rows.

The WHERE Clause

In a join, the WHERE clause specifies the join criteria.

WHERE *expression*

Where *expression* is any valid SAS condition.

63

Joining on a Common Variable

The join in the scenario requires only matching values of **ActNum**.

ActNum from **prog2.branches** = **ActNum** from **prog2.transact**

64

Identifying Variables with the Same Names

```
proc sql;
    select Transact.ActNum, Trans,
           Amnt, Branch
    from prog2.transact, prog2.branches
    where Transact.ActNum=Branches.ActNum
    ;
quit;
```

You do not need to use the table name as a prefix if the column name appears in only one table.

65

 Conceptually, SAS is selecting matching rows from the Cartesian product. However, when the code is actually processed, SAS uses the WHERE criteria to optimize the join.

Because the join outputs only rows where the values of **ActNum** match, you can select **ActNum** from either table.

```
proc sql;
    select Branches.ActNum, Trans, Amnt, Branch
        from prog2.transact, prog2.branches
        where Transact.ActNum=Branches.ActNum
    ;
quit;
```

Assigning an Alias for a SAS Table

You can also specify an alias for a SAS table. The alias replaces the table name as the column prefix.

> **FROM** *SAS-data-set-1* <AS> *alias-1,*
> *SAS-data-set-2* <AS> *alias-2 ...*

An alias can be any valid SAS name.

66

Assigning an Alias for a SAS Table

```
proc sql;
   select B.ActNum, Trans,
          Amnt, Branch
      from prog2.transact as T,
           prog2.branches as B
      where T.ActNum=B.ActNum
   ;
quit;
```

67

Usually, the table alias is used as a convenience. If you are joining two tables with the same table name but different library references, you **must** specify an alias.

Inner Join with PROC SQL

ActNum	Trans	Amnt	Branch
56891	D	126.32	N. Lincoln
56891	C	560	N. Lincoln
58876	D	14.56	W. Argyle
59987	C	371.69	E. Wacker

68

 **Exercises**

2. Performing Simple Joins Using PROC SQL (Optional)

The SAS table `prog2.rduschedule` has one row representing each time a flight attendant or pilot is scheduled to fly into RDU airport. It contains the flight number, the date of the flight, and the employee's identification number.

Partial Listing of `prog2.rduschedule`

FltID	SchDate	EmpID
IA03600	03JAN2000	E00075
IA03600	03JAN2000	E00434
IA03600	03JAN2000	E00481
IA02400	16JAN2000	E00082
IA02003	20JAN2000	E00082
IA02003	20JAN2000	E00485
IA02005	23JAN2000	E00481
IA02402	07FEB2000	E00364

The SAS table `prog2.fltspts` is a master table of all the flight attendants and pilots in the company. It contains each employee's first name, last name, identification number, and job code.

Partial Listing of `prog2.fltspts`

FirstName	LastName	ID	Job Code
DOROTHY E	MILLS	E00001	FLTAT3
J. KEVIN	COCKERHAM	E00024	FLTAT3
DESIREE	GOLDENBERG	E00031	PILOT3
ALEC	FISHER	E00033	FLTAT2
NORMA JEAN	WIELENGA	E00043	PILOT3
GREGORY J.	GOODYEAR	E00046	FLTAT1
HANS	ECKHAUSEN	E00047	FLTAT3
JOHN K.	MELTON	E00052	FLTAT2
ANNE	WHITE JR.	E00055	PILOT3

Use PROC SQL to produce a report showing all the information for the flight attendants and pilots scheduled to fly into RDU.

Partial Output

EmpID	FirstName	LastName	Job Code	FltID	SchDate
E00434	KATE	SMITH	PILOT2	IA03600	03JAN2000
E00481	BETTY A.	YANG	FLTAT2	IA03600	03JAN2000
E00481	BETTY A.	YANG	FLTAT2	IA02005	23JAN2000
E00377	DONALD T.	SZCZEPANSKI	PILOT1	IA02000	16FEB2000
E00207	ANNE H.	YANG	FLTAT2	IA02405	17FEB2000
E00432	SANDRA	SCHOBER	FLTAT2	IA02405	17FEB2000
E00052	JOHN K.	MELTON	FLTAT2	IA03400	03APR2000
E00247	CARRIE D.	DODGE	PILOT2	IA03400	03APR2000
E00120	PEGGY H.	DUNLAP	FLTAT2	IA02000	05APR2000
E00248	DAWN B.	EDWARDS	FLTAT3	IA02000	05APR2000

Hint: SQL joins do not require key columns to have the same name.

8.3 Solutions to Exercises

1. Match-Merging Two Data Sets

```
    /*Each data set must be sorted by ProdCode before
        merging*/

proc sort data=prog2.prices out=pricesort;
   by ProdCode;
run;

proc sort data=prog2.todaysales out=salesort;
   by ProdCode;
run;

data revenue
      notsold(keep=Price ProdCode)
      invalidcode(Keep=ProdCode Qty);
   merge pricesort(in=InPrice) salesort(in=InSales);
   by ProdCode;
   if InPrice and InSales then do; /*Matching ProdCodes*/
      Revenue=Qty*Price; /*Only necessary to
                             calculate revenue for matches*/
      output Revenue;
   end;
      else if InPrice and not InSales
         then output notsold;
         /*Product not in todaysales data set. */
         /*It has not sold this week*/
      else if InSales and not InPrice
         then output invalidcode;
            /*Product in todaysales that is not
              in the master price list.*/
run;

proc print data=revenue;
run;

proc print data=notsold;
run;

proc print data=invalidcode;
run;
```

2. Performing Simple Joins Using PROC SQL (Optional)

```
proc sql;
   select EmpID, FirstName, LastName,
          JobCode, FltID, SchDate
       from prog2.rduschedule, prog2.fltspts
       where EmpID=ID  /*SQL does not require
                         key variables
                         to have the same name.*/
   ;
quit;
```

Chapter 9   Learning More

9.1 Where Do I Go From Here?

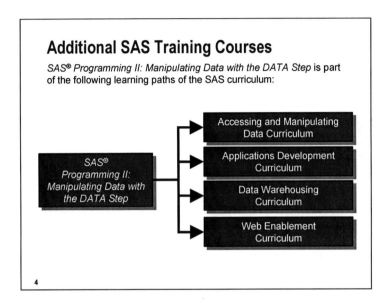

Additional learning paths include

- Data Presentation
- Data Mining
- IT Service Vision
- HR Vision
- Statistical Analysis
- JMP
- StatView.

The *SAS® Training* catalog is published annually and contains information on training services available from SAS. Included in the catalog are detailed course descriptions, course fees, and suggested learning paths, as well as information on discounts and special offers.

Specific SAS Training Courses

SAS® Programming III: Advanced Techniques

includes topics that you can use to broaden your programming skills.

SAS® Macro Language

includes topics on building complete macro-based systems using the SAS macro facility.

5

SAS Training

For additional information about other training opportunities available from SAS, refer to the SAS Training Web site:

www.sas.com/training

6

Next Steps

Consider taking a certification exam to assess your knowledge of SAS software. For a current listing of certification exams and registration information, visit **www.sas.com/certification**.

10

Other SAS Training Opportunities

Other training opportunities include

- e-Learning products that deliver training as a self-paced study directly to your desktop
- seminars and events that deliver knowledge and enable communication among SAS users.

9

---

e-Learning products include SAS OnlineTutor, which brings lessons to your standard Web browser. These lessons allow you to explore the latest SAS software and develop your SAS programming skills.

Seminars and events include the Business Knowledge Series. This series of seminars taught by industry experts provides organizations with expertise in the latest business developments

9.2   SAS Resources

SAS Services

SAS is a full-service company that provides

Consulting	short- or long-term consulting services to meet business needs
Training	instructor-based and online training options
Certification	global certification program to assess knowledge of SAS software and earn industry-recognized credentials.

12

SAS Services

SAS is a full-service company that provides

Online Help	a comprehensive online
Help system	to address many information needs
Documentation	extensive online and hardcopy reference information
Technical Support	specialists for all SAS software products and supported operating systems.

13

SAS Services

Access the SAS Web site at www.sas.com to learn more about available software, support, and services and to take advantage of these offerings.

14

You can use the SAS Web site to

- read about software, either by application or by industry
- learn about upcoming worldwide events, such as industry trade shows
- report problems to the Technical Support Division
- learn about consulting services
- identify the most appropriate learning path and register for courses online
- review the list of certification exams designed to assess knowledge of SAS software; identify test preparation options; and register online for a certification exam
- browse and order from the online version of the *SAS® Publications Catalog*
- access online versions of SAS publications.

Consulting Services

SAS offers flexible consulting options to meet short- or long-term business needs. Services such as installation, needs assessment, project scoping, prototyping, or short-term technical assistance help you reap the benefits of SAS software as quickly as possible.

Consultants provide expertise in areas such as

- data warehousing
- data mining
- business intelligence
- Web-enablement tasks
- e-intelligence
- analytical solutions
- business solutions
- custom applications
- client/server technology
- systems-related issues.

Training Services

SAS offers training services and a certification program to help you achieve business and professional goals. Whether you are a beginning or an accomplished SAS software user, training services are available to help you increase your skills and expand your knowledge.

Instructor-based Training offers both public and on-site courses that encompass the breadth of SAS software including

- the SAS programming language
- report writing
- applications development
- data warehousing
- client/server strategies
- structured query language (SQL)
- financial consolidation and reporting
- database access
- statistical analysis.

Seminars led by industry experts are also available through the Business Knowledge Series to provide you with expertise in the latest business developments.

Online Training combines the instructional quality of SAS courses with the benefits of self-paced training.

SAS OnlineTutor for Version 8: SAS Programming is the latest online training product. With thirty-five comprehensive, highly interactive lessons and also quizzes and exercises to test your comprehension, SAS OnlineTutor provides fifty to sixty hours of instruction.

The content is relevant to both novice and intermediate SAS software users. The lessons range from how to use the new features in the Version 8 SAS environment to how to write programming code to access, manage, analyze, and present your data.

For more information about training services, visit the Web at www.sas.com/training and order the complimentary *SAS® Training* catalog, published biannually.

The **SAS Certified Professional Program** was developed the recognize SAS software users who can demonstrate an in-depth understanding of SAS software.

The core-level exam, SAS Core Concepts Version 8, represents the cornerstone of the program. It measures knowledge of fundamental SAS programming skills. Core-level certification is a prerequisite to certification at a specialty level.

Version 8 certifications:

- SAS Certified Professional V8 (core-level)
- SAS Certified Developer's V8 Transition Exam (specialty-level)

Version 6 certifications:

- SAS Certified Professional V6 (core-level)
- SAS Certified Professional - Data Management V6 (specialty-level)
- SAS Certified Professional - Business Intelligence V6 (specialty-level)
- SAS Certified Professional - Application Development V6 (specialty-level)

For more information about the SAS Certified Professional Program, refer to the SAS Certification Web site:

www.sas.com/certification.

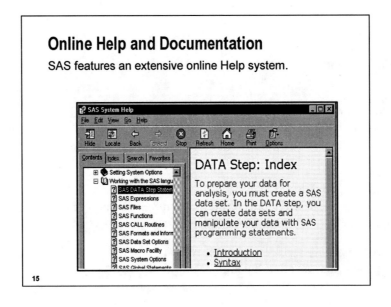

Online Help and Documentation

You can also access SAS OnlineDoc, which provides you with SAS System reference documentation.

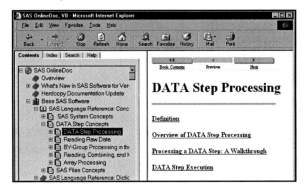

16

SAS Documentation

SAS documentation is also available in hardcopy. Some useful references are

- SAS® Language Reference: Concepts, Version 8 (order # Q57375)
- SAS® Language Reference: Dictionary, Version 8, Volumes 1 and 2 (order # Q57239)
- SAS® Procedures Guide, Version 8 (order # Q57238)

continued...

17

SAS Documentation

- The Complete Guide to the SAS® Output Delivery System, Version 8 (order # Q57241)
- SAS/GRAPH® Software: Reference, Version 8 (order # Q57263)
- SAS® SQL Query Window User's Guide, Version 8 (order # Q57280).

18

Publications Services

For a complete list of documentation available in online and hardcopy form, access the SAS Publications Web site at **www.sas.com/pubs**.

    You can order documentation using the Publications Catalog through the SAS Publications Web site or by calling **1-800-727-3228**.

SAS also publishes a number of magazines and newsletters. To view these periodicals, access the SAS Publications Web site.

SAS also offers **SelecText**, a service for U.S. colleges and universities. The SelecText service allows instructors to create custom course textbooks for teaching students to use SAS software. Access the SelecText Web site at **www.sas.com/selectext** or send e-mail to `selectext@sas.com`.

Technical Support Services

Technical Support provides you with the resources to answer any questions or solve any problems that you encounter when you use SAS software. You have access to a variety of tools to solve problems on your own and a variety of ways to contact Technical Support when you need help.

- **Free, Unlimited Support**

  Free technical support is available to all sites that license software from SAS. This includes unlimited telephone support for customers in North America by calling **1-919-677-8008**. Customers outside North America can contact their local SAS Institute office. There is also an electronic mail interface and FTP site.

- **Reported Problems**

  Although SAS software is recognized as a leader in reliability, SAS realizes that no software is problem free. We do our best to let you know about bugs or problems that have been reported to Technical Support. Information about reported problems is available in the SAS Notes and SAS/C Compiler Usage Notes, which are distributed with the software, and can also be searched via the Web interface. We also inform you about more serious problems through Alert Notes and the TSNEWS-L list server.

- **Local Support at Your Site**

  To provide the most effective response to your questions and problems, one or more people at your site are designated as local SAS Support personnel. These are knowledgeable SAS users who are provided with additional resources to assist all SAS users at your site. You can often get a quick answer to your SAS questions by contacting your local SAS consultant before calling SAS Technical Support.

To use SAS Technical Support, you must know your SAS System site number. Your site number can be found at the top of the SAS log. The site number can also be easily obtained using the SETINIT procedure, which displays information about your SAS installation in the log.

```
PROC SETINIT;
RUN;
```

SAS Users Groups

SAS Users Groups offer the opportunity to

- enhance your understanding of SAS software and services
- exchange ideas about using your software and hardware most productively
- learn of new SAS products and services as soon as they become available
- have more influence over the direction of SAS software and services
- additional information, including a list of SAS Users Groups worldwide, is available at the SAS Users Groups Web site:

www.sas.com/usergroups

Index